Essential C++

The C++ In-Depth Series

Bjarne Stroustrup, Editor

"I have made this letter longer than usual, because I lack the time to make it short."
—BLAISE PASCAL

The advent of the ISO/ANSI C++ standard marked the beginning of a new era for C++ programmers. The standard offers many new facilities and opportunities, but how can a real-world programmer find the time to discover the key nuggets of wisdom within this mass of information? The C++ In-Depth Series minimizes learning time and confusion by giving programmers concise, focused guides to specific topics.

Each book in this series presents a single topic, at a technical level appropriate to that topic. The Series' practical approach is designed to lift professionals to their next level of programming skills. Written by experts in the field, these short, in-depth monographs can be read and referenced without the distraction of unrelated material. The books are cross-referenced within the Series, and also reference *The C++ Programming Language* by Bjarne Stroustrup.

As you develop your skills in C++, it becomes increasingly important to separate essential information from hype and glitz, and to find the in-depth content you need in order to grow. The C++ In-Depth Series provides the tools, concepts, techniques, and new approaches to C++ that will give you a critical edge.

Titles in the Series

Essential C++, Stanley B. Lippman
Exceptional C++: 47 Engineering Puzzles, Programming Problems, and Exception-Safety Solutions, Herb Sutter

Forthcoming Titles

C++ Network Programming: Using the ACE Framework, Steve Huston and Douglas Schmidt
Writing Efficient C++, Stanley B. Lippman

Essential C++

Stanley B. Lippman

Dreamworks Feature Animation

ADDISON–WESLEY

An Imprint of Addison Wesley Longman, Inc.
Reading, Massachusetts • Harlow, England • Menlo Park, California
Berkeley, California • Don Mills, Ontario • Sydney
Bonn • Amsterdam • Tokyo • Mexico City

The publisher offers discounts on this book when ordered in quantity for special sales. For more information please contact:

Corporate, Government, and Special Sales
Addison Wesley Longman, Inc.
One Jacob Way
Reading, Massachusetts 01867

Copyright © 2000 Addison Wesley Longman

Library of Congress Cataloging-in-Publication Data

Lippman, Stanley B.
    Essential C++ / Stanley B. Lippman
        p.   cm.
    Includes bibliographical references and index.
    ISBN 0-201-48518-4
    1. C++ (Computer program language) I. Title.
QA76.73.C153 L577 1999
005.13'3--dc21   99–046613
                                        CIP

ISBN 0-201-48518-4

1 2 3 4 5 6 7 8 9—MA—0302010099

First printing, October 1999

To Beth,
who remains essential

—

To Danny and Anna,
hey, kids
look, it's done ...

Contents

Preface

Gosh, but this book is short. I mean, wow. My C++ *Primer* is 1237 pages counting the index, title, and dedication pages. This one weighs in at 276 — in boxing terms, we're talking bantamweight.

The first question, of course, is how come? Actually, there's a story to that.

I'd been pestering everyone at Disney Feature Animation for a number of years to let me work on a production. I asked directors, management types — even Mickey, if the truth be told. In part, it was for the glamour, I suppose. Hollywood. The big screen. Also, I hold a Master of Fine Arts as well as my Comp Sci degree, and film work seemed to promise some sort of personal synthesis. What I told management, of course, was that I needed the experience in production in order to provide usable tools. As a compiler writer, I'd always been one of my own main users. It's difficult to get defensive or feel unfairly criticized when you're one of the principal complainers about your software.

The computer effects lead on the Firebird segment of *Fantasia 2000* was interested in having me join the production. To kind of try things out, he asked me to write a tool to read the raw Disney camera information for a scene and generate a camera node that could be plugged in to the Houdini animation package. I wrote it in C++, of course. It worked. They liked it. I was invited to come on board.

Once on the production (thanks to Jinko and Chyuan), I was asked to rewrite the tool in Perl. The other TDs, it was explained, weren't heavy-duty programmers but knew Perl, Tcl, and so on. (TD is film industry jargon for technical director. I was the segment's software TD. There was also a lighting TD [hi, Mira] and a model TD [hi, Tim] as well as the actual computer effects animators [hi, Mike, Steve, and Tonya].) And oh, by the way, could I do this quickly, because, gosh, we have a proof of concept test to get out that the directors (hi, Paul and Gaetan) and effects supervisor (hi, Dave) are waiting for to pitch to the then head of Feature Animation (hi, Peter). No emergency, you understand, but ...

This left me in somewhat of a quandary. I can program reasonably quickly in C++ with confidence. Unfortunately, I didn't know Perl. I thought, OK, I'll read a book. But it can't be too big a book, at least not right now. And it had better not tell me too much, although I know I should know everything, only later. After all, this is show biz: The directors need a proof of concept, the artist needs a plug-in to prove the concept, and the producer — heck, she needs a 48-hour day. I didn't need the best book on Perl — just the right book to get me going and not steer me too far off the righteous path.

I found that book in *Learning Perl*, by Randal Schwartz. It got me up and running, and it was fun to read. Well, as much as any computer book is fun. It leaves out gobs of good stuff. At the time, though, I didn't need all that stuff — I needed to get my Perl scripts working.

Eventually, I realized sadly that the third edition of *C++ Primer* could no longer fill a similar role for someone needing to learn C++. It had just become too big. I think it's a grand book, of course — particularly with Josée Lajoie coming on board as coauthor of the third edition. But it's too comprehensive for this kind of just-in-time C++ language learning. That's why I decided to write this book.

You're probably thinking, but C++ is not Perl. That's correct. And this text is not *Learning Perl*. It's about learning C++. The real question is, How does one shed almost a thousand pages and still claim to be teaching anything?

1. **Level of detail**. In computer graphics, *level of detail* refers to how sharply an image is rendered. The invading Hun on horseback in the left front corner of the screen needs a face with eyes, hair, five o'clock shadow, clothes, and so on. The Hun way back there — no, not the rock, silly — well, we don't render both images with the same care for detail. Similarly, the level of detail in this book is clamped down considerably. *C++ Primer*, in my opinion, has the most complete but readable discussion of operator overloading in existence (I can say that because Josée was the author). However, it takes 46 pages of discussion and code examples. Here, I take 2 pages.

2. **Core language**. When I was editor of the *C++ Report*, I used to say that half the job of editing the magazine was in deciding what not to put in. The same is true for this text. The text is organized around a series of a programming problems. Language features are introduced to provide a solution to individual problems. I didn't have a problem that multiple or virtual inheritance could solve, so I do not discuss them. To implement an iterator class, however, I had to introduce nested types. Class conversion operators are easy to misuse and are complicated to explain. I therefore chose not to present them. And so on. The choice and order of presentation of language features are always open to criticism. This is my choice and my responsibility.

3. **Number of code examples**. *C++ Primer* has hundreds of pages of code that we step through in detail, including an object-oriented Text Query system and about a half-dozen fully implemented classes. Although this text is code-driven, the set of code examples is simply not as rich as that of *C++ Primer*. To help compensate, solutions to all the program exercises are provided in Appendix A. As my editor, Deborah Lafferty, said, "If you are trying to teach something quickly, it is helpful to have the answers at your fingertips to reinforce the learning."

Structure of This Book

The text consists of seven chapters and two appendixes. Chapter 1 provides a description of the predefined language in the context of writing a small interactive program. It covers the built-in data types, the predefined operators, the vector and string library classes, the conditional and looping statements, and the iostream library for input and output. I introduce the vector and string classes in this chapter because I encourage their use over the built-in array and C-style character string.

Chapter 2 explains how to design and use a function and walks through the many flavors of functions supported in C++: inline, overloaded, and template functions as well as pointers to functions.

Chapter 3 covers what is commonly referred to as the Standard Template Library (STL): a collection of container classes, such as a vector, list, set, and map, and generic algorithms to operate on those containers, such as sort(), copy(), and merge(). Appendix B presents an alphabetical listing of the most commonly used generic algorithms and provides an example of how each one is used.

As a C++ programmer, your primary activity is the delivery of classes and object-oriented class hierarchies. Chapter 4 walks through the design and use of the C++ class facility to create data types specific to your application domain. For example, at Dreamworks Animation, where I do some consulting work, we design classes to do four-channel compositing of images and so on. Chapter 5 explains how to extend class design to support families of related classes in object-oriented class hierarchies. Rather than design eight independent image compositing classes, for example, we define a compositing hierarchy using inheritance and dynamic binding.

Class templates are the topic of Chapter 6. A class template is a kind of prescription for creating a class in which one or more types or values are parameterized. A vector class, for example, may parameterize the type of element it contains. A buffer class may parameterize not only the type of element it holds but also the size of its buffer. The chapter is driven by the implementation of a binary tree template class.

Finally, Chapter 7 illustrates how to use the C++ exception handling facility and fit it into the existing standard library exception class hierarchy. Appendix A provides solutions to the programming exercises. Appendix B provides a program example and discussion of the most frequently used generic algorithms.

A Note on the Source Code

The full source code of the programs developed within the text as well as the solutions to the exercises is available on-line for downloading both at the Addison Wesley Longman Web site (www.awl.com/cseng/titles/0-201-48518-4) and at my home page (www.objectwrite.com). All the code has been executed under both Visual C++ 5.0

using the Intel C++ compiler and Visual C++ 6.0 using the Microsoft C++ compiler. You may need to modify the code slightly to have it compile on your system. If you make any modifications, send me a list of them (slippman@objectwrite.com), and I will post them, along with your name, in a modifications file attached to the solutions code. (Note that the full source code is *not* displayed within the text itself.)

Acknowledgments

Special thanks go to Josée Lajoie, coauthor of *C++ Primer*, 3rd Edition. She has been a wonderful support because of her insightful comments on the various drafts of this text and her unfailing encouragement. I also offer special thanks to Dave Slayton for going through both the text and the code examples with a razor-sharp green pencil, and to Steve Vinoski for his compassionate but firm comments on the drafts of this text.

Special thanks also go to the Addison-Wesley editorial team: Deborah Lafferty, who, as editor, supported this project from the beginning, Betsy Hardinger, who, as copyeditor, contributed greatly to the readability of the text, and John Fuller, who, as production manager, shepherded us from manuscript to bound text.

During the writing of this text, I worked as an independent consultant, multiplexing between *Essential C++* and a set of (reasonably) understanding clients. I'd like to thank Colin Lipworth, Edwin Leonard, and Kenneth Meyer for their patience and good faith.

Where to Find More Information

From a completely biased point of view, the two best one-volume introductions to C++ are Lippman and Lajoie's *C++ Primer* and Stroustrup's *The C++ Programming Language*, both in their third edition. Throughout the text I refer you to one or both of the texts for more in-depth information. The following books are cited in the text. (A more extensive bibliography can be found in both *C++ Primer* and *The C++ Programming Language*.)

[LIPPMAN98] Lippman, Stanley, and Josée Lajoie, *C++ Primer, 3rd Edition*, Addison Wesley Longman, Inc., Reading, MA (1998) ISBN 0-201-82470-1.

[LIPPMAN96a] Lippman, Stanley, *Inside the C++ Object Model*, Addison Wesley Longman, Inc., Reading, MA (1996) ISBN 0-201-83454-5.

[LIPPMAN96b] Lippman, Stanley, Editor, *C++ Gems*, a SIGS Books imprint, Cambridge University Press, Cambridge, England (1996) ISBN 0-13570581-9.

[STROUSTRUP97] Stroustrup, Bjarne, *The C++ Programming Language, 3rd Edition*, Addison Wesley Longman, Inc., Reading, MA (1997) ISBN 0-201-88954-4.

[SUTTER99] Sutter, Herb, *Exceptional C++*, Addison Wesley Longman, Inc., Reading, MA (2000) ISBN 0-201-61562-2.

Typographical Conventions

The text of the book is set in 10.5 pt. Palatino. Program text and language keywords appear in 8.5 pt. `lucida`. Functions are identified by following their name with the C++ function call operator (`()`). Thus, for example, `foo` represents a program object, and `bar()` represents a program function. Class names are set in Palatino.

1

Basic C++ Programming

In this chapter, we evolve a small program to exercise the fundamental components of the C++ language. These components consist of the following:

1. A small set of data types: Boolean, character, integer, and floating point.
2. A set of arithmetic, relational, and logical operators to manipulate these types. These include not only the usual suspects, such as addition, equality, less than, and assignment, but also the less conventional increment, conditional, and compound assignment operators.
3. A set of conditional branch and looping statements, such as the `if` statement and `while` loop, to alter the control flow of our program.
4. A small number of compound types, such as a pointer and an array. These allow us, respectively, to refer indirectly to an existing object and to define a collection of elements of a single type.
5. A standard library of common programming abstractions, such as a string and a vector.

1.1 How to Write a C++ Program

We've been asked to write a simple program to write a message to the user's terminal asking her to type in her name. Then we read the name she enters, store the name so that we can use it later, and, finally, greet the user by name.

OK, so where do we start? We start in the same place every C++ program starts — in a function called `main()`. `main()` is a user-implemented function of the following general form:

```
int main()
{
    // our program code goes here
}
```

int is a C++ language keyword. *Keywords* are predefined names given special meaning within the language. int represents a built-in integer data type. (I have much more to say about data types in the next section.)

A *function* is an independent code sequence that performs some computation. It consists of four parts: the return type, the function name, the parameter list, and the function body. Let's briefly look at each part in turn.

The *return type* of the function usually represents the result of the computation. main() has an integer return type. The value returned by main() indicates whether our program is successful. By convention, main() returns 0 to indicate success. A nonzero return value indicates something went wrong.

The *name* of a function is chosen by the programmer and ideally should give some sense of what the function does. min() and sort(), for example, are pretty good function names. f() and g() are not as good. Why? Because they are less informative as to what the functions do.

main is not a language keyword. The compilation system that executes our C++ programs, however, expects a main() function to be defined. If we forget to provide one, our program will not run.

The *parameter list* of a function is enclosed in parentheses and is placed after the name of the function. An empty parameter list, such as that of main(), indicates that the function accepts no parameters.

The parameter list is typically a comma-separated list of types that the user can pass to the function when the function is executed. (We say that the user has *called*, or *invoked*, a function.) For example, if we write a function min() to return the smaller of two values, its parameter list would identify the types of the two values we want to compare. A min() function to compare two integer values might be defined as follows:

```
int min( int val1, int val2 )
{
    // the program code goes here ...
}
```

The *body* of the function is enclosed in curly braces ({}). It holds the code sequence that provides the computation of the function. The double forward slash (//) represents a comment, a programmer's annotation on some aspect of the code. It is intended for readers of the program and is discarded during compilation. Everything following the double forward slash to the end of the line is treated as a comment.

Our first task is to write a message to the user's terminal. Input and output are not a predefined part of the C++ language. Rather, they are supported by an *object-oriented class hierarchy* implemented in C++ and provided as part of the C++ standard library.

A class is a user-defined data type. The class mechanism is a method of adding to the data types recognized by our program. An object-oriented class hierarchy defines a family of related class types, such as terminal and file input, terminal and file output, and so on. (We have a lot more to say about classes and object-oriented programming throughout this text.)

C++ predefines a small set of fundamental data types: Boolean, character, integer, and floating point. Although these provide a foundation for all our programming, they are not the focus of our programs. A camera, for example, must have a location in space, which is generally represented by three floating point numbers. A camera also has a viewing orientation, which is also represented by three floating point numbers. There is usually an aspect ratio describing the ratio of the camera viewing width to height. This is represented by a single floating point number.

On the most primitive level, that is, a camera is represented as seven floating point numbers, six of which form two x,y,z coordinate tuples. Programming at this low level requires that we shift our thinking back and forth from the manipulation of the camera abstraction to the corresponding manipulation of the seven floating point values that represent the camera in our program.

The class mechanism allows us to add layers of type abstraction to our programs. For example, we can define a Point3d class to represent location and orientation in space. Similarly, we can define a Camera class containing two Point3d class objects and a floating point value. We're still representing a camera by seven floating point values. The difference is that in our programming we are now directly manipulating the Camera class rather than seven floating point values.

The definition of a class is typically broken into two parts, each represented by a separate file: a *header file* that provides a declaration of the operations supported by the class, and a *program text file* that contains the implementation of those operations.

To use a class, we include its header file within our program. The header file makes the class known to the program. The standard C++ input/output library is called the *iostream* library. It consists of a collection of related classes supporting input and output to the user's terminal and to files. To use the iostream class library, we must include its associated header file:

```
#include <iostream>
```

To write to the user's terminal, we use a predefined class object named cout (pronounced *see out*). We direct the data we wish cout to write using the output operator (<<), as follows:

```
cout << "Please enter your first name: ";
```

This represents a C++ program *statement*, the smallest independent unit of a C++ program. It is analogous to a sentence in a natural language. A statement is terminated by a semicolon. Our output statement writes the string literal (marked by double quotation marks) onto the user's terminal. The quotation marks identify the string; they are not displayed on the terminal. The user sees

```
Please enter your first name:
```

Our next task is to read the user's input. Before we can read the name the user types, we must define an object in which to store the information. We define an object by specifying the data type of the object and giving it a name. We've already seen one data type: `int`. That's hardly a useful way of storing someone's name, however! A more appropriate data type in this case is the standard library string class:

```
string user_name;
```

This defines `user_name` as an object of the string class. The definition, oddly enough, is called a *declaration statement*. This statement won't be accepted, however, unless we first make the string class known to the program. We do this by including the string class header file: .

```
#include <string>
```

To read input from the user's terminal, we use a predefined class object named `cin` (pronounced *see in*). We use the input operator (>>) to direct `cin` to read data from the user's terminal into an object of the appropriate type:

```
cin >> user_name;
```

The output and input sequence would appear as follows on the user's terminal. (The user's input is highlighted in bold.)

```
Please enter your first name: anna
```

All we've left to do now is to greet the user by name. We want our output to look like this:

```
Hello, anna ... and goodbye!
```

I know, that's not much of a greeting. Still, this is only the first chapter. We'll get a bit more inventive before the end of the book.

To generate our greeting , our first step is to advance the output to the next line. We do this by writing a newline character literal to `cout`:

```
cout << '\n';
```

A character literal is marked by a pair of single quotation marks. There are two primary flavors of character literals: printing characters such as the alphabet (`'a'`, `'A'`, and so on), numbers, and punctuation marks (`';'`, `'-'`, and so on), and nonprinting characters such as a newline (`'\n'`) or tab (`'\t'`). Because there is no literal representation of nonprinting characters, the most common instances, such as the newline and tab, are represented by special two-character sequences.

Now that we've advanced to the next line, we want to generate our `Hello`:

```
cout << "Hello, ";
```

Next, we need to output the name of the user. That's stored in our string object, `user_name`. How do we do that? Just the same as with the other types:

```
cout << user_name;
```

Finally, we finish our greeting by saying goodbye (notice that a string literal can be made up of both printing and nonprinting characters):

```
cout << " ... and goodbye!\n";
```

In general, all the built-in types are output in the same way — that is, by placing the value on the right-hand side of the output operator. For example,

```
cout << "3 + 4 = ";
cout << 3 + 4;
cout << '\n';
```

generates the following output:

```
3 + 4 = 7
```

As we define new class types for use in our applications, we also provide an instance of the output operator for each class. (We see how to do this in Chapter 4.) This allows users of our class to output individual class objects in exactly the same way as the built-in types.

Rather than write successive output statements on separate lines, we can concatenate them into one compound output statement:

```
cout << '\n'
     << "Hello, "
     << user_name
     << " ... and goodbye!\n";
```

Finally, we can explicitly end main() with the use of a return statement:

```
return 0;
```

return is a C++ keyword. The expression following return, in this case 0, represents the result value of the function. Recall that a return value of 0 from main() indicates that the program has executed successfully.[1]

Putting the pieces together, here is our first complete C++ program:

```
#include <iostream>
#include <string>
using namespace std; // haven't explained this yet ...

int main()
{
     string user_name;
     cout << "Please enter your first name: ";
     cin >> user_name;
     cout << '\n'
          << "Hello, "
```

---

[1]   If we don't place an explicit return statement at the end of main(), a return 0; statement is inserted automatically. In the program examples in this book, I do not place an explicit return statement.

```
            << user_name
            << " ... and goodbye!\n";

        return 0;
    }
```

When compiled and executed, this code produces the following output (my input is highlighted in bold):

```
Please enter your first name: anna
Hello, anna ... and goodbye!
```

There is one statement I haven't explained:

```
using namespace std;
```

Let's see if I can explain this without scaring you off. (A deep breath is recommended at this point!) Both using and namespace are C++ keywords. std is the name of the standard library namespace. Everything provided within the standard library (such as the string class and the iostream class objects cout and cin) is encapsulated within the std namespace. Of course, your next question is, what is a namespace?

A *namespace* is a method of packaging library names so that they can be introduced within a user's program environment without also introducing name clashes. (A *name clash* occurs when there are two entities that have the same name in an application so that the program cannot distinguish between the two. When this happens, the program cannot run until the name clash is resolved.) Namespaces are a way of fencing in the visibility of names.

To use the string class and the iostream class objects cin and cout within our program, we must not only include the string and iostream header files but also make the names within the std namespace visible. The *using directive*

```
using namespace std;
```

is the simplest method of making names within a namespace visible. (To read about namespaces in more detail, check out either Section 8.5 of [LIPPMAN98] or Section 8.2 of [STROUSTRUP97].)

Exercise 1.1

Enter the main() program, shown earlier. Either type it in directly or download the program; see the Preface for how to acquire the source programs and solutions to exercises. Compile and execute the program on your system.

Exercise 1.2

Comment out the string header file:

```
// #include <string>
```

Now recompile the program. What happens? Now restore the string header and comment out

```
//using namespace std;
```

What happens?

Exercise 1.3

Change the name of `main()` to `my_main()` and recompile the program. What happens?

Exercise 1.4

Try to extend the program: (1) Ask the user to enter both a first and last name and (2) modify the output to write out both names.

1.2   Defining and Initializing a Data Object

Now that we have the user's attention, let's challenge her to a quiz. We display two numbers representing a numerical sequence and then request our user to identify the next value in the sequence. For example,

```
The values 2,3 form two consecutive
    elements of a numerical sequence.
What is the next value?
```

These values are the third and fourth elements of the Fibonacci sequence: 1, 1, 2, 3, 5, 8, 13, and so on. A Fibonacci sequence begins with the first two elements set to 1. Each subsequent element is the sum of its two preceding elements. (In Chapter 2 we write a function to calculate the elements.)

If the user enters 5, we congratulate her and ask whether she would like to try another numerical sequence. Any other entered value is incorrect, and we ask the user whether she would like to guess again.

To add interest to the program, we keep a running score based on the number of correct answers divided by the number of guesses.

Our program needs at least five objects: the string class object to hold the name of the user; three integer objects to hold, in turn, the user's guess, the number of guesses, and the number of correct guesses; and a floating point object to hold the user's score.

To define a data object, we must both name it and provide it with a data type. The name can be any combination of letters, numbers, and the underscore. Letters are case-sensitive. Each one of the names `user_name`, `User_name`, `uSeR_nAmE`, and `user_Name` refers to a distinct object.

A name cannot begin with a number. For example, `1_name` is illegal but `name_1` is OK. Also, a name must not match a language keyword exactly. For example, `delete` is a language keyword, and so we can't use it for an entity in our program. (This explains why the operation to remove a character from the string class is `erase()` and not `delete()`.)

Each object must be of a particular data type. The name of the object allows us to refer to it directly. The data type determines the range of values the object can hold and the amount of memory that must be allocated to hold those values.

We saw the definition of `user_name` in the preceding section. We reuse the same definition in our new program:

```
#include <string>
string user_name;
```

A class is a programmer-defined data type. C++ also provides a set of built-in data types: Boolean, integer, floating point, and character. A keyword is associated with each one to allow us to specify the data type. For example, to store the value entered by the user, we define an integer data object:

```
int usr_val;
```

`int` is a language keyword identifying `usr_val` as a data object of integer type. Both the number of guesses a user makes and the number of correct guesses are also integer objects. The difference here is that we wish to set both of them to an initial value of 0. We can define each on a separate line:

```
int num_tries = 0;
int num_right = 0;
```

Or we can define them in a single comma-separated declaration statement:

```
int num_tries = 0, num_right = 0;
```

In general, it is a good idea to initialize data objects even if the value simply indicates that the object has no useful value as yet. I didn't initialize `usr_val` because its value is set directly from the user's input before the program makes any use of the object.

An alternative initialization syntax, called a *constructor syntax*, is

```
int num_tries( 0 );
```

I know. Why are there two initialization syntaxes? And, worse, why am I telling you this now? Well, let's see whether the following explanation satisfies either or both questions.

The use of the assignment operator (=) for initialization is inherited from the C language. It works well with the data objects of the built-in types and for class objects that can be initialized with a single value, such as the string class:

```
string sequence_name = "Fibonacci";
```

It does not work well with class objects that require multiple initial values, such as the standard library complex number class, which can take two initial values: one for its real component and one for its imaginary component. The alternative constructor initialization syntax was introduced to handle multiple value initialization:

```
#include <complex>
complex<double> purei( 0, 7 );
```

The strange bracket notation following `complex` indicates that the complex class is a template class. We'll see a great deal more of template classes throughout the book. A template class allows us to define a class without having to specify the data type of one or all of its members.

The complex number class, for example, contains two member data objects. One member represents the real component of the number. The second member represents the imaginary component of the number. These members need to be floating point data types, but which ones? C++ generously supports three floating point size types: *single precision*, represented by the keyword `float`; *double precision*, represented by the keyword `double`; and *extended precision*, represented by the two keywords `long double`.

The template class mechanism allows the programmer to defer deciding on the data type to use for a template class. It allows the programmer to insert a placeholder that is later bound to an actual data type. In the preceding example, the user chose to bind the data type of the complex class members to `double`.

I know, this probably raises scads more questions than it answers. However, it is because of templates that C++ supports two initialization syntaxes for the built-in data types. When the built-in data types and programmer-defined class types had separate initialization syntaxes, it was not possible to write a template that supported both built-in and class data types. Making the syntax uniform simplified template design. Unfortunately, explaining the syntax seems to have become more complicated!

The user's running score must to be a floating point value because it may be some percentage. We'll define it to be of type `double`:

```
double usr_score = 0.0;
```

We also need to keep track of the user's *yes/no* responses: *Make another try? Try another sequence?*

We can store the user's response in a character data object:

```
char usr_more;
cout << "Try another sequence? Y/N? ";
cin >> usr_more;
```

The `char` keyword represents a character type. A character marked by a pair of single quotations represents a character literal: `'a'`, `'7'`, `';'`, and so on. Some special built-in character literals are the following (they are sometimes called *escape sequences*):

```
'\n'   newline
'\t'   tab
'\0'   null
'\''   single quote
'\"'   double quote
'\\'   backslash
```

For example, to generate a newline and then tab before printing the user's name, we might write

```
cout << '\n' << '\t' << user_name;
```

Alternatively, we can concatentate single characters into a string:

```
cout << ."\n\t" << user_name;
```

Typically, we use these special characters within string literals. For example, to represent a literal file path under Windows, we need to escape the backslash:

```
"F:\\essential\\programs\\chapter1\\ch1_main.cpp";
```

C++ supports a built-in Boolean data type to represent true/false values. In our program, for example, we can define a Boolean object to control whether to display the next numeric sequence:

```
bool go_for_it = true;
```

A Boolean object is specified with the `bool` keyword. It can hold one of two literal values, either `true` or `false`.

All the data objects defined so far modified during the course of our program. `go_for_it`, for example, eventually gets set to `false`. `usr_score` is potentially updated with each user guess.

Sometimes, however, we need an object to represent a constant value: the maximum number of guesses to allow a user, for example, or the value of pi. The objects holding these values should not be modified during the course of our program. How can we prevent the accidental modification of such objects? We can enlist the aid of the language by declaring these objects as `const`:

```
const int max_tries = 3;
const double pi = 3.14159;
```

A `const` object cannot be modified from its initial value. Any attempt to assign a value to a `const` object results in a compile-time error. For example:

```
max_tries = 42; // error: const object
```

1.3   Writing Expressions

The built-in data types are supported by a collection of arithmetic, relational, logical, and compound assignment operators. The arithmetic operators are unsurprising except for integer division and the remainder operator:

```
// Arithmetic Operators
+     addition        a + b
-     subtraction     a - b
*     multiplication  a * b
/     division        a / b
%     remainder       a % b
```

The division of two integer values yields a whole number. Any remainder is truncated; there is no rounding. The remainder is accessed using the % operator:

```
5 / 3 evaluates to 1 while 5 % 3 evaluates to 2
5 / 4 evaluates to 1 while 5 % 4 evaluates to 1
5 / 5 evaluates to 1 while 5 % 5 evaluates to 0
```

When might we actually use the remainder operator? Imagine that we want to print no more than eight strings on a line. If the number of words on the line is less than eight, we output a blank space following the word. If the string is the eighth word on the line, we output a newline. Here is our implementation:

```
const int line_size = 8;
int cnt = 1;

// these statements are executed many times, with
// a_string representing a different value each time
// and cnt growing by one with each execution ...
cout << a_string
     << ( cnt % line_size ? ' ' : '\n' );
```

The parenthetical expression following the output operator likely makes no sense to you unless you are already familiar with the conditional operator (?:). The result of the expression is to output either a space or a newline character depending on whether the remainder operator evaluates to a zero or a nonzero value. Let's see what sense we can make of it.

The expression

```
cnt % line_size
```

evaluates to zero whenever cnt is a multiple of line_size; otherwise, it evaluates to a nonzero value. Where does that get us? The conditional operator takes the following general form:

```
expr
  ? execute_if_expr_is_true
  : execute_if_expr_is_false;
```

If expr evaluates to true, the expression following the question mark is evaluated. If expr evaluates to false, the expression following the colon is evaluated. In our case, the evaluation is to feed either a space or a newline character to the output operator.

A conditional expression is treated as evaluating to false if its value is zero. Any nonzero value is treated as true. In this example, whenever cnt is not a multiple of eight, the result is nonzero, the true branch of the conditional operator is evaluated, and a space is printed.

A compound assignment operator provides a shorthand notation for applying an arithmetic operation on the object to be assigned. For example, rather than write

```
cnt = cnt + 2;
```

a C++ programmer typically writes

```
cnt += 2; // add 2 to the current value of cnt
```

A compound assignment operator is associated with each arithmetic operator: +=, -=, *=, /=, and %=.

When an object is being added to or subtracted by 1, the C++ programmer uses the increment and decrement operators:

```
cnt++; // add 1 to the current value of cnt
cnt--; // subtract 1 from the current value of cnt
```

There is a prefix and postfix version of the increment and decrement operators. In the prefix application, the object is either incremented (or decremented) by 1 before the object's value is accessed:

```
int tries = 0;
cout << "Are you ready for try #"
     << ++tries << "?\n";
```

In this example, `tries` is incremented by 1 before its value is printed. In the postfix application, the object's value is first used in the expression, and then incremented (or decremented) by 1:

```
int tries = 1;
cout << "Are you ready for try #"
     << tries++ << "?\n";
```

In this example, the value of `tries` is printed before it is incremented by 1. In both examples, the value 1 is printed.

Each of the relational operators evaluates to either true or false. They consist of the following six operators:

```
==    equality                    a == b
!=    inequality                  a != b
<     less than                   a < b
>     greater than                a > b
<=    less than or equal          a <= b
>=    greater than or equal       a >= b
```

Here is how we might use the equality operator to test the user's response:

```
bool usr_more = true;
char usr_rsp;

// ask the user if she wishes to continue
// read the response into usr_rsp
if ( usr_rsp == 'N' )
    usr_more = false;
```

The `if` statement conditionally executes the statement following it if the expression within parentheses evaluates to true. In this example, `usr_more` is set to `false` if `usr_rsp` is equal to `'N'`. If `usr_rsp` is not equal to `'N'`, nothing is done. The reverse logic using the inequality operator looks like this:

```
if ( usr_rsp != 'Y' )
    usr_more = false;
```

The problem with testing `usr_rsp` only for `'N'` is that the user might enter a lower-case `'n'`. We must recognize both. One strategy is to add an `else` clause:

```
if ( usr_rsp == 'N' )
    usr_more = false;
else
if ( usr_rsp == 'n' )
    usr_more = false;
```

If `usr_rsp` is equal to `'N'`, `usr_more` is set to `false` and nothing more is done. If it is not equal to `'N'`, the `else` clause is evaluated. If `usr_rsp` is equal to `'n'`, `usr_more` is set to `false`. If `usr_rsp` is not equal to either, `usr_more` is not assigned.

A common beginner programmer error is to use the assignment operator for the equality test, as in the following:

```
// oops this assigns usr_rsp the literal character 'N'
// and therefore always evaluates as true
if ( usr_rsp = 'N' )
    // ...
```

The logical OR operator (`||`) provides an alternative way of testing the truth condition of multiple expressions:

```
if ( usr_rsp == 'N' || usr_rsp == 'n' )
    usr_more = false;
```

The logical OR operator evaluates as true if either of its expressions evaluates as true. The leftmost expression is evaluated first. If it is true, the remaining expression is not evaluated. In our example, `usr_rsp` is tested for equality with `'n'` only if it is not equal to `'N'`.

The logical AND operator (`&&`) evaluates as true only if both its expressions evaluate as true. For example,

```
if ( password &&
    validate( password ) &&
    ( acct = retrieve_acct_info(password) ))
        // process account ...
```

The topmost expression is evaluated first. If it evaluates as false, the AND operator evaluates as false; the remaining expressions are not evaluated. In this example, the account information is retrieved only if the password is set and is determined to be valid.

The logical NOT operator (`!`) evaluates as true if the expression it is applied to is false. For example, rather than write

```
if ( usr_more == false )
    cout << "Your score for this session is "
         << usr_score << " Bye!\n";
```

we can write

```
if ( ! usr_more ) ...
```

Operator Precedence

There is one "gotcha" to the use of the built-in operators: When multiple operators are combined in a single expression, the order of expression evaluation is determined by a predefined precedence level for each operator. For example, the result of 5+2*10 is always 25 and never 70 because the multiplication operator has a higher precedence level than that of addition; as a result, 2 is always multiplied by 10 before the addition of 5.

We can override the built-in precedence level by placing parentheses around the operators we wish to be evaluated first. (5+2)*10, for example, evaluates to 70.

For the operators I've introduced, the precedence order is listed next. An operator has a higher precedence than an operator under it. Operators on the same line have equal precedence. In these cases, the order of evaluation is left to right.

```
logical NOT
arithmetic ( *, /, % )
arithmetic ( +, - )
relational ( <, >, <=, >= )
relational ( ==, != )
logical AND
logical OR
assignment
```

For example, to determine whether ival is an even number, we might write

```
! ival % 2 // not quite right
```

Our intention is to test the result of the remainder operator. If ival is even, the result is zero and the logical NOT operator evaluates to true; otherwise, the result is nonzero, and the logical NOT operator evaluates to false. Or at least that is our intention.

Unfortunately, the result of our expression is quite different. Our expression always evaluates to false except when ival is 0!

The higher precedence of the logical NOT operator causes it to be evaluated first. It is applied to ival. If ival is nonzero, the result is false; otherwise, the result is true. The result value then becomes the left operand of the remainder operator. false is made into 0 when used in an arithmetic expression; true is made into 1. Under default precedence, the expression becomes 0%2 for all values of ival except 0.

Although this is not what we intended, it is also not an error, or at least not a language error. It is an incorrect representation only of our intended program logic. And the compiler cannot know that. Precedence is one of the things that makes C++ programming complicated. To correctly evaluate this expression, we must make the evaluation order explicit using parentheses:

```
! ( ival % 2 ) // ok
```

To avoid this problem, you must hunker down and become familiar with C++ operator precedence. I'm not helping you in the sense that this section does not present either the full set of operators or a full treatment of precedence. This should be enough, though, to get you started. For the complete presentation, check out either Chapter 4 of [LIPPMAN98] or Chapter 6 of [STROUSTRUP97].

1.4   Writing Conditional and Loop Statements

By default, statements are executed once in sequence, beginning with the first statement of main(). In the preceding section, we had a peek at the if statement. The if statement allows us to execute conditionally one or a sequence of statements based on the truth evaluation of an expression. An optional else clause allows us to test multiple truth conditions. A looping statement allows us to repeat one or a sequence of statements based on the truth evaluation of an expression. The following pseudo-code program makes use of two looping statements (#1 and #2), one if statement (#5), one if-else statement (#3), and a second conditional statement called a switch statement (#4).

```
// Pseudo code: General logic of our program
while the user wants to guess a sequence
{ #1
    display the sequence
    while the guess is not correct and
        the user wants to guess again
    { #2
        read guess
        increment number-of-tries count
        if the guess is correct
        { #3
            increment correct-guess count
            set got_it to true
        } else {
            express regret that the user has guessed wrong
                generate a different response based on the
                current number of guesses by the user // #4
            ask the user if she wants to guess again
            read response
            if user says no // #5
                set go_for_it to false
        }
    }
}
```

Conditional Statements

The condition expression of the if statement must be within parentheses. If it is true, the statement immediately following the if statement is executed:

```
// #5
if ( usr_rsp == 'N' || usr_rsp == 'n' )
    go_for_it = false;
```

If multiple statements must be executed, they must be enclosed in curly braces following the if statement (this is called a *statement block*):

```
//#3
if ( usr_guess == next_elem )
{ // begins statement block
    num_right++;
    got_it = true;
} // ends statement block
```

A common beginner mistake is to forget the statement block:

```
// oops: the statement block is missing
// only num_cor++ is part of if statement
// got_it = true; is executed unconditionally

if ( usr_guess == next_elem )
    num_cor++;
    got_it = true;
```

The indentation of got_it reflects the programmer's intention. Unfortunately, it does not reflect the program's behavior. The increment of num_cor is associated with the if statement and is executed only when the user's guess is equal to the value of next_elem. got_it, however, is not associated with the if statement because we forgot to surround the two statements within a statement block. got_it is always set to true in this example regardless of what the user guesses.

The if statement also supports an else clause. An else clause represents one or a block of statements to be executed if the tested condition is false. For example,

```
if ( usr_guess == next_elem )
{
    // user guessed correctly
}
else
{
    // user guessed incorrectly
}
```

A second use of the else clause is to string together two or more if statements. For example, if the user guesses incorrectly, we want our response to differ based on the number of guesses. We could write the three tests as independent if statements:

```
if ( num_tries == 1 )
    cout << "Oops! Nice guess but not quite it.\n";

if ( num_tries == 2 )
    cout << "Hmm. Sorry. Wrong a second time.\n";

if ( num_tries == 3 )
    cout << "Ah, this is harder than it looks, isn't it?\n";
```

However, only one of the three conditions can be true at any one time. If one of the if statements is true, the others must be false. We can reflect the relationship among the if statements by stringing them together with a series of else-if clauses:

```
if ( num_tries == 1 )
    cout << "Oops! Nice guess but not quite it.\n";
else
if ( num_tries == 2 )
    cout << "Hmm. Sorry. Wrong again.\n";
else
if ( num_tries == 3 )
    cout << "Ah, this is harder than it looks, isn't it?\n";
else
    cout << "It must be getting pretty frustrating by now!\n";
```

The first if statement's condition is evaluated. If it is true, the statement following it is executed and the subsequent else-if clauses are not evaluated. If the first if statement's condition evaluates to false, the next one is evaluated, and so on, until one of the conditions evaluates to true, or, if num_tries is greater than 3, all the conditions are false and the final else clause is executed.

One confusing aspect of nested if-else clauses is the difficulty of organizing their logic correctly. For example, we'd like to use our if-else statement to divide the program logic into two cases: when the user guesses correctly and when the user guesses incorrectly. This first attempt doesn't work quite as we intended:

```
if ( usr_guess == next_elem )
{
    // user guessed correctly
}
else
if ( num_tries == 1 )
    // ... output response
else
if ( num_tries == 2 )
    // ... output response
else
if ( num_tries == 3 )
    // ... output response
else
    // ... output response
```

```
// now ask user if she wants to guess again
// but only if she has guessed wrong
// oops! where can we place it?
```

Each else-if clause has unintentionally been made an alternative to guessing the value correctly. As a result, we have no place to put the second part of our code to handle the user having guessed incorrectly. Here is the correct organization:

```
if ( usr_guess == next_elem )
{
    // user guessed correctly
}
else
{   // user guessed incorrectly
    if ( num_tries == 1 )
        // ...
    else
    if ( num_tries == 2 )
        // ...
    else
    if ( num_tries == 3 )
        // ...
    else // ...

    cout << "Want to try again? (Y/N) ";
    char usr_rsp;
    cin >> usr_rsp;

    if ( usr_rsp == 'N' || usr_rsp == 'n' )
        go_for_it = false;
}
```

If the value of the condition being tested is an integral type, we can replace the if-else-if set of clauses with a switch statement:

```
// equivalent to if-else-if clauses above
switch ( num_tries )
{
  case 1:
      cout << "Oops! Nice guess but not quite it.\n";
      break;

  case 2:
      cout << "Hmm. Sorry. Wrong again.\n";
      break;

  case 3:
      cout << "Ah, this is harder than it looks, isn't it?\n";
      break;
```

```
default:
    cout << "It must be getting pretty frustrating by now!\n";
    break;
}
```

The `switch` keyword is followed by an expression enclosed in parentheses (yes, the name of an object serves as an expression). The expression must evaluate to an integral value. A series of `case` labels follows the `switch` keyword, each specifying a constant expression. The result of the expression is compared against each `case` label in turn. If there is a match, the statements following the `case` label are executed. If there is no match and the `default` label is present, the statements following the `default` label are executed. If there is no match and no `default` label, nothing happens.

Why did I place a `break` statement at the end of each `case` label? Each case label is tested in turn against the expression's value. Each nonmatching `case` label is skipped in turn. When a `case` label matches the value, execution begins with the statement following the `case` label. The "gotcha" is that execution continues through each subsequent `case` statement until the end of the `switch` statement. If `num_tries` equals 2, for example, and if there was no `break` statement, the output would look like this:

```
// output if num_tries == 2 and
//    we had forgotten the break statements
Hmm. Sorry. Wrong again.
Ah, this is harder than it looks, isn't it?
It must be getting pretty frustrating by now!
```

IAfter a `case` label is matched, all the `case` labels following the matched `case` label are also executed unless we explicitly break off execution. This is what the `break` statement does. Why, you're probably asking, is the `switch` statement designed this way? Here is an example of this fall-through behavior being just right:

```
switch ( next_char )
{
  case 'a': case 'A':
  case 'e': case 'E':
  case 'i': case 'I':
  case 'o': case 'O':
  case 'u': case 'U':
      ++vowel_cnt;
      break;
  // ...
}
```

Loop Statements

A loop statement executes a statement or statement block as long as the condition expression evaluates as true. Our program requires two loop statements, one nested within the other:

```
while the user wants to guess a sequence
{
     display the sequence
     while the guess is not correct and
          the user wants to guess again
}
```

The C++ while loop maps nicely to our needs:

```
bool next_seq = true;     // show next sequence?
bool go_for_it = true;    // user wants to guess?
bool got_it = false;      // user guessed correctly?
int  num_tries = 0;       // number of user guesses
int  num_right = 0;       // number of correct answers

while ( next_seq == true )
{
        // display sequence to user
        while (( got_it == false ) &&
              ( go_for_it == true ))
        {
              int usr_guess;
              cin >> usr_guess;
              num_tries++;

              if ( usr_guess == next_elem )
              {
                   got_it = true;
                   num_cor++;
              }
              else
              {  // user guessed incorrectly
                 // tell user answer is wrong
                 // ask user if she wants to try again
                 if ( usr_rsp == 'N' || usr_rsp == 'n' )
                      go_for_it = false;
              }
        } // end of nested while loop

        cout << "Want to try another sequence? (Y/N) "
        char try_again;
        cin >> try-again;

        if ( try_again == 'N' || try_again == 'n' )
             next_seq = false;

} // end of while( next_seq == true )
```

A while loop begins by evaluating the conditional expression within parentheses. If it is true, the statement or statement block following the while loop is executed. After the statement is executed, the expression is reevaluated. This evaluation/execution cycle continues until the expression evaluates to false. Typically, some condition within the executing statement block sets the expression to false. If the expression never evaluates to false, we say that we have mistakenly fallen into an *infinite loop.*

Our outer `while` loop executes until the user says she wishes to stop:

```
bool next_seq = true;
while ( next_seq == true )
{
        // ...
        if ( try_again == 'N' || try_again == 'n' )
            next_seq = false;
}
```

Were `next_seq` initialized to false, the statement block would not be executed. The nested `while` loop allowing our user multiple guesses behaves similarly.

A loop can be terminated within the body of its code sequence by the execution of a `break` statement. In the following code fragment, for example, the `while` loop executes until `tries_cnt` equals `max_tries`. If the user guesses the correct answer, however, the loop is terminated using the `break` statement:

```
int max_tries = 3;
int tries_cnt = 0;
while ( tries_cnt < max_tries )
{
    // read user guess
    if ( usr_guess == next_elem )
        break;   // terminate loop

    tries_cnt++;
    // more stuff
}
```

The program can short-circuit execution of the current iteration of the loop by executing a `continue` statement. For example, consider the following program fragment in which all words of fewer than four characters are discarded:

```
string word;
const int min_size = 4;
while ( cin >> word )
{
    if ( word.size() < min_size )
        // terminates this iteration
        continue;

    // reach here only if the word is
    // greater than or equal min-size ...
    process_text( word );
}
```

If word is less than min_size, the continue statement is executed. The continue statement causes the current loop iteration to terminate: The remainder of the while loop
body — in this case, process_text() — is not evaluated. Rather, the loop begins again
with a new evaluation of the condition expression, which reads another string into
word. If word is greater than or equal to min_size, the entire while loop body is evaluated. In this way, all words of fewer than four characters are discarded.

1.5   How to Use Arrays and Vectors

Following are the first eight elements from six numerical sequences:

```
Fibonacci:  1, 1, 2, 3, 5, 8, 13, 21
Lucas:      1, 3, 4, 7, 11, 18, 29, 47
Pell:       1, 2, 5, 12, 29, 70, 169, 408
Triangular: 1, 3, 6, 10, 15, 21, 28, 36
Square:     1, 4, 9, 16, 25, 36, 49, 64
Pentagonal: 1, 5, 12, 22, 35, 51, 70, 92
```

Our program must display a pair of elements from a sequence and allow the user
to guess the next element. If the user guesses right and wishes to continue, the program
then displays a second pair of elements, then a third, and so on. How might we do
that?

If succeeding element pairs are taken from the same sequence, the user, recogniz-
ing one pair, recognizes them all. That is not very interesting. So we'll pick an element
pair from a different numeric sequence with each iteration of the main program loop.

For now, we'll display a maximum of six element pairs per session: one pair from
each of the six sequences. We'd like to implement this so that we can loop through the
display of the element pairs without having to know which sequence we are displaying with each loop iteration. Each iteration must have access to three values: the element pair and the element that follows them in the sequence.

The solution we discuss in this section uses a container type that can hold a contiguous sequence of integer values that we can reference not by name but by position
within the container. We store 18 values in the container as a collection of six tuples:
The first two represent the element pair to display; the third represents the next sequence element. With each iteration of the loop, we add 3 to the index value, in this
way stepping through the six tuples in turn.

In C++, we can define a container as either a built-in array or an object of the standard library vector class. In general, I recommend the use of the vector class over that
of the built-in array. However, a great deal of existing code uses the built-in array, and
it is important to understand how to use both representations.

To define a built-in array, we must specify the type of element the array is to hold,
give the array a name, and specify a dimension — that is, the number of elements the

array can hold. The dimension must be a constant expression — that is, an expression that does not require run-time evaluation. For example, the following code declares pell_seq to be an array of 18 integer elements.

```
const int seq_size = 18;
int pell_seq[ seq_size ];
```

To define a vector class object, we must first include the vector header file. The vector class is a template, so we indicate the type of its element in brackets following the name of the class. The dimension is placed in parentheses; it does not need to be a constant expression. The following code defines pell_seq as a vector class object holding 18 elements of type int. By default, each element is initialized to 0.

```
#include <vector>
vector<int> pell_seq( seq_size );
```

We access an element of either an array or a vector by specifying its position within the container. This element *indexing* uses the subscript operator ([]). One potential "gotcha" is that the first element begins at position 0 and not 1. The last element is indexed at 1 less than the size of the container. For pell_seq, the correct indexes are 0 through 17, not 1 through 18. (Getting this wrong is common enough that it has its own name: the infamous *off-by-one* error.) For example, to assign the first two elements of the Pell sequence, we write

```
pell_seq[ 0 ] = 1; // assign 1 to first element
pell_seq[ 1 ] = 2; // assign 2 to second element
```

Let's calculate the next ten elements of the Pell sequence. To *iterate over* the elements of a vector or an array, we typically use a for loop, the other primary C++ loop statement. For example,

```
for ( int ix = 2; ix < seq_size; ++ix )
    pell_seq[ ix ] = pell_seq[ ix-2 ] + 2*pell_seq[ ix-1 ];
```

The for loop consists of the following elements:

```
for ( init-statement; condition; expression )
    statement
```

The init-statement is executed once before the loop is executed. In our example, ix is initialized to 2 before the loop begins executing.

condition serves as the loop control. It is evaluated before each iteration of the loop. For as many iterations as condition evaluates as true, statement is executed. statement can be either a single statement or a statement block. If the first evaluation of condition evaluates to false, statement is never executed. In our example, condition tests whether ix is less than seq_size.

expression is evaluated after each iteration of the loop. It is typically used to modify the objects initialized within init-statement and tested in condition. If the first evaluation of condition evaluates to false, expression is never executed. In our example, ix is incremented following each iteration of the loop.

To print the elements, we iterate over the entire collection:

```cpp
cout << "The first " << seq_size
     << " elements of the Pell Series:\n\t";

for ( int ix = 0; ix < seq_size; ++ix )
     cout << pell_seq[ ix ] << ' ';

cout << '\n';
```

If we choose, we can leave out the init-statement, expression, or, less frequently, the condition portion of the for loop. For example, we could rewrite the preceding for loop as

```cpp
int ix = 0;
// ...

for ( ; ix < seq_size; ++ix )
     // ...
```

The semicolon is necessary to indicate the empty init-statement.

Our container holds the second, third, and fourth elements of each of our six sequences. How can we fill the container with the appropriate values? A built-in array can specify an initialization list, providing a comma-separated list of values for all or a subset of its elements:

```cpp
int elem_seq[ seq_size ] = {
    1, 2, 3,   // Fibonacci
    3, 4, 7,   // Lucas
    2, 5, 12, // Pell
    3, 6, 10, //Triangular
    4, 9, 16, // Square
    5, 12, 22 // Pentagonal
};
```

The number of values provided for the initialization list must not exceed the array dimension. If we provide fewer initial values than the dimension, the remaining elements are initialized to 0. If we wish, we can let the compiler calculate the array size based on the number of initial values we provide:

```cpp
// compiler computes a size of 18 elements
int elem_seq[] = {
    1, 2, 3,   3, 4, 7,   2, 5,   12,
    3, 6, 10, 4, 9, 16, 5, 12, 22
};
```

The vector class does not support an explicit initialization list. A somewhat tedious solution is to assign each element explicitly:

```
vector<int> elem_seq( seq_size );
elem_seq[ 0 ] =1;
elem_seq[ 1 ] =2;
// ...
elem_seq[ 17 ] =22;
```

One alternative is to initialize a built-in array and use that to initialize the vector:

```
int elem_vals[ seq_size ] = {
    1, 2, 3,  3, 4, 7,  2, 5,  12,
    3, 6, 10, 4, 9, 16, 5, 12, 22 };

// initialize elem_seq with values of elem_vals
vector<int> elem_seq( elem_vals, elem_vals+seq_size );
```

elem_seq is passed two values. These values are actually addresses. They mark the range of elements with which to initialize the vector. In this case, we have marked the 18 elements contained within elem_vals to be copied into elem_seq. In Chapter 3, we look at the actual details of how this works.

For now, let's see how we can use elem_seq. One difference between the built-in array and a vector class is that a vector knows its size. Our earlier for loop iterating across the built-in array looks slightly different when applied to the vector:

```
// elem_seq.size() returns the number of elements
//        contained within the vector elem_seq
cout << "The first " << elem_seq.size()
     << " elements of the Pell Series:\n\t";

for ( int ix = 0; ix < elem_seq.size(); ++ix )
    cout << pell_seq[ ix ] << ' ';
```

cur_tuple represents our index into the current sequence to display. We initialize it to 0. With each loop iteration we add 3 to cur_tuple, setting it to index the first element of the next sequence to display.

```
int cur_tuple = 0;

while ( next_seq == true &&
        cur_tuple < seq_size )
{
        cout << "The first two elements of the sequence are: "
             << elem_seq[ cur_tuple ] << ", "
             << elem_seq[ cur_tuple+1 ]
             << "\nWhat is the next element? ";

        // ...
        if ( usr_guess == elem_seq[ cur_tuple+2 ] )
            // correct!

        // ...
```

```
            if ( usr_rsp == 'N' || usr_rsp == 'n' )
                next_seq = false;
            else cur_tuple += 3;
    }
```

It would also be useful to keep track of which sequence is currently active. Let's store the name of each sequence as a string:

```
const int max_seq = 6;
string seq_names[ max_seq ] = {
    "Fibonacci",
    "Lucas",
    "Pell",
    "Triangular",
    "Square",
    "Pentagonal"
};
```

We can use seq_names as follows:

```
if ( usr_guess == elem_seq[ cur_tuple+2 ] )
{
    ++num_cor;
    cout << "Very good. Yes, "
        << elem_seq[ cur_tuple+2 ]
        << " is the next element in the "
        << seq_names[ cur_tuple/3 ] << "sequence.\n";
}
```

The expression cur_tuple/3 yields, in turn, 0, 1, 2, 3, 4, and 5, providing the index into the array of string elements that identify the active sequence.

1.6   Pointers Allow for Flexibility

Our display solution in the preceding section has two primary drawbacks. First, it has a fixed upper limit of six sequences; if the user should guess all six sequences, the program unexpectedly terminates. Second, it always displays the same six element pairs in the same order. How might we extend our program's flexibility?

One possible solution is to maintain six vectors, one for each sequence, calculated to some number of elements. With each iteration of the loop, we draw our element pair from a different vector. When using a vector a second time, we draw our element pair from a different index within the vector. This approach resolves both drawbacks.

As with our earlier solution, we'd like to access the different vectors transparently. In the preceding section, we achieve transparency by accessing each element by index rather than by name. With each loop iteration, we increment the index value by 3. Otherwise, the code remains invariant.

In this section, we achieve transparency by accessing each vector indirectly by a pointer rather than by name. A *pointer* introduces a level of indirection to a program. Rather than manipulate an object directly, we manipulate a pointer that holds the address of an object. In our program, we define a pointer that can address a vector of integers. With each loop iteration, we modify the pointer to address a different vector. The actual code that manipulates the pointer does not change.

The use of a pointer does two things to our program. It increases the program's flexibility and adds a level of complexity absent in direct object manipulation. This section should convince you of the truth of both statements.

We already know how to define an object. The following statement, for example, defines ival as an object of type int initialized to a value of 1,024:

```
int ival = 1024;
```

A pointer holds the address of an object of a particular type. To define a pointer of a particular type, we follow the type name with an asterisk:

```
int *pi; // pi is a pointer to an object of type int
```

pi is a pointer to an object of type int. How do we initialize it to point to ival? The evaluation of an object's name, such as

```
ival; // evaluates to the value of ival
```

evaluates to its associated value — 1,024 in this case. To retrieve the address of the object rather than its value, we apply the address-of operator (&):

```
&ival; // evaluates to the address of ival
```

To initialize pi to ival's address, we write the following:

```
int *pi = &ival;
```

To access the object addressed by a pointer, we must *dereference* the pointer — that is, retrieve the object sitting at the address held by the pointer. To do that, we apply an asterisk to the pointer as follows:

```
// dereference pi to access the object it addresses
if ( *pi != 1024 )   // read
     *pi = 1024;      // write
```

The initial complexity of using a pointer, as you can see, comes from its confusing syntax. The complexity in this case stems from the dual nature of a pointer: Either we can manipulate the address contained by the pointer, or we can manipulate the object to which the pointer points. When we write

```
pi; // evaluates to the address held by pi
```

we are, in effect, manipulating the pointer object. When we write

```
*pi; // evaluates to the value of the object addressed by pi
```

we are manipulating the object pi addresses.

A second complexity introduced by a pointer is the possibility that it addresses no object. For example, when we write *pi, this may or may not cause our program to fail at run-time! If pi addresses an object, our dereference of pi works exactly right. If pi addresses no object, however, our attempt to dereference pi results in undefined run-time behavior. This means that when we use a pointer, we must be sure that it addresses an object before we attempt to dereference it. How do we do that?

A pointer that addresses no object has an address value of 0 (it is sometimes called a *null* pointer). Any pointer type can be initialized or assigned a value of 0.

```
// initialize each pointer to address no object

int *pi = 0;
double *pd = 0;
string *ps = 0;
```

To guard against dereferencing a null pointer, we test a pointer to see whether its address value is zero. For example,

```
if ( pi && *pi != 1024 )
    *pi = 1024;
```

The expression

```
if ( pi && ... )
```

evaluates to true only if pi contains an address other than 0. If it is false, the AND operator does not evaluate its second expression. To test whether a pointer is null, we typically use the logical NOT operator:

```
if ( ! pi ) // true if pi is set to 0
```

Here are our six vector sequence objects:

```
vector<int> fibonacci, lucas, pell, triangular, square, pentagonal;
```

What does a pointer to a vector of integer objects look like? Well, in general, a pointer has this form:

```
type_of_object_pointed_to * name_of_pointer_object
```

Our pointer addresses the type vector<int>. Let's name it pv and initialize it to 0:

```
vector<int> *pv = 0;
```

pv can address each of the sequence vectors in turn. Of course, we can assign pv the address of an explicit sequence:

```
pv = &fibonacci;
// ...
pv = &lucas;
```

But doing the assignment this way sacrifices code transparency. An alternative solution is to store the address of each sequence within a vector. This technique allows us to access them transparently through an index:

```
const int seq_cnt = 6;

// an array of seq_cnt pointers to
//    objects of type vector<int>
vector<int> *seq_addrs[ seq_cnt ] = {
    &fibonacci,  &lucas, &pell,
    &triangular, &square, &pentagonal
};
```

seq_addrs is a built-in array of elements of type vector<int>*. seq_addrs[0] holds
the address of the fibonacci vector, seq_addrs[1] holds the address of the lucas vector, and so on. We use this to access the individual vectors through an index rather
than by name:

```
vector<int> *current_vec = 0;
// ...

for ( int ix = 0; ix < seq_cnt; ++ix )
{
    current_vec = seq_addrs[ ix ];
    // all element display is implemented
    // indirectly through current_vec
}
```

The remaining problem with this implementation is that it is totally predictable.
The sequence is always Fibonacci, Lucas, Pell, and so on. We'd like to randomize the
display order of our sequences. We can do that using the C language standard library
rand() and srand() functions:

```
#include <cstdlib>

srand( seq_cnt );
seq_index = rand() % seq_cnt;
current_vec = seq_addrs[ seq_index ];
```

rand() and srand() are standard library functions that support pseudo-random
number generation. srand() *seeds* the generator with its parameter. Each call of rand()
returns an integer value in a range between 0 and the maximum integer value an int
can represent. We must clamp that value between 0 and 5 to have it be a valid index
into seq_addrs. The remainder (%) operator ensures that our index is between 0 and 5.
The cstdlib header file contains the declaration of both functions.

We handle a pointer to a class object slightly differently than we handle a pointer
to an object of a built-in type. This is because a class object has an associated set of operations that we may wish to invoke. For example, to check whether the first element
of the fibonacci vector is set to 1, we might write

```
if ( ! fibonacci.empty() &&
     ( fibonacci[1] == 1 ))
```

How would we achieve the same tests indirectly through pv? The dot connecting fibonacci and empty() is called a *member selection operator*. It is used to select class operations through an object of the class. To select a class operation through a pointer, we use the arrow member selection operator (->):

```
! pv->empty()
```

Because a pointer can address no object, before we invoke empty() through pv we must first check that pv's address is nonzero:

```
pv && ! pv->empty()
```

Finally, to apply the subscript operator, we must dereference pv. (The additional parentheses around the dereference of pv are necessary because of the higher precedence of the subscript operator.)

```
if ( pv && ! pv->empty() && (( *pv )[1] == 1 ))
```

We look at pointers again in the discussion of the Standard Template Library in Chapter 3, and in Chapter 6, in which we design and implement a binary tree class. For a more in-depth discussion of pointers, refer to Section 3.3 of [LIPPMAN98].

1.7 Writing and Reading Files

If a user should happen to run our program a second time, it would be nice to allow her score to reflect both sessions. To do this, we must (1) write the user's name and session data to a file at the end of the session and (2) read the user's session data back into the program at the start of the next session. Let's see how we might do that.

To read and write to a file, we must include the fstream header file:

```
#include <fstream>
```

To open a file for output, we define an ofstream (an output file stream) class object, passing it the name of the file to open:

```
// seq_data.txt is opened in output mode
ofstream outfile( "seq_data.txt" );
```

What happens when we declare outfile? If it doesn't exist, the file is created and opened for output. If it does exist, it is opened for output and any existing data in the file is discarded.

If we wish to add to rather than replace the data within an existing file, we must open the file in append mode. We do this by providing an ios_base::app second value to the ofstream object. (At this point in this book, it is better that you just use this and not inquire too deeply as to what the heck it actually is!)

```
// seq_data.txt is opened in append mode
// new data is added at the end of the file
ofstream outfile( "seq_data.txt", ios_base::app );
```

A file may fail to open. Before we write to it, we must confirm that it has been opened successfully. The simplest way to check that is to test the truth value of the class object:

```
// if outfile evaluates as false,
// the file could not be opened
if ( ! outfile )
```

If the file could not be opened, the ofstream class object evaluates to false. In this example, we alert the user by writing a message to cerr. cerr represents *standard error*. cerr, like cout, directs its output to the user's terminal. The difference is that cerr's output is not buffered; it displays on the user's terminal immediately.

```
if ( ! outfile )
     // open failed for some reason ...
     cerr << "Oops! Unable to save session data!\n";

else
     // ok: outfile is open, let's write the data
     outfile << usr_name  << ' '
             << num_tries << ' '
             << num_right << endl;
```

If the file is opened successfully, we direct output to it in the same way as we do for the ostream class objects cout and cerr. In this example, we write three values to outfile, the second two separated by a space. endl is a predefined *manipulator* provided by the iostream library.

A manipulator performs some operation on the iostream rather than write or read data. endl inserts a newline character and then flushes the output buffer. Other predefined manipulators include hex, which displays an integer value in hexidecimal notation; oct, which displays an integer value in octal notation; and setprecision(n), which sets the display of floating point precision to n. (For a full list of the predefined iostream manipulators, refer to Section 20.9 of [LIPPMAN98].)

To open a file for input, we define an ifstream class object (an input file stream), passing it the name of a file. If the file cannot be opened, the ifstream class object tests as false. Otherwise, the file is positioned at the beginning of the data stored in the file.

```
// infile opened in output mode
ifstream infile( "seq_data.txt" );

int num_tries = 0;
int num_cor = 0;

if ( ! infile )
{
     // open failed for some reason ...
     // we'll presume it is a new user ...
}
```

```
    else
    {
        // ok: read each line of the input file
        //      see if user has played before ...
        // format of each line:
        //      name num_tries num_correct
        // nt: number of tries
        // nc: number of correct guesses

        string name;
        int nt;
        int nc;

        while ( infile >> name )
        {
            infile >> nt >> nc;
            if ( name == usr_name )
            {
                // match!
                cout << "Welcome back, " << usr_name
                     << "\nYour current score is " << nc
                     << " out of " << nt << "\nGood Luck!\n";

                num_tries = nt;
                num_cor = nc;
            }
        }
    }
}
```

Each iteration of the while loop reads the next line of the file until the end-of-file is reached. When we write

```
    infile >> name
```

the return value of the input statement is the class object from which we are reading — infile in this case. When the end-of-file is reached, the truth condition of the class object evaluates to false. This is why the conditional expression of the while loop terminates when end-of-file is reached:

```
    while ( infile >> name )
```

Each line of the file contains a string followed by two integers, of the form

```
    anna 24 19
    danny 16 12
    . . .
```

The line

```
    infile >> nt >> nc;
```

reads in turn the number of user guesses into nt and the number of correct guesses into nc.

If we wish to both read from and write to the same file, we define an fstream class object. To open it in append mode, we must provide a second value of the form `ios_base::in|ios_base::app`:[2]

```
fstream iofile( "seq_data.txt",
                ios_base::in|ios_base::app );

if ( ! iofile )
    // open failed for some reason ... darn!
else
{
    // reposition to front of file to begin reading
    iofile.seekg( 0 );

    // ok: everything else is the same ...
}
```

When we open a file in append mode, the current position of the file is at the end. If we try to read the file without repositioning it, we simply encounter the end-of-file. The `seekg()` operation repositions `iofile` to the beginning of the file. Because it is opened in append mode, any write operation adds the data to the end of the file.

The iostream library is rich in functionality, many of the details of which I haven't the space to cover here. For a detailed discussion of the iostream library, see Chapter 20 of [LIPPMAN98] or Chapter 21 of [STROUSTRUP97].

Exercise 1.5

Write a program to ask the user his or her name. Read the response. Confirm that the input is at least two characters in length. If the name seems valid, respond to the user. Provide two implementations: one using a C-style character string, and the other using a string class object.

Exercise 1.6

Write a program to read in a sequence of integers from standard input. Place the values, in turn, in a built-in array and a vector. Iterate over the containers to sum the values. Display the sum and average of the entered values to standard output.

Exercise 1.7

Using your favorite editor, type two or more lines of text into a file. Write a program to open the file, reading each word into a `vector<string>` object. Iterate over the vector, displaying it to `cout`. That done, sort the words using the `sort()` generic algorithm,

---

[2]   If I chose not to explain the simpler `ios_base::app` earlier, I certainly am not going to explain this guy! See [LIPPMAN98], Section 20.6, for a full explanation and detailed example.

```
#include <algorithm>
sort( container.begin(), container.end() );
```

Then print the sorted words to an output file.

Exercise 1.8

The `switch` statement of Section 1.4 displays a different consolation message based on the number of wrong guesses. Replace this with an array of four string messages that can be indexed based on the number of wrong guesses.

2

Procedural Programming

Writing an entire program in main(), as we did in Chapter 1, is not very practical except for small programs written by a single individual. Typically, we factor common operations, such as calculating the elements of the Fibonacci sequence or generating a random number, into independent functions. This approach has three primary benefits. First, our programs are simpler to understand because they are a sequence of function calls rather than the code sequence to accomplish each operation. Second, we can use the functions across multiple programs. Third, it is easier to distribute the work across multiple programmers or groups within a project.

This chapter covers the basic rules for writing independent functions. It also briefly discusses overloaded and template functions and illustrates the use of pointers to functions.

2.1   How to Write a Function

In this section, we write a function that returns the Fibonacci element at a position specified by the user. For example, if the user asks, "What is the eighth Fibonacci element?" our function answers, "21." How do we go about defining this function?

We must define the following four parts to our function:

1. **The return type of the function**. Our function returns the element value at the user-specified position. Its value is of type int, so our function's return type is also of type int. A function that does not return a value has a return type of void. A function that prints a Fibonacci sequence to the terminal, for example, is likely to declare its return type void.

2. **The name of the function**. foo() is a common name. It is not a good name, however, because it is not helpful in identifying the operation provided by the function. fibon_elem() is a somewhat better name, although no doubt you can think of an even better name.

3. **The parameter list of the function**. The parameters of a function serve as placeholders for values that are later supplied by the user during each invocation of the function. A parameter, that is, represents what varies with each invocation of a function. Our function, for example, defines one parameter: the element's position in the sequence. The user will supply this position each time our function is invoked. A parameter specifies both a type and a name. For our function, we define a single parameter of type int. A function can have an empty parameter list. For example, a function to greet the user and read in the user's name is unlikely to require parameters.

4. **The body of the function**. The body of the function implements the logic of the operation. Typically, it manipulates the named parameters of the function. The function body is enclosed in curly braces and appears after the parameter list.

Before a function can be called within our program, it must be declared. A function declaration allows the compiler to verify the correctness of its use — whether there are enough parameters, whether they are of the correct type, and so on. The function declaration specifies the return type, the name, and the parameter list but not the function body. This is called the *function prototype*.

```
// a declaration of our function
int fibon_elem( int pos );
```

A function definition consists of the function prototype plus the function body. Given an element's position, fibon_elem() must calculate its value. Here is one possible implementation. (The /*,*/ pair is a multiline form of comment. Everything from the /* up to and including the matching */ is treated as a comment.)

```
/* A second form of comment delimiter
 *
 * 1st and 2nd elements of the Fibonacci Sequence
 * are 1; each subsequent element is the sum of
 * the preceding two elements
 *
 * elem: holds value to be returned
 * n_2, n_1: holds preceding values
 * pos: element position user requested
 */

int elem = 1; // holds return value
int n_2 = 1, n_1 = 1;
for ( int ix = 3; ix <= pos; ++ix )
{
      elem = n_2 + n_1;
      n_2 = n_1; n_1 = elem;
}
```

If the user asks for the first or second element, the body of the for loop is never executed. elem is initialized to 1, which is the correct value to return. If the user asks for the third or subsequent position, the loop calculates each value until ix exceeds pos. elem contains the value of the element at pos.

To return a value from a function, we use the return statement. For our function, the return statement looks like this:

```
return elem;
```

If we are willing to trust that our user never makes a mistake and if we are willing to calculate any Fibonacci position, however large, then we are finished. Unfortunately, if we ignore both of these issues, our function is likely to fail at one time or another.

What are the mistakes a user might make? The user might enter an invalid position — perhaps a value of 0 or a negative number. If the user does that, fibon_elem() returns 1, and that is wrong. So we check for that possibility:

```
// check for invalid position
if ( pos <= 0 )
    // ok, now what?
```

What should we do if the user requests an invalid position? The most extreme thing we can do is terminate the program. The standard library exit() function does just that. We pass it a value, and that value becomes the exit status of the program:

```
// terminate program with exit status of -1
if ( pos <= 0 )
    exit( -1 );
```

To use exit(), we must include the cstdlib header file:

```
#include <cstdlib>
```

Having our small function terminate an entire program is probably too severe. One alternative is to throw an exception indicating that fibon_elem() has received an invalid position. Unfortunately, exception handling is not discussed until Chapter 7, so that solution isn't an option just now.

We could return 0 and trust that the user recognizes that zero is an invalid value within the Fibonacci sequence. In general, however, trust is not a sound engineering principle. A more reasonable choice is to change our return value to indicate whether fibon_elem() is able to calculate the value:

```
// revised function prototype
bool fibon_elem( int pos, int &elem );
```

A function can return only one value. In this case, the value returned is either true or false based on whether fibon_elem() can calculate the element's value. That leaves us with the problem of returning the element's actual value. In our revised function prototype, we solve that problem by adding a second parameter of type reference to int. This allows us in effect to have two values returned from the function. I explain the difference in behavior between the parameters pos and elem in the next section. It's a somewhat complicated idea that is best treated in a section of its own.

What happens if the user asks for the element value at position 5,000? That's a large number. When I tried to calculate it, I received the following answer:

```
element # 5000 is -1846256875
```

That's not correct. What happened? I call it the ineluctable modality of the computer. Each arithmetic type can represent only a minimum and a maximum value of all possible domain values.[1] int, for example, is a signed type. The result of fibon_elem() *overflowed* the maximum positive value it can represent. When I changed elem to be of type unsigned int, the answer became

```
element # 5000 is 2448710421
```

What would happen if the user asked for the 10,000th position? The 100,000th? The millionth? There is no end to the Fibonacci sequence. Our implementation, however, must impose an endpoint to the position value we are willing to support. How do we decide on that endpoint? Ultimately, that depends on the requirements of our users. For my purposes here, I've imposed an arbitrary but sufficient upward limit of 1,024 (it allows elem to remain an ordinary int).

Here is the final implementation of fibon_elem():

```cpp
bool fibon_elem( int pos, int &elem )
{
    // check if invalid position ...
    if ( pos <= 0 || pos > 1024 )
        { elem = 0; return false; }

    // elem is 1 for positions 1 and 2
    elem = 1;
    int n_2 = 1, n_1 = 1;

    for ( int ix = 3; ix <= pos; ++ix )
    {
        elem = n_2 + n_1;
        n_2 = n_1; n_1 = elem;
    }

    return true;
}
```

---

[1] To determine the minimum and maximum values for a particular type, we can query the standard library numeric_limits class (for more details, see [STROUSTRUP97]):

```cpp
#include <limits>
int max_int = numeric_limits<int>::max();
double min_dbl = numeric_limits<double>::min();
```

The following small program exercises `fibon_elem()`:

```cpp
#include <iostream>
using namespace std;

// forward declaration of fibon_elem()
// makes function known to compiler ...
bool fibon_elem( int, int& );

int main()
{
    int pos;
    cout << "Please enter a position: ";
    cin >> pos;

    int elem;
    if ( fibon_elem( pos, elem ))
         cout << "element # " << pos
               << " is " << elem << endl;
    else cout << "Sorry. Could not calculate element # "
               << pos << endl;
}
```

In our example, the declaration of `fibon_elem()` does not provide names for its two parameters. This is OK. The name of a parameter is necessary only if we need access to the parameter within the function. Some authors recommend always specifying the parameter names as a form of documentation. In a small program such as this, there seems little real benefit in doing so.

When the program is compiled and executed, the output looks like this (my input is highlighted in bold):

```
Please enter a position: 12
element # 12 is 144
```

A function that declares a non-void return type must return a value at each of its exit points. Each return statement within a function represents an explicit exit point. An implicit exit point follows the last statement within the function body if it is not a return statement. The following definition of `print_sequence()`, for example, fails to compile because its implicit exit point does not return a value.

```cpp
bool print_sequence( int pos )
{
    if ( pos <= 0 || pos > 1024 )
    {
        cerr << "invalid position: " << pos
              << " -- cannot handle request!\n";

        return false;
    }
```

```
cout << "The Fibonacci Sequence for "
     << pos << " positions: \n\t";

// prints 1 1 for all values except pos == 1
switch ( pos )
{
    default:
    case 2:
      cout << "1 ";
      // no break;
    case 1:
      cout << "1 ";
      break;
}

int elem;
int n_2 = 1, n_1 = 1;
for ( int ix = 3; ix <= pos; ++ix )
{
    elem = n_2 + n_1;
    n_2 = n_1; n_1 = elem;

    // print 10 elements to a line
    cout << elem << ( !( ix % 10 ) ? "\n\t" : " " );
}
cout << endl;

// compiler error is generated here:
// implicit exit point ... no return statement!
}
```

print_sequence() contains two exit points, but we have specified only one return statement. An implicit exit point occurs following the last statement. Our implementation returns a value only for an invalid position! Oops. Luckily, the compiler catches this and flags it as an error. We need to add a return true; as the last statement.

To exercise this implementation, I added a call to print_sequence() following the call to fibon_elem() in the earlier main() program. When compiled and executed, our main() program now generates the following output:

```
Please enter a position: 12
element # 12 is 144
The Fibonacci Sequence for 12 positions:
        1 1 2 3 5 8 13 21 34 55
        89 144
```

A second form of the return statement does not return a value. It is used only in functions with a void return type. It is used to terminate a function prematurely.

```
void print_msg( ostream &os, const string &msg )
{
    if ( msg.empty() )
         // nothing to print; terminate function ...
         return;

    os << msg;
}
```

In this example, a final return statement is unnecessary because no value is being returned. The implicit exit point is sufficient.

Exercise 2.1

main(), presented earlier, allows the user to enter only one position value and then terminates. If a user wishes to ask for two or more positions, she must execute the program two or more times. Modify main() to allow the user to keep entering positions until she indicates she wishes to stop.

2.2   Invoking a Function

In this section we implement a function to sort a vector of integer values so that we can explore the behavior of passing parameters both by reference and by value. The sorting algorithm is a simple bubble sort implemented by two nested for loops. The outer for loop walks through the vector elements from ix, which begins at 0 and ends at size-1. The idea is that upon completion of each iteration of the outer loop, the element indexed by ix is in its proper place. When ix is 0, the smallest element is found and placed at position 0, and when ix is 1, the second smallest element is in place, and so on. The placement is executed by the inner for loop. jx begins at ix+1 and ends at size-1. It compares the element value at ix with the element value at jx. If the element value at jx is smaller, the two element values are swapped. Our first implementation fails. The purpose of this section is to explain why. Here we go.

```
void display( vector<int> vec )
{
    for ( int ix = 0; ix < vec.size(); ++ix )
         cout << vec[ix] << ' ';
    cout << endl;
}

void swap( int val1, int val2 )
{
    int temp = val1;
    val1 = val2;
    val2 = temp;
}
```

```
void bubble_sort( vector<int> vec )
{
    for ( int ix = 0; ix < vec.size(); ++ix )
        for ( int jx = ix+1; jx < vec.size(); ++jx )
            if ( vec[ ix ] > vec[ jx ] )
                swap( vec[ix], vec[jx] );
}

int main()
{
    int ia[ 8 ] = { 8, 34, 3, 13, 1, 21, 5, 2 };
    vector<int> vec( ia, ia+8 );

    cout << "vector before sort: ";
    display( vec );

    bubble_sort( vec );

    cout << "vector after sort:  ";
    display( vec );
}
```

When this program is compiled and executed, the following output is generated, showing that the vector defined within `main()` is not sorted:

```
vector before sort: 8 34 3 13 1 21 5 2
vector after sort:  8 34 3 13 1 21 5 2
```

It's not unusual to have a program not work the first time we run it. The question is, what do we do now?

If we have a debugger available, a good next step is to step through the program's execution, examining the run-time values of the various objects in our program and watching the actual control flow of the `for` loops and `if` statement. A more practical approach in the context of this text is to add print statements to trace the control logic and display the state of the objects. So where do we begin?

The nested `for` loops represent the critical area of our program — in particular, the test of the two elements and call of `swap()`. If the sorting algorithm isn't working, this portion of the program is likely to be failing. I've instrumented it as follows:

```
ofstream ofil( "text_out1" );
void bubble_sort( vector<int> vec )
{
    for ( int ix = 0; ix < vec.size(); ++ix )
        for ( int jx = ix+1; jx < vec.size(); ++jx )
            if ( vec[ ix ] > vec[ jx ] ){
                // debugging output
                ofil << "about to call swap!"
                    << " ix: " << ix << " jx: " << jx << '\t'
```

```
                          << " swapping: " << vec[ix]
                          << " with " << vec[ jx ] << endl;

                  // ok: actual swap code ...
                  swap( vec[ix], vec[jx] );
              }
      }
```

After we compile and execute the program, the following debugging output is generated. Two things are surprising: swap() is called exactly as it should be, and the vector is nevertheless unchanged from its original order. Who said programming is fun?

```
vector before sort:  8 34 3 13 1 21 5 2
about to call swap! ix: 0 jx: 2 swapping: 8 with 3
about to call swap! ix: 0 jx: 4 swapping: 8 with 1
about to call swap! ix: 0 jx: 6 swapping: 8 with 5
about to call swap! ix: 0 jx: 7 swapping: 8 with 2
about to call swap! ix: 1 jx: 2 swapping: 34 with 3
about to call swap! ix: 1 jx: 3 swapping: 34 with 13
about to call swap! ix: 1 jx: 4 swapping: 34 with 1
about to call swap! ix: 1 jx: 5 swapping: 34 with 21
about to call swap! ix: 1 jx: 6 swapping: 34 with 5
about to call swap! ix: 1 jx: 7 swapping: 34 with 2
about to call swap! ix: 2 jx: 4 swapping: 3 with 1
about to call swap! ix: 2 jx: 7 swapping: 3 with 2
about to call swap! ix: 3 jx: 4 swapping: 13 with 1
about to call swap! ix: 3 jx: 6 swapping: 13 with 5
about to call swap! ix: 3 jx: 7 swapping: 13 with 2
about to call swap! ix: 5 jx: 6 swapping: 21 with 5
about to call swap! ix: 5 jx: 7 swapping: 21 with 2
about to call swap! ix: 6 jx: 7 swapping: 5 with 2
vector after sort:   8 34 3 13 1 21 5 2
```

An examination of swap() should convince us that it is implemented correctly. If we've started to doubt our judgment, however, we can instrument swap() to confirm that it is correctly swapping values:

```
void swap( int val1, int val2 )
{
   ofil << "swap( " << val1
        << ", " << val2 << " )\n";

   int temp = val1;
   val1 = val2;
   val2 = temp;

   ofil << "after swap(): val1 " << val1
        << "  val2: " << val2 << "\n";
}
```

In addition, after calling swap(), I added a call of display() to see the state of the vector. The output shows us that (1) everything is working correctly, and (2) nothing is coming out right:

```
vector before sort: 8 34 3 13 1 21 5 2
about to call swap! ix: 0 jx: 2swapping: 8 with 3
swap( 8, 3 )
after swap(): val1 3  val2: 8
vector after swap(): 8 34 3 13 1 21 5 2
```

The trace output shows that bubble_sort() correctly recognizes that the first and third elements, values 8 and 3, must be swapped. swap() is correctly invoked, and, within swap(), the values are correctly swapped. The vector, however, is not changed.

Unfortunately, this is not something we're just going to figure out on our own. If you're like me, you tend to be dogged about problems, hunkering down and thinking you can bull your way through. Sometimes, what we need more than a stubborn streak is someone to show us the missing bit of the puzzle.

The problem has to do with how we are passing the arguments to swap(). A way to approach this issue is to ask this question: What is the relationship between, on the one hand, the two elements of the vector passed to swap() from within bubble_sort() and, on the other hand, the two parameters manipulated within swap()?

```
void bubble_sort( vector<int> vec )
{
    // ...
    if ( vec[ ix ] > vec[ jx ] )
        swap( vec[ix], vec[jx] );
    // ...
}

void swap( int val1, int val2 )
{
    // what is the relationship between
    // the formal parameters val1, val2
    // and the actual arguments vec[ix] and vec[jx]?
}
```

What is the relationship between vec[ix] and vec[jx], passed to the call of swap(), and the two parameters of swap(), val1 and val2? If both pairs represent the same two objects, then changing val1 and val2 within swap() should change the values within vec[ix] and vec[jx]. But this is not what is happening. It is as if we were manipulating two different pairs of objects that have no relationship to each other except that both pairs hold the same values.

This, in fact, is exactly what is happening. It explains why even though we swap the values, the change is not reflected in the vector. In effect, the objects passed to swap() are copied, and there is no relationship between the two pairs of objects.

When we invoke a function, a special area of memory is set up on what is called the *program stack*. Within this special area of memory there is space to hold the value of each function parameter. (It also holds the memory associated with each object defined within the function — we call these *local* objects.) When the function completes, this area of memory is discarded. (We say that it is *popped* from the program stack.)

By default, when we pass an object to a function, such as vec[ix], its value is copied to the local definition of the parameter. (This is called *pass by value* semantics.) There is no connection between the objects manipulated within swap() and the objects passed to it within bubble_sort(). That is why our program fails.

For our program to work, we must somehow bind the swap() parameters to the actual objects being passed in. (This is called *pass by reference* semantics.) The simplest way of doing this is to declare the parameters as references:

```
/*
 * OK: by declaring val1 and val2 as references
 *       changes to the two parameters within swap()
 *       are reflected in the objects passed to swap()
 */
void swap( int & val1, int & val2 )
{
    /*
     * note that our code within swap()
     * does not change -- only the relationship
     * between the parameters of swap() and the
     * objects passed to swap() changes
     */
    int temp = val1;
    val1 = val2;
    val2 = temp;
}
```

Before I explain references, let's confirm that in fact this small change corrects our program. Here is a partial trace of a recompilation and execution of our program:

```
vector before sort: 8 34 3 13 1 21 5 2
about to call swap! ix: 0 jx: 2 swapping: 8 with 3
3 34 8 13 1 21 5 2
about to call swap! ix: 0 jx: 4 swapping: 3 with 1
1 34 8 13 3 21 5 2
about to call swap! ix: 1 jx: 2 swapping: 34 with 8
1 8 34 13 3 21 5 2
about to call swap! ix: 1 jx: 4 swapping: 8 with 3
// ...
about to call swap! ix: 5 jx: 7 swapping: 21 with 13
1 2 3 5 8 13 34 21
about to call swap! ix: 6 jx: 7 swapping: 34 with 21
1 2 3 5 8 13 21 34
vector after sort:  8 34 3 13 1 21 5 2
```

Oops. Everything is working great now except that the vector within `main()` that we pass to `bubble_sort()` is not being changed. Now that we're experienced, the first thing we look for is a parameter passed by value rather than by reference:

```
void bubble_sort( vector<int> vec ){ /* ... */ }
```

Changing `vec` to be a reference is the final correction to our program:

```
void bubble_sort( vector<int> &vec ){ /* ... */ }
```

To confirm that, let's recompile and execute:

```
vector before sort: 8 34 3 13 1 21 5 2
vector after sort:  1 2 3 5 8 13 21 34
```

Whew! That was hard. A lot of programming is like that. Often, the solution is pretty simple, but only after you understand what the problem is.

Pass by Reference Semantics

A reference serves as an indirect handle to an object. We declare a reference by sandwiching an ampersand (&) between the type's name and the name of the reference:

```
int ival = 1024;  // an object of type int
int *pi  = &ival; // a pointer to an object of type int
int &rval = ival; // a reference to an object of type int
```

When we write

```
int jval = 4096;
rval = ival;
```

we assign `ival`, the object `rval` refers to, the value stored by `jval`. We do not cause `rval` to now refer to `jval`. A reference cannot be reassigned to refer to another object. When we write

```
pi = &rval;
```

we assign `pi` the address of `ival`, the object `rval` refers to. We do not cause `pi` to point to `rval`. All manipulation of a reference acts on the object the reference refers to. This is also true when the reference is a function parameter.

When we assign `val1` with `val2` within `swap()`,

```
void swap( int &val1, int &val2 )
{
    // the actual arguments are modified ...
    int temp = val1;
    val1 = val2;
    val2 = temp;
}
```

we are really assigning `vec[ix]` with `vec[jx]`, which are the two objects `val1` and `val2` refer to in the call of `swap()` within `bubble_sort()`:

```
swap( vec[ix], vec[jx] );
```

Similarly, when val2 is assigned with temp within swap(), we are really assigning vec[jx] with the original value of vec[ix].

When an object is passed to a reference parameter, the object's value is not copied. Rather, the address of the object being passed is copied. Each access of the reference parameter within the function is an indirect manipulation of the object passed in.

One reason to declare a parameter as a reference is to allow us to modify directly the actual object being passed to the function. This is important because, as we've seen, our program otherwise may behave incorrectly.

A second reason to declare a parameter as a reference is to eliminate the overhead of copying a large object. This is a less important reason. Our program is correct; it is simply less efficient.

For example, we currently pass our vector to display() by value. This means that we copy the entire vector object each time we wish to display it. This is not wrong. The output generated is exactly what we want. It is simply faster to pass the address of the vector. Again, one way to do that is to declare the vector parameter to be a reference:

```
void display( const vector<int> &vec )
{
    for ( int ix = 0; ix < vec.size(); ++ix )
        cout << vec[ix] << ' ';
    cout << endl;
}
```

We declare it to be a reference to const vector because we do not modify it within the body of the function. It is not an error to omit the const. Having the const there informs readers of the program that we are passing the vector by reference to prevent copying it rather than to modify it within the function.

If we wish, we can pass our vector as a pointer parameter. The effect is the same: We pass the address of the object into the function rather than make a copy of the entire object. One difference, of course, is the syntax between a reference and a pointer. For example,

```
void display( const vector<int> *vec )
{
    if ( ! vec ){
        cout << "display(): the vector pointer is 0\n";
        return;
    }
    for ( int ix = 0; ix < vec->size(); ++ix )
        cout << (*vec)[ix] << ' ';
    cout << endl;
}

int main()
{
    int ia[ 8 ] = { 8, 34, 3, 13, 1, 21, 5, 2 };
```

```
vector<int> vec( ia, ia+8 );

cout << "vector before sort: ";
display( &vec ); // pass the address now

// ...
}
```

A more important difference between a pointer and a reference parameter is that a pointer may or may not actually address an object. Before we dereference a pointer, we must always make sure that it is not set to 0. A reference, however, always refers to some object, so the check for 0 is unnecessary.

In general, unless you wish to modify the parameter within the function, as we did with fibon_elem() in the preceding section,

```
bool fibon_elem( int pos, int &elem );
```

I recommend *not* passing built-in types by reference. The reference mechanism is primarily intended to support the passing of class objects as parameters to functions.

Scope and Extent
Objects defined within a function, with the requisite one exception, exist only while the function is executing. Returning the address of one of these *local* objects results in serious run-time program errors. Recall that a function is temporarily placed on the program stack in a special area of memory for the extent of its execution. Local objects are stored in this area of memory. When the function completes, this area of memory is discarded. The local objects no longer exist. Addressing a nonexisting object in general is a bad programming idiom. For example, fibon_seq() returns a vector of Fibonacci elements of some user-specified size:

```
vector<int> fibon_seq( int size )
{
    if ( size <= 0 || size > 1024 )
    {
        cerr << "Warning: fibon_seq(): "
             << size << " not supported -- resetting to 8\n";

        size = 8;
    }

    vector<int> elems( size );
    for ( int ix = 0; ix < size; ++ix )
        if ( ix == 0 || ix == 1 )
            elems[ ix ] =  1;
        else elems[ ix ] =  elems[ix-1] + elems[ix-2];

    return elems;
}
```

It would be incorrect to return `elems` by either reference or pointer because `elems` ceases to exist with the completion of `fibon_seq()`. Returning `elems` by value is OK: The copy of the object returned exists outside the function.[2]

The period of time for which memory is allocated for an object is called its *storage duration* or *extent*. The memory for `elems` is allocated each time `fibon_seq()` is executed. It is deallocated each time `fibon_seq()` terminates. We say that it has *local extent*. (Function parameters, such as `size`, also have local extent.)

The region of the program over which an object is active is called its *scope*. We say that `size` and `elems` have *local scope* within the function `fibon_seq()`. The name of an object that has local scope is not visible outside its local scope.

An object declared outside a function has *file scope*. An object that has file scope is visible from the point of its declaration to the end of the file within which it is named. An object at file scope has *static extent*. This means that its memory is allocated before the beginning of `main()` and remains allocated until the program is terminated.

An object of a built-in type defined at file scope is always initialized to 0. An object of a built-in type defined at local scope, however, is left uninitialized unless explicitly provided with an initial value by the programmer.

Dynamic Memory Management

Both local and file extent are managed for us automatically. There is a third form of storage duration called *dynamic extent*. This memory comes from the program's *free store* and is sometimes called *heap memory*. This memory must be managed explicitly by the programmer. Memory allocation is done using the `new` expression, whereas memory deallocation is done using the `delete` expression.

The `new` expression is written this way:

```
new Type;
```

Here, `Type` can be any built-in or class type known to the program, or the `new` expression can be written as

```
new Type( initial_value );
```

For example,

```
int *pi;
pi = new int;
```

assigns `pi` the address of an object of type `int` allocated in heap memory. By default, an object allocated on the heap is uninitialized. The second form of the `new` expression allows us to specify an initial value. For example,

```
pi = new int( 1024 );
```

---

[2]   A class object returned by value is optimized by most C++ compilers into an additional reference parameter. For a discussion of the *name return value* optimization, see Section 14.8 of [LIPPMAN98].

also assigns `pi` the address of an object of type `int` allocated in heap memory. This object, however, is initialized to a value of 1,024.

To allocate an array of heap elements, we write

```
int *pia = new int[ 24 ];
```

This code allocates an array of 24 integer objects on the heap. `pia` is initialized to address the first element of this array. The array elements themselves are uninitialized. There is no syntax for initializing an array of elements allocated on the heap.

A heap object is said to have dynamic extent because it is allocated at run-time through use of the `new` expression and continues to exist until explicitly deallocated through use of the `delete` expression. For example, the following delete expression causes the object addressed by `pi` to be deallocated:

```
delete pi;
```

To delete an array of objects, we add an empty subscript operator between the pointer addressing the array and the delete expression:

```
delete [] pia;
```

We do not need to check that `pi` is nonzero:

```
if ( pi != 0 ) // unnecessary -- compiler checks for us
     delete pi;
```

The compiler does this check automatically. If for some reason the programmer does not apply the `delete` expression, the heap object is never deallocated. This is called a *memory leak*. In Chapter 6, we look at why we might choose to use dynamic memory allocation in the design of our programs. We look at ways to prevent memory leaks in our discussion of exception handling in Chapter 7.

2.3   Providing Default Parameter Values

Printing a trace of our bubble sort program to `ofil` required that I make `ofil` available to the multiple functions I wished to debug. Because I was responding to unexpected and unwelcomed behavior, I chose the quickest solution to the problem of making an object visible across multiple functions: I defined `ofil` at file scope.

As a general programming rule, however, it is better to communicate between functions using parameters rather than use objects defined at file scope. One reason is that a function that is dependent on an object defined at file scope is harder to reuse in a different context. The function is also harder to modify: We must understand not only the logic specific to the function but also the logic of the objects defined at file scope.

Let's see how we might revise `bubble_sort()` to do away with its reliance on the file scope instance of `ofil`:

```
void bubble_sort( vector<int> &vec, ofstream &ofil )
{
    for ( int ix = 0; ix < vec.size(); ++ix )
        for ( int jx = ix+1; jx < vec.size(); ++jx )
            if ( vec[ ix ] > vec[ jx ] )
            {
                ofil << "about to call swap! ix: " << ix
                     << " jx: " << jx << "\tswapping: "
                     << vec[ix] << " with " << vec[ jx ] << endl;

                swap( vec[ix], vec[jx], ofil );
            }
}
```

Although this technique removes our reliance on the file scope instance of `ofil`, it introduces a number of potentially vexing problems. Every call to `bubble_sort()` now requires our user to pass in an ofstream class object. Also, we're generating this information without the user being able to turn it off. In the general case, when things are going well, no one is interested in this information.

We'd prefer not to bother the user either with having to specify an output stream or with having to turn anything off. By default, we'd like not to generate information. However, we'd like to allow the interested user to generate the information and specify the file into which the information should be stored. How might we do that?

C++ allows us to associate a default value for all or a subset of parameters. In our case, we provide the ofstream pointer parameter with a default value of 0:

```
void bubble_sort( vector<int> &vec, ofstream *ofil = 0 )
{
    for ( int ix = 0; ix < vec.size(); ++ix )
        for ( int jx = ix+1; jx < vec.size(); ++jx )
            if ( vec[ ix ] > vec[ jx ] )
            {
                if ( ofil != 0 )
                    (*ofil) << "about to call swap! ix: " << ix
                         << " jx: " << jx << "\tswapping: "
                         << vec[ix] << " with " << vec[ jx ] << endl;
                swap( vec[ix], vec[jx], ofil );
            }
}
```

This revised version of `bubble_sort()` declares its second parameter as a pointer to an ofstream object rather than as a reference. We must make this change to provide a default value of 0, indicating that no ofstream object is addressed. Unlike a pointer, a reference cannot be set to 0. A reference must always refer to some object.

An invocation of `bubble_sort()` with a single argument generates no debugging information. An invocation with a second argument that addresses an ofstream object generates the debugging information:

```
int main()
{
    int ia[ 8 ] = { 8, 34, 3, 13, 1, 21, 5, 2 };
    vector<int> vec( ia, ia+8 );

    // no debug information --
    // it is as if we invoked bubble_sort( vec, 0 );
    bubble_sort( vec );
    display( vec );

    // ok: debug information generated ...
    ofstream ofil( "data.txt" );
    bubble_sort( vec, &ofil );
    display( vec, ofil );
}
```

The implementation of display() presents a different situation. Currently, it hard-codes the output to cout. In the general case, cout is fine. In some cases, however, users are likely to prefer to supply an alternative target, such as a file. Our implementation must support both uses of display() in main(). Our solution is to make cout the default ostream parameter:

```
void display( const vector<int> &vec, ostream &os = cout )
{
    for ( int ix = 0; ix < vec.size(); ++ix )
        os << vec[ix] << ' ';
    os << endl;
}
```

There are two somewhat unintuitive rules about providing default parameters. The first rule is that default values are resolved positionally beginning with the right-most parameter. If a parameter is provided with a default value, all the parameters to its right must also have a default value. The following, for example, is illegal:

```
// error: no default value for vec
void display( ostream &os = cout, const vector<int> &vec );
```

The second rule is that the default value can be specified only once — either in the declaration or in the definition of the function, but not both. So where should we specify the default value?

Typically, a function declaration is placed in a header file. This header file is then included by files that wish to use the function. (Recall that we included the cstdlib header file to include the declaration of the exit() library function.) The definition of a function typically is placed in a program text file. This file is compiled once and is linked to our program whenever we wish to use the function. The header file, that is, provides the greater visibility of the function. (Header files are discussed in more detail in Section 2.9.)

Because of its greater visibility, we place the default value in the function declaration rather than in the function definition. For example, the declaration and definition of display() generally would look like this:

```
// header file declaration specifies default value
// let's call the header file: NumericSeq.h

void display( const vector<int>&, ostream&=cout );

// program text file definition includes header file
// the definition itself does not specify the default value

#include "NumericSeq.h"

void display( const vector<int> &vec, ostream &os )
{
    for ( int ix = 0; ix < vec.size(); ++ix )
        os << vec[ix] << ' ';
    os << endl;
}
```

2.4   Using Local Static Objects

Our fibon_seq() function of Section 2.2 calculates a Fibonacci sequence of a user-specified size with each invocation, returning a vector holding the elements. That is a bit more work than is necessary.

We really need only one Fibonacci sequence vector. The elements, after all, are invariant. The only thing that changes from one call of fibon_seq() to the next is the number of elements the user wishes to have available. Consider the following three invocations of fibon_seq():

```
fibon_seq( 24 );
fibon_seq( 8 );
fibon_seq( 18 );
```

The first call calculates all the values necessary to fulfill the request of the second and third invocations. If a fourth invocation requested 32 elements, we really need calculate only elements 25 through 32 — if we could cache the elements calculated between invocations. How might we do that?

A vector object local to the function does not provide a solution. The local object is created with each invocation of the function and is discarded as soon as the function terminates. A tempting alternative is to define a vector object at file scope. It is always tempting to introduce an object at file scope to solve a communications problem between functions. In general, however, file scope objects complicate the independence and understandability of individual functions.

An alternative solution, in this case, is a local static object. For example,

```
const vector<int>*
fibon_seq( int size )
{
    static vector< int > elems;
    // do the logic to populate it ...

    return &elems;
}
```

elems is now defined as a local static object of fibon_seq(). What does this mean? Unlike a nonstatic local object, the memory associated with a static local object persists across function invocations. elems is no longer destroyed and re-created with each invocation of fibon_seq(). This is why we can now safely return elems's address.

A local static object allows us to define a single vector to hold the elements of the Fibonacci sequence. With each invocation of fibon_seq(), we need calculate only those elements that are not as yet inserted into elems. Here is one possible implementation:

```
const vector<int>*
fibon_seq( int size )
{
    const int max_size = 1024;
    static vector< int > elems;

    if ( size <= 0 || size > max_size ){
        cerr << "fibon_seq(): oops: invalid size: "
             << size << " -- can't fulfill request.\n";
        return 0;
    }

    // if size is equal to or greater than elems.size(),
    // no calculations are necessary ...
    for ( int ix = elems.size(); ix < size; ++ix ){
        if ( ix == 0 || ix == 1 )
            elems.push_back( 1 );
        else elems.push_back( elems[ix-1]+elems[ix-2] );
    }
    return &elems;
}
```

Previously, we have always defined a vector to be of a particular size and have assigned values to existing elements. But in this version of fibon_seq(), we have no way of guessing how big a vector we'll need. Rather, we define elems to be an empty vector and insert elements as we need them. push_back() inserts the value at the back of the vector. The memory to support this is managed automatically by the vector class itself. (In Chapter 3 we look in detail at vectors and the other standard library container classes.)

2.5   Declaring a Function Inline

Recall that `fibon_elem()` returns the Fibonacci element at a user-specified position within the sequence. In our original implementation, it calculates the sequence up to the requested position with each invocation. It also tests whether the requested position is reasonable. We can simplify its implementation by factoring subtasks into separate functions:

```cpp
bool is_size_ok( int size )
{
    const int max_size = 1024;
    if ( size <= 0 || size > max_size )
    {
        cerr << "Oops: requested size is not supported : "
             << size << " -- can't fulfill request.\n";
        return false;
    }
    return true;
}

// calculate up to size elements of Fibonacci sequence
// return address of static container holding elements
const vector<int> *fibon_seq( int size )
{
    static vector< int > elems;
    if ( ! is_size_ok( size ))
        return 0;

    for ( int ix = elems.size(); ix < size; ++ix )
        if ( ix == 0 || ix == 1 )
            elems.push_back( 1 );
        else elems.push_back( elems[ix-1]+elems[ix-2] );
    return &elems;
}

// returns the Fibonacci element at position pos
// (we must adjust by 1 because first element is stored at 0)
// returns false if position is unsupported
bool fibon_elem( int pos, int &elem )
{
    const vector<int> *pseq = fibon_seq( pos );

    if ( ! pseq )
        { elem = 0; return false; }

    elem = (*pseq)[ pos-1 ];
    return true;
}
```

By factoring size checking into `is_size_ok()` and the calculation of the Fibonacci elements into `fibon_seq()`, we make `fibon_elem()` simpler to implement and understand. In addition, these two functions are now available to other applications.

The drawback is that `fibon_elem()` now requires three function calls to complete its operation, whereas previously it required only one. Is this additional overhead critical? That depends on the context of its use. If its performance should prove unacceptable, one solution is to fold the three functions back into one. In C++, an alternative solution is to declare the functions as inline.

An inline function represents a request to the compiler to expand the function at each call point. With an inline function, the compiler replaces the function call with a copy of the code to be executed. In effect, this allows us to benefit from the performance improvement of folding the functions back into `fibon_elem()` while still maintaining the three functions as independent operations.

We declare a function inline by prefixing its definition with the `inline` keyword:

```
// ok: now fibon_elem() is an inline function
inline bool fibon_elem( int pos, int &elem )
        { /* definition same as above */ }
```

The inline specification is only a request to the compiler. Whether the compiler actually honors the request is implementation-dependent. (For a discussion of why the inline specification is only a request, see Section 7.1.1 of [STROUSTRUP97].)

In general, the best candidate functions for inlining, such as `fibon_elem()` and `is_size_ok()`, are small, frequently invoked, and not computationally complex.

The definition of an inline function is usually placed within a header file. For it to be expanded, its definition must be available before its call. (This is discussed further in Section 2.9.)

2.6   Providing Overloaded Functions

Rather than have each function generate its own diagnostic messages, let's provide a general `display_message()` function. It might be used as follows:

```
bool is_size_ok( int size )
{
        const int max_size = 1024;
        const string msg( "Requested size is not supported" );

        if ( size <= 0 || size > max_size ){
            display_message( msg, size );
            return false;
        }
        return true;
}
```

Similarly, our program in Chapter 1 might use it to display its greeting to the user

```
const string
      greeting( "Hello. Welcome to Guess the Numeric Sequence" );

display_message( greeting );
```

and to display the two elements of the sequence:

```
const string seq( "The two elements of the sequence are " );
display_message( seq, elem1, elem2 );
```

In another instance, we might want to use display_message() simply to output a new-line or tab character:

```
display_message( '\n' ); display_message( '\t' );
```

Can we really pass parameters to display_message() that differ both in type and number? Yes. How? Through function overloading.

Two or more functions can be given the same name if the parameter list of each function is unique either by the type or the number of parameters. For example, the following declarations represent the four overloaded instances of display_message() invoked earlier:

```
void display_message( char ch );
void display_message( const string& );
void display_message( const string&, int );
void display_message( const string&, int, int );
```

How does the compiler know which instance of the four overloaded functions to invoke? It compares the actual arguments supplied to the function invocation against the parameters of each overloaded instance, choosing the best match. This is why the parameter list of each overloaded function must be unique.

The return type of a function by itself does not distinguish two instances of a function that have the same name. The following, for example, is illegal. It results in a compile-time error:

```
// error: parameter list not return type must be unique
ostream& display_message( char ch );
bool display_message( char ch );
```

Why isn't the return type itself sufficient to overload a function? It is because the return type cannot guarantee a sufficient context with which to distinguish instances. For example, in the following call there is really no way for the compiler to determine which instance the user wished to have invoked:

```
display_message( '\t' ); // which one?
```

Overloading a set of functions that have unique implementations but perform a similar task simplifies the use of these functions for our users. Without overloading, we would have to provide each function with a unique name.

2.7 Defining and Using Template Functions

Let's say that a colleague of ours has asked for three additional `display_message()`
instances to handle a vector of integers, a vector of doubles, and a vector of strings:

```
void display_message( const string&, const vector<int>& );
void display_message( const string&, const vector<double>& );
void display_message( const string&, const vector<string>& );
```

On completing the implementation of these three instances, we notice that the
function body for each instance is exactly the same. The only difference across these
functions is the type of the second parameter:[3]

```
void display_message( const string &msg, const vector<int> &vec )
{
    cout << msg;
    for ( int ix = 0; ix < vec.size(); ++ix )
        cout << vec[ ix ] << ' ';
}

void display_message( const string &msg, const vector<string> &vec )
{
    cout << msg;
    for ( int ix = 0; ix < vec.size(); ++ix )
        cout << vec[ ix ] << ' ';
    cout << '\n';
}

void display_message( const string&, const vector<string>&,
                      ostream& = cout );
```

There's no reason to think that another colleague won't come along asking for yet
another instance that supports a vector of some additional type. It would certainly
save us a great deal of effort if we could define a single instance of the function body
rather than duplicate the code multiple times and make the necessary minor changes
to each instance. To do that, however, we need a facility to bind that single instance to
each vector type we wish to display. The function template mechanism provides just
this facility.

A *function template* factors out the type information of all or a subset of the types
specified in its parameter list. In the case of `display_message()`, we wish to factor out
the type of the element contained within the vector. This allows us to define a single
instance of the unchanging part of the function template. It is incomplete, however,

---

[3] A more flexible implementation adds a third parameter of type ostream that by default is set to `cout`:
```
void display_message( const string&, const vector<string>&,
                      ostream& = cout );
```

because the factored-out type information is missing. This type information is supplied by the user in using a particular instance of the function template.

A function template begins with the keyword `template`. It is followed by a list of one or more identifiers that represent the types we wish to defer. The list is set off by a less-than/greater-than bracket pair (<, >). The user supplies the actual type information each time he uses a particular instance of the function. These identifiers in effect serve as placeholders for actual data types within the parameter list and body of the function template. For example,

```
template <typename elemType>
void display_message( const string &msg,
                      const vector<elemType> &vec )
{
    cout << msg;
    for ( int ix = 0; ix < vec.size(); ++ix )
    {
        elemType t = vec[ ix ];
        cout << t << ' ';
    }
}
```

The keyword `typename` specifies `elemType` as a type placeholder within the function template `display_message()`. `elemType` is an arbitrary name. I could have easily chosen `foobar` or `T`. We must defer the actual type of the vector to be displayed. We do that by placing `elemType` within the bracket pair following vector.

What about the first parameter? `msg` never varies its type with each invocation of `display_message()`. It is always a constant reference to a string class object, so there is no need to factor its type. A function template typically has a combination of explicit and deferred type specifiers in its parameter list.

How do we use a function template? It looks pretty much the same as the use of an ordinary function. For example, when we write

```
vector< int > ivec;
string msg;
// ...
display_message( msg, ivec );
```

the compiler binds `elemType` to type `int`. An instance of `display_message()` is created in which the second parameter is of type `vector<int>`. Within the function body, the local object t also becomes an object of type `int`. Similarly, when we write

```
vector< string > svec;
// ...
display_message( msg, svec );
```

`elemType` becomes bound to type `string`. An instance of `display_message()` is created in which the second parameter is of type `vector<string>`, and so on.

The function template serves as a kind of prescription for the generation of an unlimited number of function instances in which elemType is bound to a built-in or user-defined class type.

In general, we overload a function when there are multiple implementations, but each instance provides the same general service. We make a function a template when the body of the code remains invariant across a variety of types.

A function template can also be an overloaded function. For example, let's provide two instances of display_message(): one with a second parameter of type vector, and the other with a second parameter of type list. (list is another container class defined in the C++ standard library. We look at the list container class in Chapter 3.)

```
// overloaded instances of a function template
template <typename elemType>
void display_message( const string &msg, const vector<elemType> &vec );

template <typename elemType>
void display_message( const string &msg, const list<elemType> &lt );
```

2.8   Pointers to Functions Add Flexibility

We must provide a function to return a vector of elements similar to fibon_seq() for each of our other five numerical sequences. The full set of functions might be declared as follows:

```
const vector<int> *fibon_seq( int size );
const vector<int> *lucas_seq( int size );
const vector<int> *pell_seq( int size );
const vector<int> *triang_seq( int size );
const vector<int> *square_seq( int size );
const vector<int> *pent_seq( int size );
```

What about fibon_elem()? Must we also provide six separate instances of this, one for each numeric sequence? The definition of fibon_elem() is as follows:

```
bool fibon_elem( int pos, int &elem )
{
    const vector<int> *pseq = fibon_seq( pos );

    if ( ! pseq )
        { elem = 0; return false; }

    elem = (*pseq)[ pos-1 ];
    return true;
}
```

The only sequence-dependent aspect of fibon_elem() is the call to the associated sequence function to retrieve the vector of elements. If we eliminate this dependency, we eliminate the need for more than a single instance of the function. We achieve this independence using a pointer — specifically, a pointer to function.

The definition of a *pointer to function* is complicated. It must specify the return type and parameter list of the function it is addressing. In our case, the parameter list is a single int, and the return type is const vector<int>*. In addition, the definition must place a * somewhere to indicate that the object being defined is a pointer. Finally, of course, we must give the pointer a name. Let's call it seq_ptr. As usual, our first attempt is almost correct.

```
const vector<int>* *seq_ptr( int ); // almost correct
```

This code defines seq_ptr as a function that has a parameter list of a single int and has a return type of a pointer to a pointer to a const vector of elements of type int! To have seq_ptr be recognized as a pointer, we must override the default precedence of * with parentheses:

```
const vector<int>* (*seq_ptr)( int ); // ok
```

seq_ptr can address any function with the same return type and parameter list. This means that it can address each of the six numeric sequence functions. Let's rewrite fibon_elem() as the more general seq_elem() as follows:

```
bool seq_elem( int pos, int &elem,
               const vector<int>* (*seq_ptr)(int))
{
    // invoke function addressed by seq_ptr

    const vector<int> *pseq = seq_ptr( pos );
    if ( ! pseq )
        { elem = 0; return false; }

    elem = (*pseq)[ pos-1 ];
    return true;
}
```

The function addressed by a pointer to function is invoked in the same way as the function itself. That is,

```
const vector<int> *pseq = seq_ptr( pos );
```

is an indirect invocation of the function addressed by seq_ptr. We don't know (or care) what function it addresses. It might be wise, however, to confirm that it does at least address *some* function:

```
if ( ! seq_ptr )
    display_message( "Internal Error: seq_ptr is set to null!" );
```

A pointer to function can be initialized or assigned either 0 to indicate that it addresses no function

```
const vector<int>* (*seq_ptr)( int ) = 0;
```

or the address of a function. The next question is, how do we access a function's address? It's one of the least complicated operations in C++. We just name it

```
// assigns seq_ptr the address of pell_seq()
seq_ptr = pell_seq;
```

What if we wish to set seq_ptr to a different sequence function with each iteration of our display loop without having to name each function explicitly? To solve this problem, we can again resort to indexing into an array. In this case, we define an array of pointers to functions:

```
// seq_array is an array of pointers to functions
const vector<int>* (*seq_array[])( int ) = {
    fibon_seq,  lucas_seq,  pell_seq,
    triang_seq, square_seq, pent_seq
};
```

seq_array is an array of pointers to functions holding six elements. The first element is the address of fibon_seq(), the second, lucas_seq(), and so on. We can set seq_ptr with each iteration of a while loop while the user still wishes to guess another sequence:

```
int seq_index = 0;
while ( next_seq == true )
{
    seq_ptr = seq_array[ ++seq_index ];
    // ...
}
```

Alternatively, what if we wished to access the pointer explicitly to the function generating the Pell sequence? It is somewhat clumsy having to remember that the Pell instance is addressed by the third array element. A more intuitive method of indexing is to provide a set of mnemonic constant values. For example,

```
enum ns_type {
    ns_fibon, ns_lucas, ns_pell,
    ns_triang, ns_square, ns_pent
};
```

An enumerated type is defined by the keyword enum followed by an optional identifier, such as ns_type. eThe items in the comma-separated list of named values within curly braces are called *enumerators*. By default, the first enumerator is assigned a value of 0. Each subsequent enumerator is given a value that is 1 greater than its predecessor. For ns_type, ns_fib has an associated value of 0, ns_lucas, 1, ns_pell, 2, and so on through ns_pent, which has an associated value of 5.

To access a particular pointer to function explicitly, we use the associated enumerator as the index:

```
seq_ptr = seq_array[ ns_pell ];
```

2.9   Setting Up a Header File

Before I can invoke seq_elem(), I must first declare it to the program. If it is invoked in five program text files, there must be five declarations available. Rather than separately declare seq_elem() in each of the five files, we place the function declaration in a header file. The header file is then included in each program text file that wishes to use the function.

Using this convention, we need maintain only a single declaration of a function. If its parameter list or return type changes, only this one declaration needs to be modified. All users of the function automatically include the updated function declaration.

Header files by convention are given a .h suffix — except for the standard library header files, which have no suffix. We'll call our header file NumSeq.h and place in it a declaration of all the functions related to our numeric sequences:

```
// NumSeq.h
bool                seq_elem( int pos, int &elem );
const vector<int> *fibon_seq( int size );
const vector<int> *lucas_seq( int size );
const vector<int> *pell_seq( int size );
const vector<int> *triang_seq( int size );
const vector<int> *square_seq( int size );
const vector<int> *pent_seq( int size );
// and so on ...
```

There can be only one definition of a function in a program. However, there can be multiple declarations. We don't put definitions in a header file because the header file is included in multiple text files within a program.

One exception to this one-definition rule is the definition of an inline function. To expand an inline function, the definition must be available to the compiler at each invocation point. This means that we must place the inline function definitions inside a header file rather than in a separate program text file.

Objects defined at file scope are also declared in a header file if multiple files may need to access the objects. This is because an object can not be referred to until it has been declared to the program. For example, if seq_array were defined at file scope, we would likely provide a declaration within NumSeq.h. Not unexpectedly, our first try is not quite correct:

```
// This is not quite right ...
const int seq_cnt = 6;
const vector<int>* (*seq_array[seq_cnt])( int );
```

This is not correct because it is interpreted as the definition of seq_array and not as a declaration. Just as with a function, an object can be defined only once in a program. The definition of an object, as well as the definition of a function, must be placed in a program text file. We turn the definition of seq_array into a declaration by prefacing it with the keyword extern:

```
// OK: this is a declaration
extern const vector<int>* (*seq_array[seq_cnt])( int );
```

OK, granted, you might say. This is analogous to the distinction of placing function declarations in the header file but function definitions in a program text file. But. But. (You're on your feet by this point.) But if all this is true, then isn't seq_cnt also declared extern rather than explicitly defined?

Obviously, this is just to confuse you. Me. The whole gaggle of us.

A const object, like an inline function, is treated as an exception to the rule. The definition of a const object is not visible outside the file it is defined in. This means that we can define it in multiple program files without error.

Why do we want that? It is because we want the compiler to use the value of the const object in our array declarations and other situations in which a constant expression is needed, possibly across multiple files.

A file using either seq_elem() or seq_array includes the header file before a first use of either name:

```
#include "NumSeq.h"
void test_it()
{
    int elem = 0;
    if ( seq_elem( 1, elem ) && elem == 1 ) // ...
}
```

Why is NumSeq.h in quotation marks rather than angle brackets (<,>)? The short answer is that if the header file is in the same directory as the program text file including it, we use quotation marks. If it is anywhere else, we use angle brackets. The slightly more technical answer is that if the file name is enclosed by angle brackets, the file is presumed to be a project or standard header file. The search to find it examines a predefined set of locations. If the file name is enclosed by a pair of quotation marks, the file is presumed to be a user-supplied header file. The search to find it begins in the directory in which the including file is located.

Exercise 2.2

The formula for the Pentagonal numeric sequence is Pn=n*(3n-1)/2. This yields the sequence 1, 5, 12, 22, 35, and so on. Define a function to fill a vector of elements passed in to the function calculated to some user-specified position. Be sure to verify that the position specified is valid. Write a second function that, given a vector, displays its elements. It should take a second parameter identifying the type of numeric series the vector represents. Write a main() function to exercise these functions.

Exercise 2.3

Separate the function to calculate the Pentagonal numeric sequence implemented in Exercise 2.2 into two functions. One function should be inline; it checks the validity of the position. A valid position not as yet calculated causes the function to invoke a second function that does the actual calculation.

Exercise 2.4

Introduce a static local vector to hold the elements of your Pentagonal series. This function returns a const pointer to the vector. It accepts a position by which to grow the vector if the vector is not as yet that size. Implement a second function that, given a position, returns the element at that position. Write a main() function to exercise these functions.

Exercise 2.5

Implement an overloaded set of max() functions to accept (a) two integers, (b) two floats, (c) two strings, (d) a vector of integers, (e) a vector of floats, (f) a vector of strings, (g) an array of integers and an integer indicating the size of the array, (h) an array of floats and an integer indicating the size of the array, and (i) an array of strings and an integer indicating the size of the array. Again, write a main() function to exercise these functions.

Exercise 2.6

Reimplement the functions of Exercise 2.5 using templates. Modify the main() function accordingly.

3

Generic Programming

The Standard Template Library (STL) consists of two primary components: a set of container classes, including the vector, list, set, and map classes, and a set of generic algorithms to operate over these containers, including `find()`, `sort()`, `replace()`, and `merge()`.

The vector and list container classes represent sequential containers. A *sequential container* maintains a first element, a second element, and so on through a last element. We primarily iterate over a sequential container. The map and set classes represent associative containers. An *associative container* supports fast lookup of a value.

A *map* is a key/value pair: The key is used for lookup, and the value represents the data we store and retrieve. A telephone directory, for example, is easily represented by a map. The key is the individual's name. The value is the associated phone number.

A *set* contains only key values. We query it as to whether a value is present. For example, if we were to build an index of words that occur in news stories, we would want to exclude neutral words such as *the, an, but,* and so on. Before a word is entered into the index, we query an `excluded_word` set. If the word is present, we discard it; otherwise, we include the word in our index.

The generic algorithms provide a large number of operations that can be applied both to the container classes and to the built-in array. The algorithms are called generic because they are independent of both the type of element they are operating on (for example, whether it is an `int`, `double`, or string) and the type of container within which the elements are held (whether it is a vector, list, or built-in array).

The generic algorithms achieve type independence by being implemented as function templates. They achieve container independence by not operating directly on the container. Rather, they are passed an *iterator* pair (`first,last`), marking the range of elements over which to iterate. While `first` is unequal to `last`, the algorithm operates on the element addressed by `first`, increments `first` to address the next element, and then recompares `first` and `last` for equality. A good first question is, what is an iterator? The next two sections try to answer that.

3.1   The Arithmetic of Pointers

We are assigned the following programming task. We are given a vector of integers and an integer value. If the value is contained within the vector, we must return a pointer to it; otherwise, we return 0, indicating that the value is not present. Here is an implementation:

```
int* find( const vector<int> &vec, int value )
{
    for ( int ix = 0; ix < vec.size(); ++ix )
        if ( vec[ ix ] == value )
            return &vec[ ix ];
    return 0;
}
```

We test the function and are satisfied that it works. We are next assigned the task of having the function work not only with integers but also with any type in which the equality operator is defined. If you have read Section 2.7, you should recognize this task as requiring us to transform find() into a function template:

```
template <typename elemType>
elemType* find( const vector<elemType> &vec,
                const elemType &value )
{
    for ( int ix = 0; ix < vec.size(); ++ix )
        if ( vec[ ix ] == value )
            return &vec[ ix ];

    return 0;
}
```

Again, we test the function and are satisfied that it works. Our next assignment is to have find() work both for a vector and an array of elements of any type for which an equality operator is defined. Our first thought is to overload the function, providing an instance that takes a vector and an instance that takes an array.

We are advised against overloading in this case. With a little thought, we're told, we can implement find() so that a single instance can handle the elements of either a vector or a built-in array. Gosh, but that seems hard.

One strategy for solving a hard problem is to divide it into a number of smaller and hopefully simpler problems. In this example, our one big problem breaks down into (1) passing the elements of an array to find() without specifying the array and (2) passing the elements of a vector to find() without specifying the vector. Ideally, the solutions to these two problems contain a common solution to our initial problem.

Let's first solve the problem of the built-in array. How can we pass in the elements of an array to find() without specifying the array itself?

Programming a solution to a problem is immeasurably easier when we understand the problem that we are trying to solve. In our case, it will help to first understand how arrays are passed into and returned from functions. When I write

```
int min( int array[ 24 ] ) { ... }
```

it seems as if min() accepts only arrays of 24 elements and that the actual array is being passed by value. In fact, neither assumption is true: The array is not copied by value, and an array of any size can be passed to min(). I know, you're thinking *huh*?

When an array is passed into or returned from a function, only the address of the first element is passed. The following is the more accurate declaration of min():

```
int min( int *array ) { ... }
```

min() accepts integer arrays of any dimension: 1, 32, 1,024, and so on. The alternative would be vexing because it would require us to provide a separate instance of min() for each uniquely dimensioned array.

The pointer to the beginning of the array allows min() to begin reading the array. Somehow, we must indicate to min() when the reading of the array should stop. One way is to add an additional parameter that holds the size of the array. For example, here is our declaration of find() using this strategy:

```
template <typename elemType>
elemType* find( const elemType *array, int size,
                const elemType &value );
```

An alternative solution is to pass an address that, when reached, indicates that we have completed reading the elements of the array. (We call such a value a *sentinel*.)

```
template <typename elemType>
elemType* find( const elemType *first, const elemType *sentinel,
                const elemType &value );
```

One interesting aspect of this solution is that we have eliminated the declaration of the array from the parameter list — solving the first of our smaller problems.

Let's look at how each version of find() is implemented. In the first version, we access each element in turn beginning at 0 and proceeding to size-1. The first question is this: Inasmuch as the array is passed to find() as a pointer to its first element, how do we access the elements by position? Even though we are accessing the array through a pointer, we can still apply the subscript operator exactly as we did before:

```
template <typename elemType>
elemType* find( const elemType *array, int size,
                const elemType &value )
{
    if ( ! array || size < 1 )
         return 0;

    for ( int ix = 0; ix < size; ++ix )
```

```
            // we can apply subscript operator to pointer
            if ( array[ ix ] == value )
                return &array[ ix ];

        return 0; // value not found
    }
```

Although the array is passed to find() as a pointer to its first element, we see that individual elements can still be accessed through the subscript operator as if the array were an object. Why? In practice, subscripting is carried out by adding the index to the beginning address of the array to yield the address of the element. That address is then dereferenced to return the value of the element. For example,

```
        array[ 2 ];
```

returns the value of the third element of the array (indexing, remember, begins at 0). The following also returns the value of the third element:

```
        *(array + 2)
```

If the address of the first element of array is 1000, what address does array+2 yield? 1002 is a reasonable answer, but it is not the correct answer. 1002 is integer arithmetic; array+2, however, represents *pointer arithmetic*. Pointer arithmetic adds increments of the size of the type being addressed.

Let's say that array contains integer elements. array+2, then, adds the size of two integer elements to the address of array. Under pointer arithmetic, on a machine in which an integer is 4 bytes, the answer is 1008.

When we have the address of the element, we must then dereference the address to get the value of the elements. When we write array[2], the pointer arithmetic and address dereferencing are done automatically.

Here is an alternative implementation of find() in which we address each element through a pointer. To address each element of array in turn, we increment it by 1 with each iteration of our loop. To read the element addressed, we must dereference the pointer. That is, array returns the address of the element, and *array returns its value.

```
        template <typename elemType>
        elemType* find( const elemType *array, int size,
                        const elemType &value )
        {
            if ( ! array || size < 1 ) return 0;

            // ++array increments array by one elememt
            for ( int ix = 0; ix < size; ++ix, ++array )
                // *array dereferences the address
                if ( *array == value )
                    return array;
            return 0;
        }
```

In this next version, we replace the size parameter with a second pointer that serves as the sentinel address. This is the version that allows us to remove the declaration of the array from the parameter list:

```
template <typename elemType>
elemType* find( const elemType *first,
                const elemType *last, const elemType &value )
{
    if ( ! first || ! last )
        return 0;

    // while first does not equal last,
    // compare value with element addressed by first
    // if the two are equal, return first
    // otherwise, increment first to address next element

    for ( ; first != last; ++first )
        if ( *first == value )
            return first;

    return 0;
}
```

This implements the first of our two programming subtasks: we've implemented find() to access each element of our array independent of the array object the elements are contained within. How might find() be invoked? The following code uses the pointer arithmetic we illustrated earlier:

```
int    ia[8] = { 1, 1, 2, 3, 5, 8, 13, 21 };
double da[6] = { 1.5, 2.0, 2.5, 3.0, 3.5, 4.0 };
string sa[4] = { "pooh", "piglet", "eeyore", "tigger" };

int    *pi = find( ia, ia+8, ia[3] );
double *pd = find( da, da+6, da[3] );
string *ps = find( sa, sa+4, sa[3] );
```

The second address marks 1 past the last element of the array. Is that legal? Yes. If we should ever try to read or write to that address, however, all bets are off. But if all we do with that address is to compare it against other element addresses, we're fine. The address 1 past the last element of the array serves as a sentinel indicating that we have completed our iteration.

How might we implement the second programming subtask, that of accessing each element of a vector independent of the vector object the elements are contained within? A vector also holds its elements in a contiguous area of memory, so we can pass find() a begin/end pair of addresses in the same way as we do for the built-in array, except in one case. Unlike an array, a vector can be empty. For example,

```
vector<string> svec;
```

defines an empty vector of string elements. The following invocation of find(), if svec is empty, is incorrect and results in a run-time program failure:

```
find( &svec[0], &svec[svec.size()], search_value );
```

A safer implementation is first to confirm that svec is not empty.

```
if ( ! svec.empty() ) // ... ok, call find()
```

Although this is safer, it is somewhat cumbersome for the user. A more uniform way of accessing the address of the first element is to wrap the operation into a function, something like the following:

```
template <typename elemType>
inline elemType* begin( const vector<elemType> &vec )
    { return vec.empty() ? 0 : &vec[0]; }
```

A second function, end(), returns either 0 or a pointer to 1 past the last element of the vector. In this way, we can safely and uniformly invoke find() for any vector:

```
find( begin( svec ), end( svec ), search_value );
```

Moreover, this solves our original programming task of implementing find() so that a single instance can accept either a vector or a built-in array. Again, we test the function and are satisfied that it works.

Excellent, we are told. Now extend find() so that a single instance can also support the standard library list class. Now that's hard.

A list class is also a container. The difference is that the elements of a list are linked through a pair of pointers: a forward pointer addressing the next element and a backward pointer addressing the preceding element.

Pointer arithmetic doesn't work with a list. Pointer arithmetic presumes that the elements are contiguous. By adding the size of one element to the current pointer, we reset the pointer to address the next element. This is the underlying assumption of our implementation of find(). Unfortunately, that assumption doesn't hold when we access the next element of a list.

Our first thought again is to provide an overloaded second instance of find() that accepts a list object. The behaviors of the pointers of a built-in array, a vector, and a list are, we claim, simply too different to achieve a uniform syntax for next element access.

Yes and no. Yes, the behavior of the underlying pointers is too different for a uniform syntax. And no, we don't need to provide a second instance to support the list class. In fact, we don't need to alter the implementation of find() at all, except for its parameter list.

The solution is to provide a layer of abstraction over the behavior of the underlying pointers. Rather than program the underlying pointers directly, we program the layer of abstraction. We place the unique handling of the underlying pointers within that layer, shielding it from our users. This technique allows us to handle any of the standard library container classes with a single instance of find().

3.2   Making Sense of Iterators

The obvious question is, how do we implement this layer of abstraction? We need a collection of objects that support the same set of operators as the built-in pointer (++, *, ==, !=) but allow us to provide a unique implementation of those operators. *We can do exactly this with the C++ class mechanism.* We'll design a set of *iterator* classes that are programmed using the same syntax as that of a pointer. For example, if first and last are list class iterators, we can write

```
// first and last are iterator class objects
while ( first != last )
{
        cout << *first << ' ';
        ++first;
}
```

the same as if first and last are actual pointers. The difference is that the dereference operator (*), the inequality operator (!=), and the increment operator (++) represent inline function calls associated with the iterator classes. For the list class iterator, for example, the associated increment function advances to the next element by following the list pointer. For the vector class iterator, the increment function advances to the next element by adding the size of one element to the current address.

In Chapter 4 we look at how to implement an iterator class, including how to provide function instances of particular operators. In this section, we look at how to define and use the iterators associated with the standard library container classes.

Where do we get iterators? Each container class provides a begin() operation that returns an iterator that addresses the first element of the container and an end() operation that returns an iterator that addresses 1 past the last element of the container. For example, disregarding how we define an iterator object for the moment, we assign, compare, increment, and dereference an iterator as follows:

```
for ( iter = svec.begin();
      iter != svec.end(); ++iter )
        cout << *iter << ' ';
```

Before we look at how to define an iterator, let's think for a moment about the information its definition must provide: the type of the container over which it iterates, which determines how it accesses the next element; and the type of the element being addressed, which determines the value returned from a dereference of the iterator.

One possible syntax for an iterator definition might be to pass these two types as parameters to an iterator class:

```
// one possible iterator syntax
// note: not actually used in the STL
iterator< vector, string > iter;
```

The actual syntax looks considerably more complicated, at least at first sight. It also provides a more elegant solution, although that may not be apparent, or at least not until we implement and use an iterator class in Chapter 4.

```
vector<string> svec;

// the standard library iterator syntax
// iter addresses vector elements of type string
// it is initialized to the first element of svec

vector<string>::iterator iter = svec.begin();
```

iter is defined to be an iterator for vectors of string elements. It is initialized to address the first element of svec. (The double colon [::] indicates that iterator is a type nested within the string vector definition. This will make more sense when you read Chapter 4 and we implement our own iterator class. For now, we'll just use the iterator.) For a const vector, such as

```
const vector<string> cs_vec;
```

we traverse the elements using a const_iterator:

```
vector<string>::const_iterator = cs_vec.begin();
```

A const_iterator allows us to read the vector elements but not write to them.

To access the element through the iterator, we dereference it just as we do a built-in pointer:

```
cout << "string value of element: " << *iter;
```

Similarly, to invoke an operation of the underlying string element through iter, we use the member selection arrow syntax:

```
cout << "( " << iter->size() << " ): " << *iter << endl;
```

Here is a reimplementation of display() as a function template using iterators rather than the subscript operator:

```
template <typename elemType>
void display( const vector<elemType> &vec, ostream &os )
{
    vector<elemType>::const_iterator iter = vec.begin();
    vector<elemType>::const_iterator end_it = vec.end();

    // if vec is empty, iter and end_it are equal
    // and the for-loop never executes
    for ( ; iter != end_it; ++iter )
        os << *iter << ' ';
    os << endl;
}
```

Our reimplementation of find() supports either a pair of built-in pointers, or a pair of iterators to a container of a particular type:

```
template <typename IteratorType, typename elemType >
IteratorType
find( IteratorType first, IteratorType last,
      const elemType &value )
{
   for ( ; first != last; ++first )
        if ( value == *first )
            return first;

   return last;
}
```

Let's see how we might use this reimplementation of find() with a built-in array, a vector, and a list:

```
const int asize = 8;
int ia[ asize ] = { 1, 1, 2, 3, 5, 8, 13, 21 };

// initialize the list and vector with the 8 elements of ia
vector<int> ivec( ia, ia+asize );
list<int>   ilist( ia, ia+asize );

int *pia = find( ia, ia+asize, 1024 );
if ( pia != ia+asize )
     // found ...

vector< int >::iterator it;
it = find( ivec.begin(), ivec.end(), 1024 );
if ( it != ivec.end() )
     // found ...

list< int >::iterator iter;
iter = find( ilist.begin(), ilist.end(), 1024 );
if ( iter != ilist.end() )
     // found ...
```

Not bad. We've carried the generality of find() pretty far — a lot further than we imagined we could when we began the preceding section. This is not the end of the story, however, although it is pretty much the end of this section.

find()'s implementation uses the equality operator of the underlying element type. If the underlying element type does not provide an equality operator or if the user wished to define element equality differently, this instance of find() proves too inflexible. How can we add that flexibility? One solution is to replace the use of the equality operator with a function passed in as a pointer to function. A second solution is something called a *function object*, a special class implementation. In Chapter 4 we look at how to design a function object.

What we've accomplished in our successive iterations of find() is to evolve it into the generic find() algorithm. (find_if() provides the additional flexibility of passing in a pointer to function or function object in place of using the equality operator of the underlying element.)

There are more than 60 generic algorithms. The following represents a partial listing (the full listing and an example of using each one can be found in Appendix B).

- **Search algorithms**: `find()`, `count()`, `adjacent_find()`, `find_if()`, `count_if()`, `binary_search()`, and `find_first_of()`.

- **Sorting and general ordering algorithms**: `merge()`, `partial_sort()`, `partition()`, `random_shuffle()`, `reverse()`, `rotate()`, and `sort()`.

- **Copy, deletion, and substitution algorithms**: `copy()`, `remove()`, `remove_if()`, `replace()`, `replace_if()`, `swap()`, and `unique()`.

- **Relational algorithms**: `equal()`, `includes()`, and `mismatch()`.

- **Generation and mutation algorithms**: `fill()`, `for_each()`, `generate()`, and `transform()`.

- **Numeric algorithms**: `accumulate()`, `adjacent_difference()`, `partial_sum()`, and `inner_product()`.

- **Set algorithms**: `set_union()` and `set_difference()`.

The algorithms ending with the `_if` suffix take either a pointer to function or a function object to determine equality. In addition, algorithms that modify the container, such as `replace()` and `unique()`, come in two versions: an in-place version that changes the original container and a version that returns a copy of the modified container. There are, for example, both a `replace()` and a `replace_copy()` algorithm.

3.3   Operations Common to All Containers

The following operations are common to all the container classes (as well as the string class):

- The equality (`==`) and inequality (`!=`) operators return true or false.
- The assignment (`=`) operator copies one container into another.
- `empty()` returns true if the container holds no elements.
- `size()` returns a count of the elements currently held within the container.
- `clear()` deletes all the elements.

The following function exercises each of these operations:

```
void comp( vector<int> &v1, vector<int> &v2 )
{
        // are the two vectors equal?
        if ( v1 == v2 )
            return;
```

```
            // is either vector empty?
            if ( v1.empty() || v2.empty() ) return;

            // no point defining it unless we are going to use it!
            vector<int> t;

            // assign t the largest vector
            t = v1.size() > v2.size() ? v1 : v2;

            // ... use t ...

            // ok. empty t of its elements
            // t.empty() will now return true
            // t.size() will now return 0
            t.clear();

            // ... ok, fill up t and use it some more ...
        }
```

Each container supports a `begin()` and an `end()` operation to return, respectively, an iterator to the first element of the container, and 1 past the last valid element:

- `begin()` returns an iterator to the first element.
- `end()` returns an iterator that addresses 1 past the last element.

Typically, we iterate across a container starting at `begin()` and stopping when we reach `end()`. All containers support an `insert()` operation to add elements and an `erase()` operation to delete elements.

- `insert()` adds one or a range of elements to a container.
- `erase()` deletes one or a range of elements from a container.

The behavior of `insert()` and `erase()` vary depending on whether the container is sequential or associative. Sequential containers are discussed in the next section.

3.4   Using the Sequential Containers

A sequential container holds an ordered collection of elements of a single type. There is a first element, a second element, and so on, until the last element. The vector and the list are the two primary sequential containers. A vector holds its elements in a contiguous area of memory. Random access — for example, accessing element 5, then 17, and then 9 — is efficient; each element is a fixed offset from the beginning of the vector. Insertion of an element at any position other than the end of the vector, however, is inefficient; each element to the right of the inserted element must be shifted one by copying the value of each element in turn. Similarly, the deletion of any element other than the last element of a vector is inefficient.

A list represents noncontiguous memory double-linked to allow both forward and backward traversal. Each element of a list contains three fields: the value, a back pointer to the preceding element of the list, and a front pointer to the next element of the list. Insertion and deletion of elements at any position within the list is efficient. The list must simply set the appropriate back and front pointers. Random access, on the other hand, is less efficiently supported. To access element 5, then 17, and then 9 requires traversal of the intervening elements. (Think of the difference between a CD and a cassette tape in going from one track to another.)

To represent the elements of a numeric sequence, a vector is the more appropriate container. Why? There is a great deal of random access of the elements. `fibon_elem()`, for example, indexes into the container based on the position passed to it by the user. Moreover, we never delete elements, and the elements are always inserted at the end of the vector.

When is a list more appropriate? If we were reading test scores from a file and wished to store each score in ascending order, we are likely to be randomly inserting into the container with each score we read. In this case, the list container is preferred.

A third sequential container is a *deque* (pronouced *deck*). A deque behaves pretty much like a vector — the elements are stored contiguously. Unlike a vector, however, a deque supports efficient insertion and deletion of its front element (as well as its back element). If, for example, we need to insert elements at the front of the container and delete them from the back, a deque is the most appropriate container type. (The standard library queue class is implemented using a deque to hold the queue's elements.)

To use a sequential container, we must include its associated header file, one of the following:

```
#include <vector>
#include <list>
#include <deque>
```

There are five ways to define a sequential container object:

1. Create an empty container:

    ```
    list< string > slist;
    vector< int >  ivec;
    ```

2. Create a container of some size. Each element is initialized to its default value. (Recall that the default value for the built-in arithmetic types such as `int` and `double` is zero.)

    ```
    list< int >       ilist( 1024 );
    vector< string > svec( 32 );
    ```

3. Create a container of a given size and specify an initial value for each element:

    ```
    vector< int >  ivec( 10, -1 );
    list< string > slist( 16, "unassigned" );
    ```

4. Create a container, providing an iterator pair marking a range of elements with which to initialize the container:

```
int ia[ 8 ] =
    { 1, 1, 2, 3, 5, 8, 13, 21 };

vector< int > fib( ia, ia+8 );
```

5. Create a container, providing a second container object. The new container is initialized by copying the second:

```
list< string > slist;   // empty
// fill slist ...
list< string > slist2( slist ); // copy of slist ...
```

Two special operations support insertion and deletion at the back of the container: push_back() and pop_back(). push_back() inserts an element at the back. pop_back() deletes the element. In addition, the list and deque containers (but not the vector) support push_front() and pop_front(). The pop_back() and pop_front() operations do not return the deleted value. To read the front value, we use front(), and to read the back value, we use back(). For example,

```
#include <deque>
deque<int> a_line;
int ival;
while ( cin >> ival )
{
        // insert ival at back of a_line
        a_line.push_back( ival );

        // ok: read the value at front of a_line
        int curr_value = a_line.front();

        // ... do something ...

        // delete the value at front of a_line
        a_line.pop_front();
}
```

push_front() and push_back() are specialized insertion operations. There are four variations of the more general insert() operation supported by each of the containers.

*   iterator insert(iterator position, elemType value) inserts value before position. It returns an iterator addressing the inserted element. For example, the following inserts ival in sorted order within ilist:

```
list<int> ilist;
// ... fill up ilist

list<int>::iterator it = ilist.begin();
```

```
while ( it != ilist.end() )
    if ( *it >= ival )
    {
        ilist.insert( it, ival );
        break; // exit loop
    }

if ( it == ilist.end() )
    ilist.push_back( ival );
```

- void insert(iterator position, int count, elemType value) inserts count elements of value before position. For example,

```
string sval( "Part Two" );
list<string> slist;
// ... fill slist ...

list<string>::iterator
    it = find( slist.begin(), slist.end(), sval );

slist.insert( it, 8, string( "dummy" ));
```

- void insert(iterator1 position, iterator2 first, iterator2 last) inserts the range of elements marked by first, last before position:

```
int ia1[7] = { 1, 1, 2, 3, 5, 55, 89 };
int ia2[4] = { 8, 13, 21, 34 };
list<int> elems( ia1, ia1+7 );

list<int>::iterator
    it = find( elems.begin(), elems.end(), 55 );

elems.insert( it, ia2, ia2+4 );
```

- iterator insert(iterator position) inserts an element before position. The element is initialized to the default value of its type.

pop_front() and pop_back() are specialized element erase operations. There are two versions of the more general erase() operation.

- iterator erase(iterator posit) erases the element addressed by posit. For example, using the slist defined earlier, let's erase() the first instance of str:

```
list<string>::iterator
    it = find( slist.begin(), slist.end(), str );

slist.erase( it );
```

- iterator erase(iterator first, iterator last) erases the elements starting with first up to but not including last. For example, again using the slist defined earlier, let's erase() the num_times instances of str:

```
list<string>::iterator
    first = slist.begin(),
    last = slist.end();

// it1: first element to erase,
// it2: first element beyond elements to erase
list<string>::iterator it1 = find( first, last, str );
list<string>::iterator it2 = find( first, last, sval );

slist.erase( it1, it2 );
```

The returned iterator in both instances of erase() addresses the element following the element or element range deleted.

The list class does not support offset arithmetic of its iterators. This is why we do not write

```
// error: offset arithmetic is not
// supported for list class
slist.erase( it1, it1+num_tries );
```

but instead provide erase() with both it1 and it2.

3.5   Using the Generic Algorithms

To use the generic algorithms, we must include the associated algorithm header file:

```
#include <algorithm>
```

Let's exercise the generic algorithms with our numeric sequence vector. is_elem() must return true if a value is an element in the sequence; otherwise, it returns false. Four possible generic search algorithms are as follows:

1. find() searches an unordered collection marked by the iterator pair first,last for some value. If the value is found, find() returns an iterator addressing the value; otherwise, it returns an iterator addressing last.

2. binary_search() searches a sorted collection. It returns true if the value is found; otherwise, it returns false. binary_search() is more efficient than find().

3. count() returns a count of the number of elements matching some value.

4. search() matches a subsequence within a container. For example, given the sequence {1,3,5,7,2,9}, a search for the subsequence {5,7,2} returns an iterator to the beginning of the subsequence. If the subsequence is not present, an iterator to the end of the container is returned.

Because our vector is guaranteed to be in ascending order, our best choice is the binary_search():

```
#include <algorithm>
bool is_elem( vector<int> &vec, int elem )
{
    // if the elem passed in is 34, the 9th element of
    // the Fibonacci sequence, but the stored sequence
    // only holds the first 6 elements: 1,1,2,3,5,8
    // our search will not succeed.
    // Before we invoke binary_search(),
    // we must check here if we need to grow the sequence

    return binary_search( vec.begin(), vec.end(), elem );
}
```

As the comment before the invocation of binary_search() explains, we must be sure that the numeric series contains element values sufficient to include elem were it a member of the series. One way to do that is to test the largest element in the sequence against elem. If the largest element is smaller than elem, we expand the sequence until its largest element equals or exceeds elem.

One strategy for determining the largest element of the series is to use the max_element() generic algorithm. max_element() is passed an iterator pair marking the range of elements to traverse. It returns the largest element within the vector. Here is our revised is_elem():

```
#include <algorithm>

// forward declaration
extern bool grow_vec( vector<int>&, int );

bool is_elem( vector<int> &vec, int elem )
{
    int max_value = max_element( vec.begin(), vec.end() );
    if ( max_value < elem )
        return grow_vec( vec, elem );

    if ( max_value == elem )
        return true;

    return binary_search( vec.begin(), vec.end(), elem );
}
```

grow_vec() adds elements to the vector until an element in the sequence is either equal to or greater than elem. If the sequence element is equal to elem, it returns true; otherwise, it returns false.

Of course, because our vector is in ascending order, we don't really need to use max_element() to find the largest element; it is guaranteed to be at position vec.size()-1 for a non-empty vector:

```
int max_value = vec.empty() ? 0 : vec[vec.size()-1];
```

binary_search() requires that the container be sorted, but it is left to the programmer to guarantee that. If we are unsure, we can copy() our container into a second container:

```
vector<int> temp( vec.size() );
copy( vec.begin(), vec.end(), temp.begin() );
```

Now we sort() our temporary container before invoking binary_search():

```
sort( temp.begin(), temp.end() );
return binary_search( temp.begin(), temp.end(), elem );
```

copy() takes two iterators that mark the range of elements to copy. A third iterator points to the first element of the target container. The elements are then assigned in turn. It is our responsibility to make sure that the target container is large enough to hold each element to be copied. If we are not sure, we can use an inserter to override default assignment with insertion (see Section 3.9 for a discussion).

Appendix B provides an example of using each generic algorithm.

3.6   How to Design a Generic Algorithm

Here is our task. We are given a vector of integer values. We are asked to return a new vector holding all the values that are less than 10. A quick but inflexible solution is the following:

```
vector<int> less_than_10( const vector<int> &vec )
{
    vector<int> nvec;
    for ( int ix = 0; ix < vec.size(); ++ix )
        if ( vec[ ix ] < 10 )
            nvec.push_back( vec[ ix ] );
    return nvec;
}
```

If the user wants all the elements less than 11, we must either create a new function or generalize this one to allow the user to specify a value against which to compare the elements. For example,

```
vector<int> less_than( const vector<int> &vec, int less_than_val );
```

But our next task is actually somewhat more difficult. We must allow the user to specify an alternative operation, such as greater-than, less-than, and so on. How can we parameterize an operation?

One solution is to replace the less-than operator with a function call. We add a third parameter, pred, specifying a pointer to function having a parameter list of two integers and returning a bool. less_than() isn't the right name any longer, so let's call it filter():

```
vector<int> filter( const vector<int> &vec,
                    int filter_value,
                    bool (*pred)( int, int ));
```

For our user's convenience, we also define a number of relational functions that can be passed to filter():

```
bool less_than( int v1, int v2 )
    { return v1 < v2 ? true : false; }

bool greater_than( int v1, int v2 )
    { return v1 > v2 ? true : false; }
```

and so on. The user can then either pass one or the other of these functions to an invocation of filter() or define her own relational function. The only constraint is that the function passed must return bool and accept two integers in its parameter list. Here is how filter() might be invoked:

```
vector<int> big_vec;
int value;
// ... fill big_vec and value
vector<int> lt_10 = filter( big_vec, value, less_than );
```

The only task left for us is actually to implement filter():

```
vector<int> filter( const vector<int> &vec,
                    int filter_value,
                    bool (*pred)( int, int ))
{
    vector<int> nvec;

    for ( int ix = 0; ix < vec.size(); ++ix )
            // invokes the function addressed by pred
            // tests element vec[ix] against filter_value
            if ( pred( vec[ ix ], filter_value ))
                nvec.push_back( vec[ ix ] );

    return nvec;
}
```

This implementation of filter() explicitly iterates across each element using a for loop. Let's replace the use of the for loop with the find_if() generic algorithm. We repeatedly apply find_if() to the sequence to identify each element that meets the criteria defined by the user-specified pointer to function. How might we do that?

Let's start with finding every element equal to 10. The find() generic algorithm takes three arguments: the two iterators marking the first and 1 past the last element to examine, and the value we are looking for. In the following code, count_occurs() illustrates how to apply find() repeatedly to a container without looking at any element twice:

```
int count_occurs( const vector<int> &vec, int val )
{
    vector<int>::const_iterator iter = vec.begin();
    int occurs_count = 0;
    while (( iter = find( iter, vec.end(), val )) != vec.end() )
    {
        ++occurs_count;
        ++iter; // address next element
    }
    return ocurs_count;
}
```

The while loop assigns iter the return value of find(). find() returns an iterator addressing an element equal to val or, if no matching element is found, an iterator equal to vec.end(). When iter is equal to vec.end(), the loop terminates.

The success of the while loop depends on our advancing iter 1 past the matching element with each iteration of the loop. For example, let's say that vec contains the following elements: {6,10,8,4,10,7,10}. The declaration statement

```
vector<int>::const_iterator iter = vec.begin();
```

initializes iter to address the first element of the vector that holds the value 6. find() returns an iterator addressing the second element. Before we reinvoke find(), we must advance iter by 1. find() is next invoked with iter addressing the third element. find() returns an iterator addressing the fifth element, and so on.

Function Objects

Before we reimplement filter() to support find_if(), let's look at the predefined function objects provided by the standard library. A *function object* is an instance of a class that provides an overloaded instance of the function call operator. Overloading the call operator allows a function object to be used just as if it were a function.

A function object implements what we would otherwise define as an independent function. Why do we bother? The primary reason is efficiency. We can inline the call operator, thereby eliminating the function call overhead that comes with invoking the operation through a pointer to function.

The standard library predefines a set of arithmetic, relational, and logical function objects. In the following list, type is replaced by a built-in or class type in an actual use of the function object:

- Six arithmetic function objects: plus<type>, minus<type>, negate<type>, multiplies<type>, divides<type>, modulus<type>

- Six relational function objects: less<type>, less_equal<type>, greater<type>, greater_equal<type>, equal_to<type>, not_equal_to<type>

- Three logical function objects, using the &&, ||, and ! operators, respectively: logical_and<type>, logical_or<type>, and logical_not<type>

To use the predefined function objects, we must include the associated header file:

```
#include <functional>
```

For example, by default, `sort()` orders its elements in ascending order using the less-than operator of the underlying element type. If we pass `sort()` the greater-than function object, the elements are now sorted in descending order:

```
sort( vec.begin(), vec.end(), greater<int>() );
```

The syntax

```
greater<int>()
```

causes an unnamed greater class template object to be created and passed into `sort()`.

`binary_search()` expects the elements it searches to be sorted by the less-than operator. For it to search our vector correctly, we must now pass it an instance of the function object used to sort our vector:

```
binary_search( vec.begin(), vec.end(), elem, greater<int>() );
```

Let's display the Fibonacci series in a series of increasingly inpenetrable disguises: each element added to itself, each element multipled by itself, each element added to its associated Pell series element, and so on. One way to do this is by using the `transform()` generic algorithm and the function objects `plus<int>` and `multiplies<int>`.

`transform()` must be passed (1) a pair of iterators to mark the element range to transform, (2) an iterator to point to the beginning of the container from which to fetch the values to apply to the transformation, (3) an iterator to point to the beginning of the container where we are to place the result of each transformation, and (4) the function object (or pointer to function) representing the operation to apply. For example, here is our addition of the Pell elements to those of the Fibonacci:

```
transform( fib.begin(), fib.end(), // (1)
           pell.begin(),           // (2)
           fib_plus_pell.begin(),  // (3)
           plus< int >() );        // (4)
```

In this example, the target vector, `pell`, must be at least as large as `fib`, or else the `transform()` algorithm will overflow `pell`.

In this next call of `transform()`, we multiply each element by itself and store the result by overriding the original element:

```
transform( fib.begin(), fib.end(),    // (1)
           fib.begin(), fib.begin(),  // (2), (3)
           multiplies< int >() );     // (4)
```

Function Object Adapters

These function objects do not quite work with what we need to do with `find_if()`. The `less<type>` function object, for example, expects two values. It evaluates to true if the first value is less than the second. In our case, each element must be compared against the value specified by the user. Ideally, what we need to do is to turn less<type> into a unary operator by binding the second value to that specified by the user. In this way, less<type> compares each element against that value. Can we actually do that? Yes. The standard library provides an *adapter* mechanism to do just that.

A function object adapter modifies a function object. A *binder* adapter converts a binary function object into a unary object by binding one of the arguments to a particular value. This is just what we need. There are two binder adapters: bind1st, which binds the value to the first operand, and bind2nd, which binds the value to the second. Here is a possible modification of filter() using the bind2nd adapter:

```
vector<int> filter( const vector<int> &vec,
                    int val, less<int> &lt )
{
    vector<int> nvec;
    vector<int>::const_iterator iter = vec.begin();

    // bind2nd( less<int>, val )
    // binds val to the second value of less<int>
    // less<int> now compares each value against val

    while (( iter =
            find_if( iter, vec.end(),
                     bind2nd( lt, val ))) != vec.end() )
    {
            // each time iter != vec.end(),
            // iter addresses an element less than val
            nvec.push_back( *iter );
            iter++;
    }
    return nvec;
}
```

How might we generalize filter() further to eliminate its dependence both on the element type of the vector and on the vector container itself? To eliminate the dependency on the element type, we turn filter() into a template function and add the type to our template declaration. To eliminate the vector container dependency, we pass in a first, last iterator pair. Instead, we add another iterator to the parameter list indicating where we should begin copying the elements. Here is our reimplementation:

```
template <typename InputIterator, typename OutputIterator,
          typename ElemType, typename Comp>
OutputIterator
filter( InputIterator first, InputIterator last,
        OutputIterator at, const ElemType &val, Comp pred )
{
    while (( first =
             find_if( first, last,
                      bind2nd( pred, val ))) != last )
```

```
        {
                // just to see what is going on ...
                cout << "found value: " << *first << endl;

                // assign value, then advance both iterators
                *at++ = *first++;
        }
        return at;
    }
```

Can you see how you might actually call filter()? Let's write a small program to test it using both a built-in array and a vector. We need two of each container type: one to hold the values to be filtered, and one to hold the elements that get filtered. For the moment, we define the target container to be the same size as the original container. In Section 3.9, we look at an alternative solution using insert iterator adapters.

```
int main()
{
    const int elem_size = 8;

    int ia[ elem_size ] = { 12, 8, 43, 0, 6, 21, 3, 7 };
    vector<int> ivec( ia, ia+elem_size );

    // containers to hold the results of our filter()
    int ia2[ elem_size ];
    vector<int> ivec2( elem_size );

    cout << "filtering integer array for values less than 8\n";
    filter( ia, ia+elem_size, ia2, elem_size, less<int>() );

    cout << "filtering integer vector for values greater than 8\n";
    filter( ivec.begin(), ivec.end(), ivec2.begin(),
            elem_size, greater<int>() );
}
```

When compiled and executed, this program generates the following output:

```
filtering integer array for values less than 8
found value: 0
found value: 6
found value: 3
found value: 7

filtering integer vector for values greater than 8
found value: 12
found value: 43
found value: 21
```

A *negator* adapter reverses the truth value of a function object. not1 reverses the truth value of a unary function object. not2 reverses the truth value of a binary function

object. For example, to identify the elements greater than or equal to 10, we can negate
the result of the `less<int>()` function object:

```
while (( iter =
        find_if( iter, vec.end(),
               not1( bind2nd( less<int>, 10 ))))
              != vec.end() )
```

In general, there is no one solution to a problem. Our approach to finding all the
elements less than a value, for example, involves looking at each element in turn and
copying each value if it is less than the specified value. That solves our problem but is
not the only approach we might have taken.

An alternative approach is the following: First, we sort the vector. Next, using
`find_if()`, we locate the first element that is greater than the value. Finally, we delete
all the elements from that found element to the end of the vector. Actually, we'll sort
a local copy of the vector. Users might not appreciate our changing the element order
of their vector. Here is a nontemplate version of this solution:

```
vector<int> sub_vec( const vector<int> &vec, int val )
{
    vector<int> local_vec( vec );
    sort( local_vec.begin(), local_vec.end() );

    vector<int>::iterator iter =
          find_if( local_vec.begin(),
                 local_vec.end(),
                 bind2nd( greater<int>, val ));

    local_vec.erase( iter, local_vec.end() );
    return local_vec;
}
```

OK, whew. This is an intense section, and making sense of it might require a second reading and possibly writing some code. A good exercise is to try your hand at
turning `sub_vec()` into a template function along the lines of `filter()`. Let me summa-
rize what we've done.

We start with a function to find the elements in a vector of integers that have a value less than 10. We decide that hard-coding the value is too restrictive.

We first add a value parameter to allow the user to indicate a value against which
to compare the vector elements.

We next add a pointer to function parameter to allow the user to indicate which
comparison filter to apply.

We then introduce function objects, which provide an alternative, more efficient
method of passing an operation into a function. We briefly review the built-in function
objects provided by the standard library. (In Chapter 4 we look at how to write our
own function objects.)

Finally, we reimplement the function as a template function. To support multiple container types, we pass an iterator pair marking the first and 1 past the last element to traverse. To support multiple element types, we parameterize the element type. To support both pointers to functions and function objects, we parameterize the comparison operation to apply to the elements.

Our function is now independent of the element type, the comparison operation, and the container. In short, we have transformed our original function into a generic algorithm.

3.7   Using a Map

A *map* is defined as a pair of values: a key, typically a string that serves as an index and a value associated with that key. A dictionary is one example of a map. A program analyzing the occurrence count of words in a text keeps a map with a string key and an integer value representing an occurrence count:

```
#include <map>
#include <string>
map<string,int> words;
```

The simplest way to enter a key/value pair is

```
words[ "vermeer" ] = 1;
```

For our word occurrence program, we can write the following:

```
string tword;
while ( cin >> tword )
        words[tword]++;
```

The expression

```
words[tword]
```

retrieves the value associated with the string tword contains. If tword is not present in the map, it is entered into the map with a default value of 0. The increment operator increments that value by 1.

The following for loop prints the word and its occurrence count:

```
map<string,int>::iterator it = words.begin();
for ( ; it != words.end(); ++it )
        cout << "key: "    << it->first
             << "value: " << it->second << endl;
```

The member named first accesses the map's key, in this case the string representing the word. The member named second accesses the value, in this case the word's occurrence count.

There are three ways to query a map as to whether a key is present. The obvious way is to apply the key as an index:

```
int count = 0;
if ( !( count = words[ "vermeer" ] ))
        // vermeer not present
```

The disadvantage is that indexing a map *inserts* the key into the map if it is not already present. Its value is given the default value associated with its type. If "vermeer" is not present, for example, this form of search enters it into the map with an occurrence count of zero.

A second way to query the map is to use the find() operation associated with a map (this is not the find() generic algorithm). find() is invoked with the key value:

```
words.find( "vermeer" );
```

If the key value is present, find() returns an iterator to the key/value pair. Otherwise, it returns end():

```
int count = 0;
map<string,int>::iterator it;

it = words.find( "vermeer" );
if ( it != words.end() )
    count = it->second;
```

A third alternative is to query the map using the count() operation associated with a map. count() returns the number of occurrences of the item within the map:

```
int count = 0;
string search_word( "vermeer" );

if ( words.count( search_word )) // ok: present ...
    count = words[ search_word ];
```

A map can have only one occurrence of each key. If we need to store multiple instances of a key, we must use a *multimap*. (I don't discuss multimaps in this text. See [LIPPMAN98], Section 6.15, for a discussion and example of use.)

3.8   Using a Set

A set is a collection of key values. A set is used when we need to know whether a value is present. In a graph traversal algorithm, for example, we might use a set to hold each visited node. Before we move to the next node, we query the set to see whether the node has already been visited.

The word occurrence program of the preceding section, for example, may choose not to count common words. To do this, we define a word-exclusion set of type string:

```
#include <set>
#include <string>
set<string> word_exclusion;
```

Before entering a word into our map, we check whether it is present within the word_exclusion set:

```
while ( cin >> tword )
{
    if ( word_exclusion.count( tword ))
            // present in the set of excluded words?
            // then skip the rest of this iteration
            continue;

        // ok: if here, not an excluded word
        words[ tword ]++;
}
```

The continue statement causes the loop to skip the remaining statements of the current loop iteration. In this case, if tword is within the word_exclusion set, the

```
words[ tword ]++;
```

statement is never executed. The while loop instead begins the next loop iteration by evaluating

```
while ( cin >> tword )
```

A set contains only one instance of each key value. (To store multiple key values, we must use a *multiset*. Again, see [LIPPMAN98], Section 6.15, for a discussion and an example of use.)

By default, the elements are ordered using the less-than operator of the underlying element type. For example, given

```
int ia[ 10 ] = { 1, 3, 5, 8, 5, 3, 1, 5, 8, 1 } ;

vector< int > vec( ia, ia+10 );
set<int>      iset( vec.begin(), vec.end() );
```

the elements contained in iset are {1,3,5,8}.

Individual elements of a set are added using the single argument insert():

```
iset.insert( ival );
```

A range of elements is added using the insert() operation taking two iterators:

```
iset.insert( vec.begin(), vec.end() );
```

Iteration over a set is as you might expect:

```
set<int>::iterator it = iset.begin();
for ( ; it != iset.end(); ++it )
        cout << *it << ' ';

cout << endl;
```

The generic algorithms provide a number of set algorithms: set_intersection(), set_union(), set_difference(), and set_symmetric_difference().

3.9   How to Use Iterator Inserters

In our implementation of `filter()` back in Section 3.6, we assign each element of the source container that matches the predicate test into the target container:

```
while (( first =
            find_if( first, last, bind2nd( pred, val ))) != last )
        *at++ = *first++;
```

This requires that the target container be large enough to hold each assigned value. `filter()` has no way of knowing whether, after each increment, at continues to address a valid container slot. It is up to the programmer to ensure that the target container pointed to by at is large enough. In our test program of Section 3.6, we ensure that by defining the target container to be the same size as the source container:

```
int ia[ elem_size ] = { 12, 8, 43, 0, 6, 21, 3, 7 };
vector<int> ivec( ia, ia+elem_size );

int ia2[ elem_size ];
vector<int> ivec2( elem_size );
```

The problem with this solution is that in most cases the target container is too large. An alternative approach is to define an empty container and expand it as needed through element insertion. Unfortunately, `filter()` is currently implemented to assign into an existing container slot. If we reimplement `filter()` to do insertion, what happens to our existing programs using the assignment implementation of `filter()`? Moreover, what sort of insertion should we provide?

The generic algorithms that copy elements, such as `copy()`, `copy_backwards()`, `remove_copy()`, `replace_copy()`, `unique_copy()`, and so on, are similar in implementation to `filter()`. Each is passed an iterator that marks the position within a container to begin copying. With each element copy, the value is assigned and the iterator incremented. Each copy requires that we guarantee that the target container is of a sufficient size to hold the set of assigned elements. With these algorithms we don't have the option of reimplementing them.

Does this mean that we must always pass in a fixed-size container for those algorithms? That's hardly in the spirit of the STL. Rather, the standard library provides three insertion adapters. These adapters allow us to override a container's assignment operator.

- `back_inserter()` causes the container's `push_back()` operator to be invoked in place of the assignment operator. This is the preferred inserter for vectors. The argument to `back_inserter` is the container:

```
vector<int> result_vec;
unique_copy( ivec.begin(), ivec.end(),
                back_inserter( result_vec ));
```

- `inserter()` causes the container's `insert()` operation to be invoked. `inserter()` takes two arguments: the container, and an iterator into the container indicating the position at which insertion should begin. For a vector, we would write the following:

```
vector<string> svec_res;
unique_copy( svec.begin(), svec.end(),
             inserter( svec_res, svec_res.end() ));
```

- `front_inserter()` causes the container's `push_front()` operator to be invoked. This inserter can be used only with the list and deque containers:

```
list<int> ilist_clone;
copy( ilist.begin(), ilist.end(),
      front_inserter( ilist_clone ));
```

To use these adapters, we must include the `iterator` header file:

```
#include <iterator>
```

These adapters, however, cannot be used with a built-in array. The built-in array provides no support for element insertion. Here is a reimplementation of the program in Section 3.6 making use of a `back_inserter` for the vector use of `filter()`:

```
int main()
{
    const int elem_size = 8;

    int ia[ elem_size ] = { 12, 8, 43, 0, 6, 21, 3, 7 };
    vector<int> ivec( ia, ia+elem_size );

    // built-in arrays do not support insertion ...
    int ia2[ elem_size ];
    vector<int> ivec2;

    cout << "filtering integer array for values less than 8\n";
    filter( ia, ia+elem_size, ia2,
            elem_size, less<int>() );

    cout << "filtering integer vector for values greater than 8\n";
    filter( ivec.begin(), ivec.end(),
            back_inserter( ivec2 ),
            elem_size, greater<int>() );
}
```

`filter()` assigns each element in turn to the target vector — in this case, `ivec2`. In this example, we have not initialized `ivec2` to an element size, so an assignment would result in a run-time failure. By passing in `ivec2` using an inserter adapter, we turn the element assignment into an insertion. Because insertion into a vector is efficient only at the back, we choose to use a `back_inserter`.

3.10   Using the iostream Iterators

Imagine that we have been given the task of reading a sequence of string elements
from standard input, storing them into a vector, sorting them, and then writing the
words back to standard output. A typical solution looks like this:

```cpp
#include <iostream>
#incluse <string>
#include <vector>
#include <algorithm>
using namespace std;

int main()
{
    string word;
    vector<string> text;

    // ok: let's read each word in turn until done
    while ( cin >> word )
            text.push_back( word );

    // ok: sort it
    sort( text.begin(), text.end() );

    // ok: let's write them back
    for ( int ix = 0; ix < text.size(); ++ix )
        cout << text[ ix ] << ' ';
}
```

The standard library defines both input and output iostream iterator classes, called
istream_iterator and ostream_iterator, that provide a shorthand method of reading
and writing elements of a single type. To use either iterator class, we must include the
iterator header file:

```cpp
#include <iterator>
```

For example, let's see how we can use the istream_iterator class to read our string
sequence from standard input. As with all iterators, we need a first, last pair of
istream_iterators that mark the range of elements. The definition

```cpp
istream_iterator<string> is( cin );
```

provides us with a first iterator. It defines is as an istream_iterator bound to standard input that reads elements of type string. We also need a last iterator that represents 1 past the last element to be read. For standard input, end-of-file represents 1
past the last element to be read. How do we indicate that? The definition of an
istream_iterator without an istream object, such as eof,

```cpp
istream_iterator<string> eof;
```

represents end-of-file. How do we actually use this pair? In the following example, we pass them to the generic algorithm copy() together with the vector to store the string elements. Because we don't know what size to make the vector, we adapt it with a back_inserter:

```
copy( is, eof, back_inserter( text ));
```

Now we need an ostream_iterator to mark where to write each string element. We stop when there are no more elements to write out. The following defines os to be an ostream_iterator tied to standard output that holds elements of type string.

```
ostream_iterator<string> os( cout, " " );
```

The second argument is either a C-style character string or a string literal that indicates the delimiter to output between the elements. By default, the elements are written without any delimiter between them. In this example, I've chosen to output each element separated by a space. Here is how we might use it:

```
copy( text.begin(), text.end(), os );
```

copy() writes each element stored within text to the ostream indicated by os. Each element is separated by a space. Here is the complete program:

```
#include <iostream>
#include <iterator>
#include <algorithm>
#include <vector>
#include <string>
using namespace std;

int main()
{
    istream_iterator< string > is( cin );
    istream_iterator< string > eof;

    vector< string > text;
    copy( is, eof, back_inserter( text ));

    sort( text.begin(), text.end() );

    ostream_iterator<string> os( cout, " " );
    copy( text.begin(), text.end(), os );
}
```

Often, rather than read from standard input or write to standard output, we read from and write to a file. How can we do that? We simply bind the istream_iterator to an ifstream class object and the ostream_iterator to an ofstream class object:

```
#include <iostream>
#include <fstream>
#include <iterator>
```

```
#include <algorithm>
#include <vector>
#include <string>
using namespace std;

int main()
{
    ifstream in_file( "as_you_like_it.txt" );
    ofstream out_file( "as_you_like_it_sorted.txt" );

    if ( ! in_file || ! out_file )
    {
        cerr << "!!unable to open the necessary files.\n";
        return -1;
    }

    istream_iterator< string > is( in_file );
    istream_iterator< string > eof;

    vector< string > text;
    copy( is, eof, back_inserter( text ));

    sort( text.begin(), text.end() );

    ostream_iterator<string> os( out_file, " " );
    copy( text.begin(), text.end(), os );I
}
```

Exercise 3.1

Write a program to read a text file. Store each word in a map. The key value of the map
is the count of the number of times the word appears in the text. Define a word exclusion set containing words such as *a, an, or, the, and,* and *but.* Before entering a word in
the map, make sure it is not present in the word exclusion set. Display the list of words
and their associated count when the reading of the text is complete. As an extension,
before displaying the text, allow the user to query the text for the presence of a word.

Exercise 3.2

Read in a text file — it can be the same one as in Exercise 3.1 — storing it in a vector.
Sort the vector by the length of the string. Define a function object to pass to sort(); it
should accept two strings and return true if the first string is shorter than the second.
Print the sorted vector.

Exercise 3.3

Define a map for which the index is the family surname and the key is a vector of the children's names. Populate the map with at least six entries. Test it by supporting user queries based on a surname and printing all the map entries.

Exercise 3.4

Write a program to read a sequence of integer numbers from standard input using an istream_iterator. Write the odd numbers into one file using an ostream_iterator. Each value should be separated by a space. Write the even numbers into a second file, also using an ostream_iterator. Each of these values should be placed on a separate line.

4

Object-Based Programming

Although we've yet to write a class of our own, we've used classes extensively since Chapter 1: the string and vector classes, the iostream classes supporting input and output, and so on. In this chapter, we design and implement our own classes.

What do we know about classes from our use of them? Before we can use a class, we must make it known to the program because the class is not built into the language. Usually, we do this by including a header file:

```
#include <string>
string pooh[ 4 ] =
    { "winnie", "robin", "eeyore", "piglet" };
```

The class name serves as a type name in the same way as the built-in type names such as int and double. Often, there are multiple ways to initialize an object of a class:

```
#include <vector>

string dummy( "dummy" );
vector< string > svec1( 4 );
vector< string > svec2( 4, dummy );
vector< string > svec3( pooh, pooh+4 );
```

Each class provides a set of operations we can apply to objects of the class. These operations typically consist of named functions, such as size() and empty(), and overloaded instances of the predefined operators, such as inequality and assignment:

```
if ( svec2 != svec3 && ! svec3.empty() )
    svec2 = svec3;

if ( svec2.size() == 4 )
    // all is well ...
```

What we don't know, generally, is how the class is implemented. Does the string class calculate its size at each request, or does it store the size within each class object? Are the elements of the vector stored within the vector object, or are the elements stored elsewhere and addressed within the vector object by a pointer?

In general, a class consists of two parts: a public set of operations and operators, and a private implementation. These operations and operators are called class *member functions* and represent the *public interface* of the class. As users of a class, we can access only the public interface. This, in fact, is how we have used the string class, the vector class, and so on. For example, all we know about the size() member function of string is its prototype: It has a void parameter list and returns an integer value.

The private implementation of a class consists of the member function definitions and any data associated with the class. For example, if the string class object calculates the length of its string with each invocation of size(), no associated data is required and the definition of size() is likely to involve a for loop walking the length of the string. If the string class object stores the length of its string, a private *data member* must be defined within each class object. This definition of size() returns the value of that member. Each time the length of the string is modified, the data member must be updated.

These kinds of implementation details are usually of no concern to the user of the class. As users, we simply program to the public interface. In this way, as long as the interface does not change, our code using that interface also does not need to change, even if the underlying implementation is reengineered.

In this chapter, we turn from just using classes to providing classes for ourselves and others to use. Designing and implementing classes are the primary activities of C++ programmers.

4.1   How to Implement a Class

OK, where do we start? In general, we start with an abstraction. Consider a stack. A stack is a fundamental abstraction of computer science. It allows for the nesting and retrieval of values in a last-in, first-out sequence. We nest values by *pushing* a new value onto the stack, and we retrieve them by *popping* the last value pushed on the stack. Other operations that users often require are to ask whether a stack is *full* or *empty* and to determine the *size* of the stack. A stack may also support *peeking* at the last value pushed on the stack.

In the description of a stack I italicized the words that represent operations that users will likely want to apply to objects of our stack class.

What type of elements should we store? A general stack should store all types. We do this by defining the stack as a class template. Because class templates are the topic of Chapter 6 and we're only in Chapter 4, we'll define a nontemplate stack class to hold string class objects.

A class declaration begins with the keyword class followed by a user-specified class name:

```
class Stack;
```

This statement serves as a forward declaration of the Stack class; it introduces the class name to the compiler but provides no details of the operations it supports or the data members it contains. A forward declaration allows us to define class pointers and to use the class as a type specifier for class declarations:

```
// ok: these uses require a forward declaration of the class
Stack *pt = 0;
void process( const Stack& );
```

The class definition is necessary before we can define an actual Stack class object or refer to any members of the class. The skeleton of a class definition looks like this:

```
class Stack {
public:
    // ... public interface
private:
    // ... private implementation
};
```

The definition of a class consists of the class declaration followed by the class body enclosed in curly braces and terminated by a semicolon. The `public` and `private` keywords within the class body control access to the members declared within each section. Public members can be accessed from anywhere within the program. Private members can be accessed only by the member functions and *friends* of the class — later I explain what a friend is (or at least what a friend within the C++ language is). Here is the beginning of our Stack class definition:

```
class Stack {
public:
    // each operation returns true if able to be carried out
    // pop and peek place the string value within elem
    bool    push( const string& );
    bool    pop(  string &elem );
    bool    peek( string &elem );

    bool    empty();
    bool    full();

    // definition of size() is placed within class
    // other members are simply declared ...
    int     size() { return _stack.size(); }
private:
    vector<string> _stack;
};
```

Our Stack class definition supports the six operations we identified at the start of this section. The elements themselves are stored in a vector of strings we've named _stack. (My coding convention is to prepend data members with an underscore.) Here is how we might define and use a Stack class object:

```
void fill_stack( Stack &stack, istream &is = cin )
{
    string str;
    while ( is >> str && ! stack.full() )
            stack.push( str );

    cout << "Read in " << stack.size() << " elements\n";
}
```

All member functions must be declared within the class definition. Optionally, a member function can also be defined inside the class definition. If defined within the body of the class, the member function is automatically treated as being inline. size(), for example, is an inline member of Stack.

To define a member function outside the class definition, we use a special declaration syntax. Its purpose is to identify the function as a member of a particular class. If the function is intended to be inline, the inline keyword must be specified:

```
inline bool
Stack::empty()
{
    return _stack.empty();
}

bool
Stack::pop( string &elem )
{
    if ( empty() )
        return false;

    elem = _stack.back();
    _stack.pop_back();
    return true;
}
```

The syntax

```
Stack::empty()
```

tells the compiler (and reader) that we are referring to the member empty() of the Stack class — as opposed, say, to that of the vector or the string class. The name of the class followed by the double colon (Stack::) is called the *class scope operator*.

There is no difference in the treatment of an inline function if it is defined within or outside the class definition. As with the definition of a nonmember inline function, an inline member function should be placed in a header file. The class definition and the inline member functions are typically placed in a header file given the name of the class. For example, the Stack class definition and the definition of empty() would be placed inside a header file named Stack.h. This is what the user includes whenever he wishes to use our class.

The non-inline member functions are defined within a program text file, usually given the name of the class followed by one of the following suffixes: .C, .cc, .cpp, and .cxx (the x represents the reclining +). Microsoft Visual C++, for example, uses .cpp by default. The convention at Disney Feature Animation is to use .C. The convention at Dreamworks Animation is to use .cc.

Here are the remaining Stack member function definitions. full() compares the current size of the underlying vector with max_size(), the largest possible size of the vector. push() inserts an element provided that the _stack is not full.

```
inline bool Stack::full()
    { return _stack.size() == _stack.max_size(); }

bool Stack::peek( string &elem )
{
    if ( empty() )
        return false;

    elem = _stack.back();
    return true;
}
bool Stack::push( const string &elem )
{
    if ( full() )
        return false;

    _stack.push_back( elem );
    return true;
}
```

Although we've provided definitions for the full set of user operations, this is not yet a complete Stack class definition. In the next section, we walk through how to provide special initialization and deinitialization functions called the class *constructor* and *destructor*.

Exercise 4.1

Create a Stack.h and a Stack.suffix, where suffix is whatever convention your compiler or project follows. Write a main() function to exercise the full public interface, and compile and execute it. Both the program text file and main() must include Stack.h:

```
#include "Stack.h"
```

Exercise 4.2

Extend the Stack class to support both a find() and a count() operation. find() returns true or false depending on whether the value is found. count() returns the number of occurrences of the string. Reimplement the main() of Exercise 4.1 to invoke both functions.

4.2   What Are Class Constructors and the Class Destructor?

Each of our numeric sequences is a good candidate for a class. A numeric sequence class object represents a range of elements within its associated sequence. By default, the beginning position is 1. For example,

```
Fibonacci fib1( 7, 3 );
```

defines a Fibonacci class object of 7 elements beginning at position 3, and

```
Pell pel( 10 );
```

defines a Pell class object of 10 elements beginning at the default position of 1. Finally,

```
Fibonacci fib2( fib1 );
```

initializes fib2 to a copy of fib1.

Each class must keep track both of its length — how many elements of the series are represented — and of a beginning position. A 0 or negative beginning position or length is not permitted. We store both the length and the beginning position as integers. For the moment, we define a third member, _next, which keeps track of the next element to iterate over:

```
class Triangular {
public:
   // ...
private:
   int _length; // number of elements
   int _beg_pos; // beginning position of range
   int _next;    // next element to iterate over
};
```

The data members are stored within each Triangular class object. When I write

```
Triangular tri( 8, 3 );
```

tri contains an instance of _length (initialized to 8), _beg_pos (initialized to 3), and _next (initialized to 2 because the third element is indexed within the vector at position 2). Notice that it doesn't contain an instance of the actual vector holding the triangular sequence elements. Why? It's because we don't want a copy of that vector in each class object; one instance is enough for all class objects. (In Section 4.5 we look at how to support that.)

How do these data members get initialized? No, magic is not an option; the compiler does not do it for us. However, if we provide one or more special initialization functions, the compiler does invoke the appropriate instance each time a class object is defined. These special initialization functions are called *constructors*.

We identify a constructor by giving it the same name as the class. The syntactic rules are that the constructor must not specify a return type nor return a value. It can be overloaded. For example, here are three possible Triangular class constructors:

```
class Triangular {
public:
    // overloaded set of constructors
    Triangular(); // default constructor
    Triangular( int len );
    Triangular( int len, int beg_pos );

    // ...
};
```

A constructor is invoked automatically based on the values supplied to the class object being defined. For example,

```
Triangular t;
```

causes the default constructor to be applied to t. Similarly,

```
Triangular t2( 10, 3 );
```

causes the two-argument constructor to be applied. The values in parentheses are treated as the values to be passed to the constructor. Similarly,

```
Triangular t3 = 8;
```

causes the one-argument integer constructor to be applied.

Surprisingly, the following does *not* define a Triangular class object:

```
Triangular t5(); // not what it seems :-)
```

Rather, this defines t5 to be a function with an empty parameter list and returning a Triangular object. Obviously, this is a weird interpretation. Why is it interpreted this way? It's because C++ once needed to be compatible with the C language, and in C the parentheses following t5 in this case identify it as a function. The correct declaration of t5 is the same as t, shown earlier:

```
Triangular t5; // ok
```

The simplest constructor is the *default constructor*. A default constructor requires no arguments. This means one of two things. Either it takes no arguments:

```
Triangular::Triangular()
{   // default constructor
    _length = 1;
    _beg_pos = 1;
    _next = 0;
}
```

or, more commonly, it provides a default value for each parameter:

```
class Triangular {
public:
    // also a default constructor
    Triangular( int len = 1, int bp = 1 );
    // ...
};
```

```
Triangular::Triangular( int len, int bp )
{
    // _length and _beg_pos both must be at least 1
    // best not to trust the user to always be right
    _length = len > 0 ? len : 1;
    _beg_pos = bp > 0 ? bp  : 1;
    _next = _beg_pos-1;
}
```

Because we provide a default value for both integer parameters, the single default constructor instance supports the original three constructors:

```
Triangular tri1;          // Triangular::Triangular( 1, 1 );
Triangular tri2( 12 );    // Triangular::Triangular( 12, 1 );
Triangular tri3( 8, 3 ); // Triangular::Triangular( 8, 3 );
```

The Member Initialization List

A second initialization syntax within the constructor definition uses the *member initialization list*:

```
Triangular::Triangular( const Triangular &rhs )
    : _length ( rhs._length  ),
      _beg_pos( rhs._beg_pos ),_next( rhs._beg_pos-1 )
{} // yes, empty!
```

The member initialization list is set off from the parameter list by a colon. It is a comma-separated list in which the value to be assigned the member is placed in parentheses following the member's name; it looks like a constructor call.

In this example, the two alternative constructor definitions are equivalent. There is no significant benefit in choosing one form over the other.

The member initialization list is used primarily to pass arguments to member class object constructors. For example, let's redefine the Triangular class to contain a string class member:

```
class Triangular {
public:
    // ...
private:
    string _name;
    int    _next, _length, _beg_pos;
};
```

To pass the string constructor the value with which to initialize _name, we use the member initialization list.For example,

```
Triangular::Triangular( int len, int bp )
    : _name( "Triangular" )
{
    _length = len > 0 ? len : 1;
```

```
            _beg_pos = bp > 0 ? bp   : 1;
            _next = _beg_pos-1;
    }
```

Complementing the constructor mechanism is that of the destructor. A *destructor* is a user-defined class member function that, if present, is applied automatically to a class object before the end of its lifetime. The primary use of a destructor is to free resources acquired within the constructor or during the lifetime of the object.

A destructor is given the name of the class prefixed by a tilde (~). It must not specify a return value and must declare an empty parameter list. Because it has an empty parameter list, the class destructor cannot be overloaded.

Consider the following Matrix class. Within its constructor, the new expression is applied to allocate an array of doubles from the heap. The destructor is used to free that memory:

```
class Matrix {
public:
    Matrix( int row, int col )
           : _row( row ), _col( col )
    {
            // constructor allocates a resource
            // note: no error checking is shown
            _pmat = new double[ row * col ];
    }

    ~Matrix()
    {
            // destructor frees the resource
            delete [] _pmat;
    }

    // ...

private:
    int      _row, _col;
    double *_pmat;
};
```

In effect, we have automated the heap memory management within the Matrix class through the definition of its constructor and destructor. For example, consider the following statement block:

```
    {
        Matrix mat( 4, 4 );
        // constructor applied here

        // ...
        // destructor applied here
    }
```

The compiler applies the Matrix class constructor implicitly following the definition of mat. Internally, _pmat is initialized with the address of an array of 16 doubles allocated on the program's free store. Just before the closing brace of the statement block, the Matrix destructor is applied implicitly by the compiler. Internally, the array of 16 doubles addressed by _pmat is freed through the delete expression. Users of the Matrix class do not need to know any of the memory management details. This arrangment loosely mimics the design of the standard library container classes.

It is not always necessary to define a destructor. In our Triangular class, for example, the three data members are stored by value. They come into existence when the class object is defined and are deallocated automatically when the lifetime of the class object ends. There is no real work for the Triangular destructor to do. We are under no obligation to provide a destructor. The hard part is to understand when one is or is not necessary.

Memberwise Initialization

By default, when we initialize one class object with another, as in

```
Triangular tri1( 8 );
Triangular tri2 = tri1;
```

the data members of the class are copied in turn. In our example, _length, _beg_pos, and _next are copied in turn from tri1 to tri2. This is called *default memberwise initialization.*

In the case of the Triangular class, default memberwise initialization correctly copies the class data members and there is nothing we need to do explicitly. In the case of the Matrix class introduced earlier, the default memberwise behavior is not adequate. For example, consider the following:

```
{
    Matrix mat( 4, 4 );
    // constructor applied here
    {
        Matrix mat2 = mat;
        // default memberwise copy applied
        // ... use mat2 here
        // destructor applied here for mat2
    }
    // ... use mat here
    // destructor applied here for mat
}
```

The default initialization of the _pmat member of mat2 with that of mat,

```
mat2._pmat = mat._pmat;
```

causes the two instances of _pmat to address the same array in heap memory. When the Matrix destructor is applied to mat2, the array is deallocated. Unfortunately, the _pmat member of mat continues to address and manipulate the now deallocated array. This is a serious program bug.

How can we fix this? In this case, we must override the default memberwise behavior. We do that by providing an explicit instance of the Matrix class copy constructor. (By *we* I mean the designer of the Matrix class. The users of the Matrix class just presume we have done the right thing.)

If the designer of the class provides an explicit instance of the copy constructor, that instance is used in place of default memberwise initialization. The source code of the user need not change, although it must be recompiled.

What does our copy constructor look like? Its single argument is a const reference to an object of the Matrix class:

```
Matrix::Matrix( const Matrix &rhs ){
    // what should go here?
}
```

How should it be implemented? Let's create a separate copy of the array so that the destruction of one class object does not interfere with the behavior of the second:

```
Matrix::Matrix( const Matrix &rhs )
    : _row( rhs._row ), _col( rhs._col )
{ // create a "deep copy" of the array addressed by rhs._pmat
    int elem_cnt = _row * _col;
    _pmat = new double[ elem_cnt ];

    for ( int ix = 0; ix < elem_cnt; ++ix ]
        _pmat[ ix ] = rhs._pmat[ ix ];
}
```

When we design a class, we must ask ourselves whether the default memberwise behavior is adequate for the class. If it is, we need not provide an explicit copy constructor. If it is not, we *must* define an explicit instance and within it implement the correct initialization semantics.

If our class requires a copy constructor, it also requires a copy assignment operator (see Section 4.8). For a more detailed discussion of class constructors and destructors see [LIPPMAN98], Chapter 14, and [LIPPMAN96a], Chapters 2 and 5.

4.3   What Are **mutable** and **const**?

Consider the following small function:

```
int sum( const Triangular &trian )
{
    int beg_pos = trian.beg_pos();
    int length  = trian.length();
    int sum = 0;
```

```
        for ( int ix = 0; ix < length; ++ix )
            sum += trian.elem( beg_pos+ix );
        return sum;
    }
```

trian is a const reference parameter. The compiler, therefore, must guarantee that trian is not modified within sum(). Potentially, trian is modified within any member function that it invokes. To be certain that trian is not modified, the compiler must be sure that beg_pos(), length(), and elem() do not change the class object that invokes them. How does the compiler know that? The class designer must tell the compiler by labeling as const each member function that does not modify the class object:

```
class Triangular {
public:
    // const member functions
    int length()        const { return _length;  }
    int beg_pos()       const { return _beg_pos; }
    int elem( int pos ) const;

    // non-const member functions
    bool next( int &val );
    void next_reset() { _next = _beg_pos - 1; }

    // ...
private:
    int _length; // number of elements
    int _beg_pos; // beginning position of range
    int _next;    // next element to iterate over

    // static data members are covered in Section 4.5
    static vector<int> _elems;
};
```

The const modifier follows the parameter list of the function. A const member function defined outside the class body must specify the const modifier in both its declaration and definition. For example,

```
int Triangular::elem( int pos ) const
    { return _elems[ pos-1 ]; }
```

Although the compiler does not analyze each function to determine whether it is a const or a non-const member function, it does examine each const member function to make sure that it doesn't modify the class object. For example, if we were to declare the following instance of next() as a const member function, that declaration would be flagged as an error because it clearly modifies the class object that invokes it.

```
bool Triangular::next( int &value ) const
{
    if ( _next < _beg_pos + _length - 1 )
    {
```

```
                // error: modifying _next
            value = _elems[ _next++ ];
            return true;
        }
        return false;
    }
```

In the following class, the val() member function does not directly modify the
_val data member, but it does return a non-const reference to _val. Can val() still be
declared as const?

```
    class val_class {
    public:
        val_class( const BigClass &v )
            : _val( v ){}

        // is this ok?
        BigClass& val() const { return _val; }

    private:
        BigClass _val;
    };
```

No. Returning a non-const reference to _val in effect opens it to modification in the
general program. Because a member function can be overloaded based on its const-
ness, one solution to this problem is to provide two definitions — a const and a non-
const version — such as the following:

```
    class val_class {
    public:
        const BigClass& val() const { return _val; }
        BigClass& val(){ return _val; }
        // ...
    };
```

For a non-const class object, the non-const instance of val() is invoked. For a const
class object, the const instance is invoked. For example,

```
    void example( const BigClass *pbc, BigClass &rbc )
    {
        pbc->val(); // invokes const instance
        rbc.val();    // invokes non-const instance
        // ...
    }
```

When you design a class, it is important to identify the const member functions. If
you forget, each const reference class parameter will be unable to invoke the non-const
portion of the class interface. Users may become abusive. Retrofitting const onto a
class is challenging, particularly if there is widespread invocation of one member function by another.

Mutable Data Member

Here is an alternative implementation of sum() using the next() and next_reset() member functions to iterate across the elements of trian.

```cpp
int sum( const Triangular &trian )
{
    if ( ! trian.length() )
        return 0;

    int val, sum = 0;
    trian.next_reset();
    while ( trian.next( val ))
            sum += val;

    return sum;
}
```

Will this code compile? No, at least not yet. trian is a const class object. next_reset() and next() are not const member functions because both functions modify _next. Their invocation by trian, therefore, is flagged as an error.

If we are to use this implementation of sum(), both next() and next_reset() must become const member functions. We can do that by making a fine distinction.

_length and _beg_pos support the attributes of the numeric series abstraction. If we change the length or beginning position of trian, in a sense we change its identity. It is no longer equal to what it was before the change. _next, however, supports our implementation of an iterator mechanism; it does not itself support the numeric sequence abstraction. Changing the value of _next does not semantically change the class object and, one might claim, does not violate the const-ness of the object. (I said we would be making a fine distinction.) The mutable keyword provides us with a way of making just such a claim. By identifying _next as mutable, we are saying that changes to it do not violate the const-ness of our class object.

```cpp
class Triangular {
public:
    bool next( int &val ) const;
    void next_reset() const { _next = _beg_pos - 1; }
    // ...

private:
    mutable int _next,
    int _beg_pos;
    int _length;
};
```

next() and next_reset() can now modify _next and still be declared as const member functions, allowing our alternative implementation of sum(). Here is a small program that exercises sum() on three Triangular class objects:

```
int main()
{
      Triangular tri( 4 );
      cout << tri << " -- sum of elements: "
           << sum( tri ) << endl;

      Triangular tri2( 4, 3 );
      cout << tri2 << " -- sum of elements: "
           << sum( tri2 ) << endl;

      Triangular tri3( 4, 8 );
      cout << tri3  << " -- sum of elements: "
           << sum( tri3 ) << endl;

}
```

When compiled and executed, it generates the following output:

```
( 1 , 4 ) 1 3 6 10  -- sum of elements: 20
( 3 , 4 ) 6 10 15 21  -- sum of elements: 52
( 8 , 4 ) 36 45 55 66  -- sum of elements: 202
```

4.4   What Is the this Pointer?

We must implement a copy() member function that initializes one Triangular class object with another. For example, given

```
Triangular tr1( 8 );
Triangular tr2( 8, 9 );
```

the invocation of

```
tr1.copy( tr2);
```

assigns tr1 the length and beginning position of tr2. In addition, copy() must return the class object that is the target of the copy. In our example, tr1 is both the target and the object that must be returned. How can we do that? For example, here is an implementation of copy():

```
Triangular& Triangular::
copy( const Triangular &rhs )
{
   _length = rhs._length;
   _beg_pos = rhs._beg.pos;
   _next = rhs._beg_pos-1;

   return ??? what exactly ???;
};
```

rhs is bound to tr2 in our example. In the assignment

```
_length = rhs._length;
```

_length refers to the member associated with tr1. We need a way of referring to the tr1 class object as a whole. The this pointer provides us with that handle.

Within a member function, the this pointer addresses the class object that invokes the member function. In our example, tr1 is addressed by the this pointer. How does that get done? Internally, the compiler adds the this pointer as an argument to each class member function. copy(), for example, is transformed as follows:

```
// Pseudo Code: Internal Member Function Transformation

Triangular& Triangular::
copy( Triangular *this, const Triangular &rhs )
{
   this->_length  = rhs._length;
   this->_beg_pos = rhs._beg.pos;
   this->_next = rhs._beg_pos-1;
};
```

This transformation requires a second transformation: Each invocation of copy() must now provide two arguments. To accomplish this, our original invocation

```
tr1.copy( tr2);
```

is internally transformed into

```
// internal code transformation:
// tr1 becomes the class object addressed by the this pointer
copy( &tr1, tr2);
```

Inside a class member function, the this pointer provides access to the class object through which the member function is invoked. To return tr1 from within copy(), we simply dereference the this pointer as follows:

```
// returns the class object addressed by the this pointer
return *this;
```

When you copy one class object with another, it is a good practice to first check to make sure that the two class objects are not the same. To do this, we again use the this pointer:

```
Triangular& Triangular::
copy( const Triangular &rhs )
{
   // check that the two objects are not the same
   if ( this != &rhs )
   {
      _length = rhs._length;
      _beg_pos = rhs._beg_pos;
      _next = rhs._beg_pos-1;
   }
   return *this;
}
```

4.5   Static Class Members

In our procedural implementation of Chapter 2, we maintain one container instance to hold the elements of the Fibonacci sequence through use of a local `static` vector. Our class implementation also needs only one container instance to hold the elements of each numeric sequence. The `static` keyword again provides the solution, although it means something different when used within a class.

A static data member represents a single, shared instance of that member that is accessible to all the objects of that class. In the following class definition, for example, we declare `_elems` as a static data member of the Triangular class:

```
class Triangular {
public:
    // ...
private:
    static vector<int> _elems;
};
```

Because only a single instance of a static data member exists, we must provide an explicit definition of that instance within a program text file. The definition looks like the global definition of an object except that its name is qualified with the class scope operator:

```
// placed in program text file, such as Triangular.cpp
vector<int> Triangular::_elems;
```

An initial value, if desired, can also be specified:

```
int Triangular::_initial_size = 8;
```

The member functions of the class can access a static data member the same as if it were an ordinary data member:

```
Triangular::Triangular( int len, int beg_pos )
    : _length( len > 0 ? len : 1 ),
      _beg_pos( beg_pos > 0 ? beg_pos : 1 )
{
    _next = _beg_pos-1;
    int elem_cnt = _beg_pos + _length;

    if ( _elems.size() < elem_cnt )
         gen_elements( elem_cnt );
}
```

A `const static int` data member, such as `buf_size`, next, is the one instance in which a class member can be explicitly initialized within its declaration:

```
class intBuffer {
public:
    // ...
```

```
private:
    static const int _buf_size = 1024;  // ok
    int _buffer[ _buf_size ];           // ok
};
```

Static Member Functions

Consider the following implementation of is_elem(). Given a value, it returns true or false depending on whether the value is an element of the Triangular sequence:

```
bool Triangular::
is_elem( int value )
{
    if ( ! _elems.size() ||
         _elems[ _elems.size()-1 ] < value )
            gen_elems_to_value( value );

    vector<int>::iterator found_it;
    vector<int>::iterator end_it = _elems.end();

    found_it = find( _elems.begin(), end_it, value );
    return found_it != end_it;
}
```

Ordinarily, a member function must be invoked through an object of the class. The object is bound to the member function's this pointer. It is through the this pointer that a member function accesses the nonstatic data members stored within each class object.

is_elem(), however, does not access any nonstatic data members. Its operation is independent of any particular class object, and it would be convenient to invoke it as a freestanding function. We can't write

```
if ( is_elem( 8 )) ...
```

however, because there is no way for the compiler or reader to know which is_elem() we want to invoke. Use of the class scope operator clears up that ambiguity:

```
if ( Triangular::is_elem( 8 )) ...
```

A static member function can be invoked independently of a class object in exactly this way. A member function can be declared as static only if it does not access any nonstatic class members. We make it static by prefacing its declaration within the class definition with the keyword static:

```
class Triangular {
public:
    static bool is_elem( int );
    static void gen_elements( int length );
    static void gen_elems_to_value( int value );
    static void display( int len, int beg_pos, ostream &os = cout );
    // ...
```

```
    private:
       static const int   _max_elems = 1024;
       static vector<int> _elems;
       // ...
    };
```

When defined outside the class body, the static keyword is not repeated (this is also true of static data members):

```
    void Triangular::
    gen_elems_to_value( int value )
    {
       int ix = _elems.size();
       if ( ! ix )
       {
            _elems.push_back( 1 );
            ix = 1;
       }

       while ( _elems[ ix-1 ] < value &&
               ix < _max_elems )
       {
          // cout << "elems to value: " << ix*(ix+1)/2 << endl;
          _elems.push_back( ix*(ix+1)/2 );
          ++ix;
       }

       if ( ix == _max_elems )
          cerr << "Triangular Sequence: oops: value too large "
               << value << " --  exceeds max size of "
               << _max_elems << endl;
    }
```

Here is an example of how we might independently invoke is_elem():

```
    #include <iostream>
    #include "Triangular.h"
    using namespace std;

    int main()
    {
       char ch;
       bool more = true;

       while ( more )
       {
            cout << "Enter value: ";
            int ival;
            cin >> ival;

            bool is_elem = Triangular::is_elem( ival );
```

```
        cout << ival
            << ( is_elem ? " is " : " is not " )
            << "an element in the Triangular series.\n"
            << "Another value? (y/n) ";

    cin >> ch;
    if ( ch == 'n' || ch == 'N' )
        more = false;
    }
}
```

When the program is compiled and executed, it generates the following output (my input is highlighted in bold):

```
Enter value: 1024
1024 is not an element in the Triangular series.
Another value? (y/n) y
Enter value: 0
0 is not an element in the Triangular series.
Another value? (y/n) y
Enter value: 36
36 is an element in the Triangular series.
Another value? (y/n) y
Enter value: 55
55 is an element in the Triangular series.
Another value? (y/n) n
```

For completeness, here is the definition of gen_elements():

```
void Triangular::
gen_elements( int length )
{
    if ( length < 0 || length > _max_elems ){
        // issue error message and return
    }

    if ( _elems.size() < length )
    {
        int ix = _elems.size() ? _elems.size()+1 : 1;
        for ( ; ix <= length-1; ++ix )
            _elems.push_back( ix*(ix+1)/2 );
    }
}
```

4.6   Building an Iterator Class

To illustrate how to overload a set of operators for a class, let's walk through the implementation of an iterator class. We must support the following usage:

```
Triangular trian( 1, 8 );
Triangular::iterator
            it = trian.begin(),
            end_it = trian.end();

while ( it != end_it )
{
    cout << *it << ' ';
    ++it;
}
```

For this to work, of course, the operators !=, *, and ++ must be defined for objects of the iterator class. How do we do this? We define them as operator member functions. An operator function looks like an ordinary function except that rather than provide the function with a name, we specify the keyword operator followed by the operator we wish to overload. For example,

```
class Triangular_iterator
{
public:
// set _index to index-1 in order not to subtract 1 with
// each element access ...
    Triangular_iterator( int index ) : _index( index-1 ){}
    bool operator==( const Triangular_iterator& ) const;
    bool operator!=( const Triangular_iterator& ) const;
    int  operator*() const;
    int& operator++();        // prefix version
    int  operator++( int );   // postfix version
private:
    void check_integrity() const;
    int _index;
};
```

The Triangular_iterator class maintains an index into the Triangular class static data member, _elems, which holds the sequence elements. (For this to work, the Triangular class must grant special access permission to the member functions of the Triangular_iterator class. In Section 4.7 we see how to grant access privilege through the friend mechanism.) Two Triangular_iterator class objects are equal if the two _index members are equal:

```
inline bool Triangular_iterator::
operator==( const Triangular_iterator &rhs ) const
          { return _index == rhs._index; }
```

An operator is applied directly to the class object(s):

```
if ( trian1 == trian2 ) ...
```

If we wish to apply the operator to a class object addressed by a pointer, we must first dereference the pointer to gain access to the class object:

```
if ( *ptri1 == *ptri2 ) ...
```

The complement of an operator is typically implemented in terms of its associated operator. For example,

```
inline bool Triangular_iterator::
operator!=( const Triangular_iterator &rhs ) const
        { return !( *this == rhs ); }
```

The rules governing operator overloading are as follows:

- We cannot introduce new operators. All the predefined operators can be overloaded except the four operators ., .*, ::, and ?:.

- The predefined *arity* of the existing operators cannot be overridden. Every binary operator must be provided with two operands, and every unary operator with only one. We cannot define the binary equality operator, for example, to take either more or fewer parameters than its predefined two.

- The predefined precedence of the existing operators cannot be overridden. For example, the division operator always takes precedence over addition.

- An operator function must take at least one class type as an argument. That is, we cannot redefine existing operators or introduce operators for nonclass types, such as pointers.

An operator can be defined either as a member operator function,

```
inline int Triangular_iterator::
operator*() const
{
    check_integrity();
    return Triangular::_elems[ _index ];
}
```

or as a nonmember operator function,

```
inline int
operator*( const Triangular_iterator &rhs )
{
    rhs.check_integrity();

    // note: the non-member instance has no
    // access privilege to nonpublic members
    return Triangular::_elems[ rhs.index() ];
}
```

The parameter list of a nonmember operator always defines one more parameter than its member operator counterpart. In a member operator, the this pointer implicitly represents the left operand.

The check_integrity() member function ensures that _index is not larger than _max_elems and that _elems holds the necessary elements.

```
inline void Triangular_iterator::
check_integrity() const
{
    // we'll look at the throw expression in Chapter 7 ...
    if ( _index > Triangular::_max_elems )
        throw iterator_overflow();

    // grow vector if necessary ...
    if ( _index > Triangular::_elems.size() )
        Triangular::gen_elements( _index );
}
```

We must provide a prefix (++trian) and postfix (trian++) instance of the increment operator. The prefix instance is defined with an empty parameter list:

```
inline int& Triangular_iterator::
operator++()
{   // prefix instance
    ++_index;
    check_integrity();
    return Triangular::_elems[ _index ];
}
```

Ordinarily, the postfix instance would also be defined with an empty parameter list. However, each overloaded operator must have a unique parameter list. The language solution is to require that we define the postfix instance with a single integer parameter:

```
inline int Triangular_iterator::
operator++( int )
{
    // postfix instance
    check_integrity();
    return Triangular::_elems[ _index++ ];
}
```

Both the prefix and the postfix instance of the increment (and decrement) operator can be applied directly to an object of the class:

```
++it; // prefix
it++; // postfix
```

Where is the single integer argument for the postfix instance? The compiler generates that for us automatically to force the postfix instance of the operator to be called. Happily, the user does not need to bother about it.

Our next task is to provide a begin() and end() pair of member functions for the Triangular class as well as to support the definition of iterator. The iterator support requires that I introduce the topic of *nested types*, which is discussed soon.

First, however, here are the necessary modifications to the Triangular class definition:

```
#include "Triangular_iterator.h"

class Triangular {
public:
    // this shields users from having to know
    // the actual name of the iterator class ...
    typedef Triangular_iterator iterator;

    Triangular_iterator begin() const
    {
        return Triangular_iterator( _beg_pos );
    }

    Triangular_iterator end() const
    {
        return Triangular_iterator( _beg_pos+_length );
    }
    // ...

private:
    int    _beg_pos;
    int    _length;
    // ...
};
```

Nested Types

A typedef introduces an alternative name for a type, and takes this general form:

```
typedef existing_type new_name;
```

Here, existing_type can be a built-in, compound, or class type. In our example, we provide iterator as a synonym for the Triangular_iterator class in order to simplify its use. The syntax for defining an object of type iterator

```
Triangular::iterator it = trian.begin();
```

uses the class scope operator to direct the compiler to look in the Triangular class definition for the declaration of iterator. If we simply write

```
iterator it = trian.begin(); // error
```

the compiler does not know to look within the Triangular class for the declaration of iterator, so the definition of it is flagged as an error.

By nesting iterator within each class that supports the iterator abstraction, we can provide multiple definitions with the same name but at the cost of a more complex declaration syntax.

```
Fibonacci::iterator     fit = fib.begin();
Pell::iterator          pit = pel.begin();
vector<int>::iterator   vit = _elems.begin();
string::iterator        sit = file_name.begin();
```

4.7   Collaboration Sometimes Requires Friendship

The nonmember instance of `operator*()` directly accesses both the private member `_elems` of the Triangular class and the private member function `check_integrity()` of the Triangular_iterator class.

```
inline int operator*( const Triangular_iterator &rhs )
{
    rhs.check_integrity();
    return Triangular::_elems[ rhs.index() ];
}
```

Why does this compile? A class can designate functions and classes as friends. The *friends* of a class can access the private members of that class in the same way as the member functions of that class. For this instance of `operator*()` to compile, it must be a friend to both the Triangular and the Triangular_iterator class:

```
class Triangular {
    friend int operator*( const Triangular_iterator &rhs );
    // ...
};

class Triangular_iterator {
    friend int operator*( const Triangular_iterator &rhs );
    // ...
};
```

We declare a function a friend to a class by prefacing its prototype with the `friend` keyword. The declaration can appear anywhere in the class definition. It is not affected by the `private` or `public` access levels of the class. (To make multiple instances of an overloaded function friends of a class, we must explicitly list each instance.)

The Triangular_iterator instance of `operator*()`, as well as its `check_integrity()` member function, both directly access the private members of the Triangular class. We can declare both instances as friends of the Triangular class:

```
class Triangular {
    friend int Triangular_iterator::operator*();
    friend void Triangular_iterator::check_integrity();
    // ...
};
```

For this to compile successfully, the Triangular_iterator class definition must be provided before its two member functions are declared as friends. Otherwise, the compiler hasn't enough information to confirm the correct prototype of the two member functions or even that one or both are member functions of the class.

Alternatively, we can grant friendship to the class itself, in turn conferring friendship on all the member functions of that class. For example,

```
class Triangular {
    // confers friendship on all the
    // member functions of Triangular_iterator
    friend class Triangular_iterator;

    // ...
};
```

This form of class friendship does not require that the definition of the class be seen before the friend declaration.

Friendship, however, is not always required. For example, consider the definition of check_integrity():

```
inline void Triangular_iterator::
check_integrity()
{
    if ( _index < Triangular::_max_elems )
        throw iterator_overflow();

    if ( _index > Triangular::_elems.size() )
        Triangular::gen_elements( _index );
}
```

If the Triangular class provides a public access function to _max_elems and a public function to return the current size of _elems, then check_integrity() does not need the proffered friendship. For example,

```
class Triangular {
public:
    static int elem_size() { return _elems.size(); }
    static int max_elems() { return _max_elems;    }
    // ...
};

// no longer needs to be a friend
inline void Triangular_iterator::
check_integrity()
{
    if ( _index < Triangular::max_elems() )
        throw iterator_overflow();

    // grow vector if necessary ...
    if ( _index > Triangular::elems_size() )
        Triangular::gen_elements( _index );
}
```

Friendship is generally required for performance reasons, such as the multiplication of a Point and Matrix in a nonmember operator function. For a simple read or write of a data member, an inline public access function is usually an adequate alternative to friendship.

Here is a small program to exercise our iterator class:

```
int main()
{
    Triangular tri( 20 );
    Triangular::iterator it = tri.begin();
    Triangular::iterator end_it = tri.end();

    cout << "Triangular Series of " << tri.length() << " elements\n";
    while ( it != end_it )
    {
        cout << *it << ' ';
        ++it;
    }

    cout << endl;
}
```

When compiled and executed, this program generates the following output:

```
Triangular Series of 20 elements
3 6 10 15 21 28 36 45 55 66 78 91 105 120 136 153 171 190 210 231
```

4.8   Implementing a Copy Assignment Operator

By default, when we assign one class object with another, as in

```
Triangular tri1( 8 ), tri2( 8, 9 );
tri1 = tri2;
```

the data members of the class are copied in turn. In our example, _length, _beg_pos, and _next are copied from tri2 to tri1. This is called default memberwise copy.

In the case of the Triangular class, the default memberwise copy semantics are sufficient; there is nothing we need to do explicitly. In the case of the Section 4.2 Matrix class, however, the default memberwise behavior is not adequate. The reasons for this are discussed in the Default Memberwise Initialization subsection of Section 4.2.

The Matrix class requires both a copy constructor and a copy assignment operator. Here is how we might define the Matrix copy assignment operator:

```
Matrix& Matrix::
operator=( const Matrix &rhs )
{
    if ( this != &rhs )
    {
        _row = rhs._row; _col = rhs._col;
        int elem_cnt = _row * _col;

        delete [] _pmat;
        _pmat = new double[ elem_cnt ];
```

```
            for ( int ix = 0; ix < elem_cnt; ++ix ]
                  _pmat[ ix ] = rhs._pmat[ ix ];
        }

    return *this;
};
```

If the class designer provides an explicit instance of the copy assignment operator, that instance is used in place of default memberwise initialization. The source code of the user need not change, although it must be recompiled.

(Strictly speaking, this implementation is not exception-safe. See [SUTTER99] for a discussion.)

4.9   Implementing a Function Object

In Section 3.6, we looked at the predefined function objects of the standard library. In this section, we look at how to implement our own function objects. A function object is a class that provides an overloaded instance of the function call operator.

When the compiler encounters what appears to be a function call, such as

```
    lt( ival );
```

lt can be the name of a function, a pointer to function, or an object of a class that has provided an instance of the function call operator. If lt is a class object, the compiler internally transforms the statement as follows:

```
    lt.operator()( ival ); // internal transformation
```

The function call operator can take any number of parameters: none, one, two, and so on. It is used, for example, to support multidimensional subscripting of a Matrix class because the actual subscript operator is limited to accepting one parameter.

Let's implement an overloaded instance of the call operator to test whether a value passed to it is less than some other value. We'll call the class LessThan. Each object must be initialized with a value against which to compare. In addition, we support read and write access of that value. Here's our implementation:

```
class LessThan {
public:
    LessThan( int val ) : _val( val ){}
    int  comp_val() const    { return _val; }
    void comp_val( int nval ){ _val = nval; }

    bool operator()( int value ) const;

private:
    int _val;
};
```

The implementation of the function call operator looks like this:

```
inline bool LessThan::
operator()( int value ) const { return value < _val; }
```

We can explicitly define a LessThan class object in the same way as any other class object:

```
LessThan lt10( 10 );
```

We invoke the overloaded call operator function by applying the call operator (()) to the class object. For example,

```
int count_less_than( const vector<int> &vec, int comp )
{
    LessThan lt( comp );

    int count = 0;
    for ( int ix = 0; ix < vec.size(); ++ix )
        if ( lt( vec[ ix ] ))
            ++count;

    return count;
}
```

More typically, we pass a function object as an argument to a generic algorithm:

```
void print_less_than( const vector<int> &vec,
                      int comp, ostream &os = cout )
{
    LessThan lt( comp );
    vector<int>::const_iterator iter = vec.begin();
    vector<int>::const_iterator it_end = vec.end();

    os << "elements less than " << lt.comp_val() << endl;
    while (( iter = find_if( iter, it_end, lt )) != it_end )
    {
        os << *iter << ' ';
        ++iter;
    }
}
```

Here's a small program to exercise these two functions:

```
int main()
{
    int ia[16] = { 17, 12, 44, 9, 18, 45, 6, 14,
                   23, 67, 9, 0, 27, 55, 8, 16 };
    vector<int> vec( ia, ia+16 );
    int comp_val = 20;

    cout << "Number of elements less than "
         << comp_val << " are "
```

```
            << count_less_than( vec, comp_val ) << endl;
        print_less_than( vec, comp_val );
    }
```

When compiled and executed, the program generates the following output:

```
Number of elements less than 20 are 10
elements less than 20
17 12 9 18 6 14 9 0 8 16
```

Appendix B provides additional examples of function object definitions.

4.10   Providing Class Instances of the iostream Operators

Often, we wish to both read and write objects of a class. For example, to display our
trian class object, we want to be able to write

```
    cout << trian << endl;
```

To support this, we must provide an overloaded instance of the output operator:

```
    ostream& operator<<( ostream &os, const Triangular &rhs )
    {
        os << "( " << rhs.beg_pos() << ", "
            << rhs.length()        << " ) ";

        rhs.display( rhs.length(), rhs.beg_pos(), os );
        return os;
    }
```

We return the same ostream object passed into the function. This allows multiple
output operators to be concatenated. Both objects are passed by reference. The ostream
operand is not declared as const because each output operation modifies the internal
state of the ostream object. The class object to be output, such as rhs, is declared as
const because we are passing it by reference for efficiency rather than to modify the
object itself. For example, given the object

```
    Triangular tri( 6, 3 );
```
the statement
```
    cout << tri << '\n';
```
generates
```
    ( 3 , 6 ) 6 10 15 21 28 36
```

Why is the output operator a nonmember function? A member function requires
that its left operand be an object of the class. Were the output operator a member function, then the tri class object would need to be placed to the left of the output operator:

```
    tri << cout << '\n';
```

This would certainly confuse users of the class!

The following input operator reads only the first four elements representing the Triangular class. The beginning position and its length are the only unique aspects of a Triangular class object. The actual element values are invariant; they are not stored within a particular class object.

```
istream&
operator>>( istream &is, Triangular &rhs )
{
    char ch1, ch2;
    int bp, len;

    // given the input: ( 3 , 6 ) 6 10 15 21 28 36
    // ch1 == '(', bp == 3, ch2 == ',', len == 6
    is >> ch1 >> bp
       >> ch2 >> len;

    // set the three data members of rhs ...
    rhs.beg_pos( bp );
    rhs.length( len );
    rhs.next_reset();

    return is;
}
```

Here is a small program to test our input and output operators:

```
int main()
{
    Triangular tri( 6, 3 );
    cout << tri << '\n';

    Triangular tri2;
    cin >> tri2;

    // let's see what we got ...
    cout << tri2;
}
```

When compiled and executed, it generates the following output (my input is highlighted in bold):

```
( 3 , 6 ) 6 10 15 21 28 36
( 4 , 10 )
( 4 , 10 ) 10 15 21 28 36 45 55 66 78 91
```

Input operators are generally more complicated to implement because of the possibility of invalid data being read. For example, what if the left parenthesis was missing? For this example, I do not consider the possibility of invalid input. For a more realistic example of an input operator and a discussion of possible iostream error states, see [LIPPMAN98], Chapter 20.

4.11   Pointers to Class Member Functions

The classes supporting the Fibonacci, Pell, Lucas, Square, and Pentagonal sequences
are identical to those of the Triangular class except for the algorithm to generate the
element sequence. In Chapter 5 we organize these classes into an object-oriented class
hierarchy. In this section, we implement a general sequence class, num_sequence, to
support all six sequences in a single class object. Here is our `main()` program:

```
int main()
{
    num_sequence ns;
    const int pos = 8;
    for ( int ix = 1; ix < num_sequence::num_of_sequences(); ++ix )
    {
        ns.set_sequence( num_sequence::nstype( ix ));
        int elem_val = ns.elem( pos );
        display( cout, ns, pos, elem_val );
    }
}
```

ns is our general sequence class object. With each iteration of the for loop, we reset
ns to represent a different numeric sequence using set_sequence() and the ns_type()
return value. num_of_sequences() returns a count of the numeric sequences currently
supported. Both num_of_sequences() and ns_type() are inline static member functions.
elem() returns the element at the requested position. When the program is compiled
and executed, it generates the following output:

```
The element at position 8 for the fibonacci sequence is 21
The element at position 8 for the pell sequence is 408
The element at position 8 for the lucas sequence is 47
The element at position 8 for the triangular sequence is 36
The element at position 8 for the square sequence is 64
The element at position 8 for the pentagonal sequence is 92
```

The key to the design of the num_sequence class is the pointer to member function
facility. A pointer to member function looks much the same as a pointer to nonmember
function (introduced in Section 2.8). Both of them specify the return type and parameter list. A pointer to member function, however, must also indicate the class to which
it is a member. For example,

```
void (num_sequence::*pm)( int ) = 0;
```

declares pm to be a pointer to member function of the num_sequence class. The member function pm addresses must have a return type of void and must take a single
parameter of type int. pm is initialized to 0, indicating that it does not currently
address a member function.

If the syntax seems overly complex, we can hide it behind a typedef. For example,

```
typedef void (num_sequence::*PtrType)( int );
PtrType pm = 0;
```

declares PtrType as an alternative typedef name for a pointer to member function of the num_sequence class returning void and taking a single parameter of type int. The two declarations of pm are equivalent.

The six numeric sequences are the same except for the algorithm to generate the sequence elements. The num_sequence class provides the following six member functions, each of which can be addressed by our PtrType pointer to member function:

```
class num_sequence {
public:
    typedef void (num_sequence::*PtrType)( int );

    // _pmf addresses one of these
    void fibonacci( int );
    void pell( int );
    void lucas( int );
    void triangular( int );
    void square( int );
    void pentagonal( int );
    // ...
private:
    PtrType      _pmf;
};
```

To take the address of a class member function, we apply the address-of operator (&) to the member function name qualified by its class scope operator. The return type and parameter list of the function are not specified. For example, to define and initialize a pointer to member to the fibonacci() member function, we write

```
PtrType pm = &num_sequence::fibonacci;
```

Similarly, to assign pm, we write

```
pm = &num_sequence::triangular;
```

Each invocation of set_sequence() assigns _pmf the address of one of the six functions. For simplicity, we can store the addresses of the six member functions in a static array. To prevent recalculating the elements of each sequence, we also keep a static vector of six element vectors:

```
class num_sequence {
public:
    typedef void (num_sequence::*PtrType)( int );
    // ...
private:
    vector<int>* _elem;          // points to the current vector
    PtrType      _pmf;           // points to the current algorithm
```

```
        static const int          num_seq = 7; //!
        static PtrType            func_tbl[ num_seq ];
        static vector<vector<int> > seq;
};
```

The most complicated member definition here is that of seq:

```
static vector<vector<int> > seq;
```

This says that seq is a vector in which each element is a vector of integer elements. For example, it can hold the element vectors of each of our six numeric sequences. If we forget the space between the two greater-than symbols,

```
// does not compile!
static vector<vector<int>> seq;
```

the definition does not compile. This is because of the *maximal munch* compilation rule. This rule requires that a symbol sequence always be interpreted as the maximal legal sequence of symbols. Because >> is a legal operator sequence, the two symbols are always grouped together in the absence of the space. Similarly, when we write a+++p, under the maximal munch rule it is always interpreted as

```
a++ + p
```

We must provide a definition of each static data member. Because PtrType is a nested type, any reference to it outside the num_sequence class must be qualified with the class scope operator. The value of num_seq is specified within the class definition, so we do not repeat it here.

```
const int num_sequence::num_seq;
vector<vector<int> > num_sequence::seq( num_seq );

num_sequence::PtrType
    num_sequence::func_tbl[ num_seq ] =
    {  0,
        &num_sequence::fibonacci,
        &num_sequence::pell,
        &num_sequence::lucus,
        &num_sequence::triangular,
        &num_sequence::square,
        &num_sequence::pentagonal
    };
```

If you find the nested type syntax confusing, you can hide it with a typedef:

```
typedef num_sequence::PtrType PtrType;
PtrType num_sequence::func_tbl[ num_seq ] = ...
```

_elem and _pmf are set as a unit within set_sequence(). _elem addresses the vector that holds the elements for the numeric sequence. _pmf, of course, addresses the member function to generate additional elements of that sequence. (The actual implementation of set_sequence() is deferred until Section 5.2.)

Unlike a pointer to function, a pointer to member function must be invoked through an object of the member function's class. The object becomes the `this` pointer of the member function that is invoked.

For example, suppose we are given the following definitions:

```
num_sequence ns;
num_sequence *pns = &ns;
PtrType pm = &num_sequence::fibonacci;
```

To invoke pmf through ns, we write

```
// equivalent to ns.fibonacci( pos )
(ns.*pm)( pos )
```

The .* pair of symbols is the pointer to member selection operator for class objects. The parentheses are necessary for it to be evaluated correctly. The pointer to member selection operator for a pointer to class operator is the ->* pair of symbols:

```
// equivalent to pns->fibonacci( pos )
(pns->*pm)( pos )
```

Following is the implementation of elem(). If the position requested by the user is valid and if the number of elements currently stored does not include that position, the necessary elements are generated through an invocation of the function addressed by _pmf.

```
int num_sequence::elem( int pos )
{
    if ( ! check_integrity( pos ))
        return 0;

    if ( pos > _elem->size() )
        ( this->*_pmf )( pos-1 );

    return (*_elem)[ pos-1 ];
}
```

This is all the implementation we need to discuss at this point. In Chapter 5 we look at the programming details that allow each num_sequence class object to know its numeric sequence type at any point in its lifetime. Then we look at simpler ways to support these kinds of multiple type manipulations through object-oriented programming.

Exercise 4.3

Consider the following global data:

```
string program_name;
string version_stamp;
int version_number;
```

```
int tests_run;
int tests_passed;
```

Write a class to wrap around this data.

Exercise 4.4

A user profile consists of a login, the actual user name, the number of times logged on, the number of guesses made, the number of correct guesses, the current level — one of beginner, intermediate, advanced, or guru — and the percentage correct (this latter may be computed or stored). Provide a UserProfile class. Support input and output, equality and inequality. The constructors should allow for a default user level and default login name of "guest." How might you guarantee that each guest login for a particular session is unique?

Exercise 4.5

Implement a 4x4 Matrix class supporting at least the following general interface: addition and multiplication of two Matrix objects, a `print()` member function, a compound += operator, and subscripting supported through a pair of overloaded function call operators, as follows:

```
float& operator()( int row, int column );
float  operator()( int row, int column ) const;
```

Provide a default constructor taking an optional 16 data values and a constructor taking an array of 16 elements. You do not need a copy constructor, copy assignment operator, or destructor for this class (these are required in Chapter 6 when we reimplement the Matrix class to support arbitrary rows and columns).

5

Object-Oriented Programming

As you saw in Chapter 4, the primary use of a class is to introduce a new type that more directly represents an entity in our application domain. In a library check-out application, for example, it is generally easier to program the classes Book, Borrower, and DueDate directly than to translate the program logic to the underlying character, arithmetic, and Boolean data types.

The object-based programming model proves cumbersome when our application begins to be filled with class types that represent an *is-a-kind-of* instance of a type. For example, imagine that over time our library check-out application must add support for a RentalBook class, an AudioBook class, and an InteractiveBook class in addition to the original Book class. Each class is likely to share data members and the member functions to manage the data. Each class also requires additional unique data members to represent its state. Each class may (or may not) have a separate check-out and over-due fine algorithm, although each class shares the same interface.

The object-based class mechanisms of Chapter 4 cannot easily model both the commonality and the differences of these four *are-a-kind-of* Book classes. Why? It's because this model does not provide support for specifying relationships among classes. For this kind of support, we need the *object-oriented programming* model.

5.1   Object-Oriented Programming Concepts

The two primary characteristics of object-oriented programming are inheritance and polymorphism. *Inheritance* allows us to group classes into families of related types, allowing for the sharing of common operations and data. *Polymorphism* allows us to program these families as a unit rather than as individual classes, giving us greater flexibility in adding or removing any particular class.

Inheritance defines a parent/child relationship. The *parent* defines the public interface and private implementation that are common to all its children. Each *child* adds to or overrides what it inherits to implement its own unique behavior. An AudioBook child class, for example, in addition to the title and author it inherits from its parent Book class, introduces support for a speaker and a count of the number of cassettes. In addition, it overrides the inherited check_out() member function of its parent.

In C++, the parent is called the *base* class and the child is called the *derived* class. The relationship between the parent or base class and its children is called an *inheritance hierarchy*. At a design review meeting, for example, we might say, "We intend to implement an AudioBook derived class. It will override the check_out() method of its Book base class. However, it will reuse the inherited Book class data members and member functions to manage its shelf location, author's name, and title."

Figure 5.1 pictures a portion of a possible library lending material class hierarchy. The root of the class hierarchy is an abstract base class, LibMat. LibMat defines all the operations that are common to all the different types of library lending materials: check_in(), check_out(), due_date(), fine(), location(), and so on. LibMat does not represent an actual lending material object; rather, it is an artifact of our design. In fact, it is the key artifact. We call it an abstract base class.

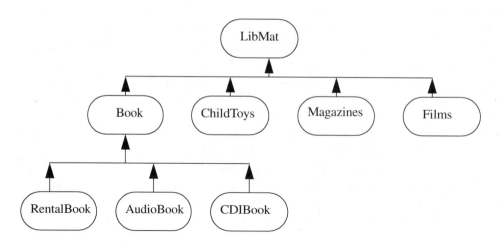

Figure 5.1 Portion of Library Lending Material Class Hierarchy

In an object-oriented program, we indirectly manipulate the class objects of our application through a pointer or reference of an abstract base class rather than directly manipulate the actual derived class objects of our application. This allows us to add or remove a derived class without the need for any modification to our existing program. For example, consider the following small function:

```
void loan_check_in( LibMat &mat )
{
    // mat actually refers to a derived class object
    // such as Book, RentalBook, Magazines, and so on ...
```

```
        mat.check_in();

        if ( mat.is_late() )
            mat.assess_fine();

        if ( mat.waiting_list();
            mat.notify_available();
    }
```

There are no LibMat objects in our application, only Book, RentalBook, AudioCDs, and so on. How does this function actually work? What happens, for example, when the check_in() operation is invoked through mat? For this function to make sense, mat must somehow refer to one of the actual class objects of our application each time loan_check_in() is executed. In addition, the check_in() member function that is invoked must somehow resolve to the check_in() instance of the actual class object mat refers to. This is what happens. The question is, how does it work?

The second unique aspect of object-oriented programming is polymorphism: the ability of a base class pointer or reference to refer transparently to any of its derived class objects. In our loan_check_in() function, for example, mat always addresses some object of one of the classes derived from LibMat. Which one? That cannot be determined until the actual execution of the program, and it is likely to vary with each invocation of loan_check_in().

Dynamic binding is a third aspect of object-oriented programming. In non-object-oriented programming, when we write

```
        mat.check_in();
```

the instance of check-in() to be executed is determined at compile-time based on mat's class type. Because the function to invoke is resolved before the program begins running, this is called *static binding*.

In object-oriented programming, the compiler cannot know which instance of check_in() to invoke. This can be determined only during program execution based on the actual derived class object mat addresses each time loan_check_in() is invoked. The actual resolution of which derived class instance of check_in() to invoke each time must be delayed until run-time. This is what we mean by dynamic binding.

Inheritance allows us to define families of classes that share a common interface, such as our library lending materials. Polymorphism allows us manipulate objects of these classes in a type-independent manner. We program the common interface through a pointer or reference of an abstract base class. The actual operation to invoke is not determined until run-time based on the type of the object actually addressed. (Yes, polymorphism and dynamic binding are supported only when we are using a pointer or reference. I say more about that later.)

If the library decides no longer to loan interactive books, we simply remove that class from the inheritance hierarchy. The implementation of loan_check_in() need not change. Similarly, if the library decides to charge a rental fee for certain audio books, we can implement a derived AudioRentalBook. loan_check_in() still does not need to change. If the library decides to loan laptop computers or video game equipment and cartridges, our inheritance hierarchy can accommodate that.

5.2   A Tour of Object-Oriented Programming

Let's implement a simple three-level class hierarchy to introduce the C++ language constructs and programming idioms that support object-oriented programming. We root our class hierarchy with the abstract LibMat base class. We derive a Book class from LibMat and in turn derive an AudioBook class from Book. We limit our interface to a single function, print(), together with a constructor and destructor. I've instrumented each member function to output its presence so that we can trace the behavior of the program.

By default, a member function is resolved statically at compile-time. To have a member function resolved dynamically during run-time, we preface its declaration with the virtual keyword. The LibMat class declares its destructor and print() to be virtual:

```
class LibMat {
public:
    LibMat(){ cout << "LibMat::LibMat() default constructor!\n"; }

    virtual ~LibMat(){ cout << "LibMat::~LibMat() destructor!\n"; }
    virtual void print() const
            { cout << "LibMat::print() -- I am a LibMat object!\n"; }
};
```

Let's now define a nonmember print() function that takes as a single parameter a const LibMat reference:

```
void print( const LibMat &mat )
{
    cout << "in global print(): about to print mat.print()\n";

    // this resolves to a print() member function
    //       based on the actual object mat refers to ...
    mat.print();
}
```

Within our main() program, we repeatedly invoke print(), passing it, in turn, a LibMat class object, a Book class object, and an AudioBook class object as its parameter. Based on the actual object mat refers to within each invocation of print(), the appropriate LibMat, Book, or AudioBook print() member function is invoked. Our first invocation looks like this:

```
cout << "\n" << "Creating a LibMat object to print()\n";
LibMat libmat;
print( libmat );
```

Here is a trace of its execution:

```
Creating a LibMat object to print()

// the construction of Libmat libmat
LibMat::LibMat() default constructor!

// the handling of print( libmat )
in global print(): about to print mat.print()
LibMat::print() -- I am a LibMat object!

// the destruction of Libmat libmat
LibMat::~LibMat() destructor!
```

I hope there is nothing surprising in this. The definition of libmat is followed by the default constructor invocation. Within print(), mat.print() resolves to LibMat::print(). This is followed by the LibMat destructor invocation. Things become a bit more surprising when we pass print() a Book object:

```
cout << "\n" << "Creating a Book object to print()\n";
Book b( "The Castle", "Franz Kafka" );
print( b );
```

Here is an annotated trace of the execution:

```
Creating a Book object to print()

// the construction of Book b
LibMat::LibMat() default constructor!
Book::Book( The Castle, Franz Kafka )  constructor

// the handling of print( b )
in global print(): about to print mat.print()
Book::print() -- I am a Book object!
My title is: The Castle
My author is: Franz Kafka

// the destruction of Book b
Book::~Book() destructor!
LibMat::~LibMat() destructor!
```

A first observation is that the virtual invocation through mat.print() actually works! The function invoked is Book::print() and not LibMat::print(). The second interesting thing is that both the base and the derived class constructors are invoked when the derived class object is defined. (When the derived class object is destroyed, both the derived and the base class destructors are invoked.)

How do we actually implement the derived Book class? To indicate that our new class is inheriting from an existing class, we follow its name with a colon (:) followed by the public keyword[1] and the name of the base class:

```cpp
class Book : public LibMat {
public:
    Book( const string &title, const string &author )
        : _title( title ), _author( author ){
        cout << "Book::Book( " << _title
            << ", " << _author << " )  constructor\n";
    }

    virtual ~Book(){
        cout << "Book::~Book() destructor!\n";
    }

    virtual void print() const {
        cout << "Book::print() -- I am a Book object!\n"
            << "My title is: "  << _title  << '\n'
            << "My author is: " << _author << endl;
    }

    const string& title()  const { return _title;  }
    const string& author() const { return _author; }

protected:
    string _title;
    string _author;
};
```

The print() instance within Book *overrides* the LibMat instance. This is the function invoked by mat.print(). The two access functions title() and author() are nonvirtual inline member functions. We haven't seen the protected keyword before. A member declared as protected can be directly accessed by the derived classes but cannot be directly accessed by the general program.

Let's next derive a specialized AudioBook class from our Book class. An Audio-Book, in addition to a title and author, has a narrator. Before we look at its implementation, let's first pass print() an AudioBook class object:

```cpp
cout << "\n" << "Creating an AudioBook object to print()\n";
AudioBook ab( "Man Without Qualities",
            "Robert Musil", "Kenneth Meyer" );
print( ab );
```

---

[1]   A base class can be specified as public, protected, or private. Public inheritance is the only form of inheritance covered in this text. For a discussion of protected and private inheritance see Section 18.3 of [LIPPMAN98].

What should we expect from a trace of its execution? We should expect (1) that AudioBook::print() is invoked through mat.print() and (2) that ab is constructed by, in turn, the LibMat, Book, and AudioBook constructors. This is what the trace shows:

```
Creating an AudioBook object to print()

// the construction of AudioBook ab
LibMat::LibMat() default constructor!
Book::Book( Man Without Qualities, Robert Musil )  constructor
AudioBook::AudioBook( Man Without Qualities, Robert Musil,
                      Kenneth Meyer )  constructor

// the resolution of print( ab )
in global print(): about to print mat.print()
// oops: need to handle a Book and an AudioBook!
AudioBook::print() -- I am a AudioBook object!
My title is: Man Without Qualities
My author is: Robert Musil
My narrator is: Kenneth Meyer

// the destruction of AudioBook ab
AudioBook::~AudioBook() destructor!
Book::~Book() destructor!
LibMat::~LibMat() destructor!
```

How do we implement the AudioBook derived class? We have only to program those aspects of an AudioBook that are different from those of its base Book class: the print() function, of course, support for the name of the AudioBook narrator, and the class constructor and destructor. The Book class data members and member functions that support the author and title can be used directly within the AudioBook class in the same way as if they had been defined within it rather than being inherited.

```
class AudioBook : public Book {
public:
    AudioBook( const string &title,
            const string &author, const string &narrator )
        : Book( title, author ),
          _narrator( narrator )
    {
        cout << "AudioBook::AudioBook( " << _title
            << ", " << _author
            << ", " << _narrator
            << " )  constructor\n";
    }

    ~AudioBook()
    {
        cout << "AudioBook::~AudioBook() destructor!\n";
    }
```

```
    virtual void print() const {
        cout << "AudioBook::print() -- I am an AudioBook object!\n"
            // note the direct access of the inherited
            // data members _title and _author
            << "My title is: "    << _title << '\n'
            << "My author is: "   << _author << '\n'
            << "My narrator is: " << _narrator << endl;
    }
    const string& narrator() const { return _narrator; }
protected:
    string _narrator;
};
```

Users of the derived class need not distinguish between inherited members and members actually defined within the derived class. The use of both is transparent:

```
int main()
{
    AudioBook ab( "Mason and Dixon",
                  "Thomas Pynchon", "Edwin Leonard" );

    cout << "The title is "    << ab.title()    << '\n'
        << "The author is "   << ab.author()   << '\n'
        << "The narrator is " << ab.narrator() << endl;
}
```

I hope that this section has given you a sense of how object-oriented programming is supported in C++. Literally, all that's missing is the details, which we deal with in the rest of the chapter. A good exercise at this point might be the following: (1) Download the source code from the Addison Wesley Longman site. (2) Look in the Chapter 5 directory for the LibMat class hierarchy and the main() program that exercises it. (3) Derive a Magazine class from LibMat and add an invocation of print(), passing in a Magazine class object.

5.3   Polymorphism without Inheritance

The num_sequence class of Section 4.10 simulates polymorphism. Each class object can be made into any of the six numerical sequences at any point in the program through the set_sequence() member function:

```
for ( int ix = 1; ix < num_sequence::num_of_sequences(); ++ix )
{
    ns.set_sequence( num_sequence::nstype( ix ));
    int elem_val = ns.elem( pos );
    // ...
}
```

The ability to change the sequence type of ns is supported through programming rather than through direct support of the language. Each class object contains an _isa data member that identifies the current numeric sequence that it represents:

```
class num_sequence {
public:
    // ...

private:
    vector<int> *_elem; // addresses current element vector
    PtrType     _pmf;  // addresses current element generator
    ns_type     _isa;  // identifies current sequence type
    // ...
};
```

_isa is set to a named constant value that represents one of the supported numeric sequence types. The constant values are grouped in an enumerated type I've named ns_type:

```
class num_sequence {
public:
    enum ns_type {
        ns_unset, ns_fibonacci, ns_pell, ns_lucas,
        ns_triangular, ns_square, ns_pentagonal
    };

    // ...
};
```

nstype() verifies that its integer parameter represents a valid numeric sequence value. If it does, it returns the associated enumerator; otherwise, it returns ns_unset:

```
class num_sequence {
public:
    // ...

    static ns_type nstype( int num )
    {
        return num <= 0 || num >= num_seq
            ? ns_unset  // invalid value
            : static_cast< ns_type >( num );
    }
};
```

The static_cast is a special conversion notation. It converts the integer num to its associated ns_type enumerator. The result of nstype() is passed to set_sequence():

```
        ns.set_sequence( num_sequence::nstype( ix ));
```

set_sequence() does the work of setting _pmf, _isa, and _elem data members to the correct numeric sequence:

```
void num_sequence::
set_sequence( ns_type nst )
{
    switch ( nst )
    {
      default:
          cerr << "invalid type: setting to 0\n";
          // deliberate fall-through

      case ns_unset:
          _pmf = 0;
          _elem = 0;
          _isa = ns_unset;
          break;

      case ns_fibonacci:  case ns_pell:    case ns_lucas:
      case ns_triangular: case ns_square: case ns_pentagonal:
           // func_tbl: table of pointer to member functions
           // seq: vector of vectors holding sequence elements
           _pmf = func_tbl[ nst ];
           _elem = &seq[ nst ];
           _isa = nst;
           break;
    }
}
```

To support a query as to the numeric sequence to which an object is currently set, I provide a what_am_i() operation that returns a character string identifying the current numeric sequence. For example,

```
inline void display( ostream &os, const num_sequence &ns, int pos )
{
    os << "The element at position "
        << pos << " for the "
        << ns.what_am_i() << " sequence is "
        << ns.elem( pos ) << endl;
}
```

what_am_i() indexes _isa into a static character string array that lists the supported numeric sequence names in the order of the ns_type enumerators:

```
const char* num_sequence::
what_am_i() const
{
    static char *names[ num_seq ] = {
        "notSet",
        "fibonacci",  "pell",
        "lucas",      "triangular",
        "square",     "pentagonal"
    };
```

```
        return names[ _isa ];
    }
```

This is quite a lot of work, particularly in terms of maintenance. Each time we wish to add to or delete a numeric sequence type, all the following must be updated correctly: the vector of element vectors, the array of pointer to member functions, the what_am_i() string array, the switch statement of set_sequence(), the value of num_seq, and so on. Under the object-oriented programming model, this sort of explicit programming overhead is eliminated, making our code simpler and more extensible.

5.4   Defining an Abstract Base Class

In this section we redesign the num_sequence class of the preceding section into an abstract base class from which we inherit each of the numeric sequence classes. How do we go about that?

The first step in defining an abstract base class is to identify the set of operations common to its children. For example, what are the operations common to all numeric sequence classes? These operations represent the public interface of the num_sequence base class. Here is a first iteration:

```
class num_sequence {
public:
    // elem( pos ): return element at pos
    // gen_elems( pos ): generate the elements up to pos
    // what_am_i() : identify the actual sequence
    // print( os ) : write the elements to os
    //check_integrity( pos ) : is pos a valid value?
    // max_elems() : returns maximum position supported
    int         elem( int pos );
    void        gen_elems( int pos );
    const char* what_am_i() const;
    ostream&    print( ostream &os = cout ) const;
    bool        check_integrity( int pos );
    static int  max_elems();
    // ...
};
```

elem() returns the element at the user-requested position. max_elems() returns the maximum number of elements supported by our implementation. check_integrity() determines whether pos is a valid position. print() displays the elements. gen_elems() generates the elements for the sequence. what_am_i() returns a character string identifying the sequence.

The next step in the design of an abstract base class is to identify which operations are type-dependent — that is, which operations require separate implementations based on the derived class type. These operations become the virtual functions of the class hierarchy. For example, each numeric sequence class must provide a separate implementation of gen_elems(). check_integrity(), on the other hand, is type-invariant. It must determine whether pos is a valid element position. Its algorithm is independent of the numeric sequence. Similarly, max_elems() is type-invariant. All the numeric sequences hold the same maximum number of elements.

Not every function is this easy to distinguish. what_am_i() may or may not be type-dependent depending on how we choose to implement our inheritance hierarchy. The same is true of elem() and print(). For now, we'll presume that they are type-dependent. Later, we'll see an alternative design that turns them into type-invariant functions. A static member function cannot be declared as virtual.

The third step in designing an abstract base class is to identify the access level of each operation. If the operation is to be available to the general program, we declare it as public. For example, elem(), max_elems(), and what_am_i() are public operations.

If the operation is not meant to be invoked outside the base class, we declare it as private. A private member of the base class cannot be accessed by the classes that inherit from the base class. In this example, all the operations must be available to the inheriting classes, so we do not declare any of them as private.

IA third access level, protected, identifies operations that are available to the inheriting classes but not to the general program. check_integrity() and gen_elems(), for example, are operations that the inheriting classes, but not the general program, must invoke. Here is our revised num_sequence class definition:

```
class num_sequence {
public:
    virtual ~num_sequence(){};

    virtual int         elem( int pos ) const = 0;
    virtual const char* what_am_i() const = 0;
    static  int         max_elems(){ return _max_elems; }
    virtual ostream&    print( ostream &os = cout ) const = 0;

protected:
    virtual void        gen_elems( int pos ) const = 0;
    bool                check_integrity( int pos ) const;

    const static int    _max_elems = 1024;
};
```

Each virtual function either must be defined for the class that declares it or, if there is no meaningful implementation of that function for that class (such as gen_elems()), must be declared as a *pure* virtual function. The assignment of 0 indicates that the virtual function is pure:

```
virtual void gen_elems( int pos ) = 0;
```

Because its interface is incomplete, a class that declares one or more pure virtual functions cannot have independent class objects defined in the program. It can serve only as the subobject of a derived class, which, in effect, completes it by providing concrete implementations for each of its pure virtual functions.

What data, if any, should the num_sequence class declare? There is no hard and fast rule. In this class design, num_sequence does not declare any class data members. This design provides an interface for the numeric sequence hierarchy but defers the implementation to its derived classes.

What about constructors and a destructor? Because there are no nonstatic data members within the class to initialize, there is no real benefit to providing a constructor. We will, however, provide a destructor. As a general rule, a base class that defines one or more virtual functions should always define a virtual destructor. For example,

```
class num_sequence {
public:
    virtual ~num_sequence();
    // ...
};
```

Why? Consider the following code sequence:

```
num_sequence *ps = new Fibonacci( 12 );
// ... use the sequence
delete ps;
```

ps is a num_sequence base class pointer, but it addresses a Fibonacci-derived class object. When the delete expression is applied to a pointer to a class object, the destructor is first applied to the object addressed by the pointer; then the memory associated with the class object is returned to the program's free store. A nonvirtual function is resolved at compile-time based on the type of the object through which it is invoked.

In this case, the destructor invoked through ps must be the Fibonacci class destructor and not the destructor of the num_sequence class. That is, which destructor to invoke must be resolved at run-time based on the object actually addressed by the base class pointer. To have this occur, we must declare the destructor virtual.

However, I don't recommend having the destructor declared as a pure virtual function in the base class — even if there is no meaningful implementation. For the destructor, it is better to provide an empty definition, such as the following:[2]

```
inline num_sequence::~num_sequence(){}
```

For completeness, here are the implementations of the num_sequence instance of the output operator and of check_integrity():

---

[2]   See the introduction to Chapter 5 of [LIPPMAN96a] for the explanation of why a virtual destructor is best not declared as a pure virtual function.

```
bool num_sequence::
check_integrity( int pos ) const
{
    if ( pos <= 0 || pos > _max_elems )
    {
        cerr << "!! invalid position: " << pos
             << " Cannot honor request\n";
        return false;
    }

    return true;
}

ostream& operator<<( ostream &os, const num_sequence &ns )
     { return ns.print( os ); }
```

Although this completes the definition of the abstract num_sequence base class, the class itself is incomplete. It provides an interface for the subsequently derived classes. IEach derived class provides the implementation that completes the num_sequence base class definition.

5.5   Defining a Derived Class

IThe derived class consists of two parts: the subobject of its base class (consisting of the nonstatic base class data members, if any) and the derived class portion (consisting of the nonstatic derived class data members). (Think of a blue Lego block snapped together with a red one.) This composite nature of the derived class is reflected in its declaration syntax:

```
// the header file contains the base class definition
#include "num_sequence.h"

class Fibonacci : public num_sequence {
public:
    // ...
};
```

The derived class name is followed by a colon, the public keyword, and the name of the base class.[3] The only rule is that the base class definition must be present before a class can inherit from it (this is why the header file containing the num_sequence class definition is included).

---

[3] As I mentioned in Section 5.1, there is also support for private and protected inheritance, as well as multiple and virtual inheritance. These are complicated, advanced design topics that I do not cover here. See Chapter 18 of [LIPPMAN98] for a complete discussion.

The Fibonacci class must provide an implementation of each of the pure virtual functions inherited from its base class. In addition, it must declare those members that are unique to the Fibonacci class. Here is the class definition:

```
class Fibonacci : public num_sequence {
public:
    Fibonacci( int len = 1, int beg_pos = 1 )
                : _length( len ), _beg_pos( beg_pos ){}

    virtual int         elem( int pos ) const;
    virtual const char* what_am_i() const { return "Fibonacci"; }
    virtual ostream&    print( ostream &os = cout ) const;
    int                 length()  const { return _length;  }
    int                 beg_pos() const { return _beg_pos; }
protected:
    virtual void        gen_elems( int pos ) const;
    int                 _length;
    int                 _beg_pos;
    static vector<int>  _elems;
};
```

In this design, length and beginning position are data members of each derived class. The read access functions length() and beg_pos() are declared as nonvirtual because there is no base class instance to override. Because they are not part of the base class interface, they cannot be accessed when we're programming through a base class pointer or reference. For example,

```
num_sequence *ps = new Fibonacci( 12, 8 );

// ok: invokes Fibonacci::what_am_i() through virtual mechanism
ps->what_am_i();

// ok: invokes inherited num_sequence::max_elems();
ps->max_elems();

// error: length() is not part of num_sequence interface
ps->length();

// ok: invokes Fibonacci destructor through virtual mechanism
delete ps;
```

If the inaccessibility of length() and beg_pos() through the base class interface turns out to be a problem for our users, we'll need to go back and modify the base class interface. One redesign is to introduce length() and beg_pos() as pure virtual functions within the num_sequence base class. This automatically turns the derived class instances of beg_pos() and length() into virtual functions. This is one reason that the derived class instances of a virtual function are not required to specify the virtual keyword. If the keyword were required, retrofitting a base class virtual function such as beg_pos() would be difficult to get right: Every derived class instance would need to be redeclared.

An alternative redesign might be to factor the storage of the length and beginning position from the derived classes into the base class. In this way, length() and beg_pos() become inherited inline nonvirtual functions. (We consider the ramifications of this design in Section 5.6.)

My point in bringing this up is that the challenge of an object-oriented design is not so much in the programming as it is in the factoring of the base and derived classes and determining the interface and members that belong to each. In general, this is an iterative process that evolves through experience and feedback from users.

Here is the implementation of elem(). The derived class virtual function must exactly match the function prototype of the base class instance. The virtual keyword is not specified in a definition that occurs outside the class.

```
int Fibonacci::
elem( int pos ) const
{
    if ( ! check_integrity( pos ))
        return 0;

    if ( pos > _elems.size() )
        Fibonacci::gen_elems( pos );

    return _elems[ pos-1 ];
}
```

Notice that elem() invokes the inherited member check_integrity() exactly as if it were a member of its class. In general, the inherited public and protected base class members, regardless of the depth of an inheritance hierarchy, are accessed as if they are members of the derived class. The public base class members are also public in the derived class and are available to users of the derived class. The protected base class members are protected within the derived class. They are available to classes inheriting from the derived class but not to users of the class. The derived class, however, has no access privilege to the private base class members.

Notice that before the element at pos is returned, a check is made whether _elems holds sufficient elements. If it does not, elem() invokes gen_elems() to fill _elems up to pos. The invocation is written as Fibonacci::gen_elems(pos) rather than the simpler gen_elems(pos). A good question might be, why?

Within elem(), we know exactly which instance of gen_elems() we want to invoke. Inside the Fibonacci instance of elem(), we want to invoke the Fibonacci instance of gen_elems(). Delaying the resolution of gen_elems() until run-time for this invocation is unnecessary. In effect, we'd like to override the virtual mechanism and have the function resolved at compile-time rather than run-time. This is what the explicit invocation of gen_elems() does. By qualifying the call of a virtual function with the class scope operator, we are telling the compiler which instance to invoke. The run-time virtual mechanism is overridden.

Here are the implementations of gen_elems() and print():

```
void Fibonacci::
gen_elems( int pos ) const
{
      if ( _elems.empty() )
           { _elems.push_back( 1 ); _elems.push_back( 1 ); }

      if ( _elems.size() < pos )
           {
                int ix  = _elems.size();
                int n_2 = _elems[ ix-2 ];
                int n_1 = _elems[ ix-1 ];

                for ( ; ix < pos; ++ix )
                 {
                      int elem = n_2 + n_1;
                      _elems.push_back( elem );
                      n_2 = n_1; n_1 = elem;
                 }
           }
}

ostream& Fibonacci::
print( ostream &os ) const
{
     int elem_pos = _beg_pos-1;
     int end_pos = elem_pos + _length;

     if ( end_pos > _elems.size() )
          Fibonacci::gen_elems( end_pos );

     while ( elem_pos < end_pos )
             os << _elems[ elem_pos++ ] << ' ';

     return os;
}
```

Notice that both elem() and print() check that _elems contains sufficient elements, and, if it does not, they invoke gen_elems(). How might we retrofit check_integrity() to make that test as well as check the validity of pos? One possibility is to provide the Fibonacci class with a check_integrity() member function:

```
class Fibonacci : public num_sequence {
public:
     // ...
```

```
protected:
    bool check_integrity( int pos ) const;
    // ...
};
```

Within the Fibonacci class, every reference to check_integrity() now resolves to the derived class instance of the function. Within elem(), for example, the call of check_integrity() now invokes the Fibonacci member.

```
int Fibonacci::
elem( int pos ) const
{
    // now resolves to Fibonacci's instance
    if ( ! check_integrity( pos ))
        return 0;

    // ...
}
```

Whenever a member of the derived class reuses the name of an inherited base class member, the base class member becomes lexically hidden within the derived class. That is, each use of the name within the derived class resolves to the derived class member. To access the base class member within the derived class, we must qualify its reference with the class scope operator of the base class. For example,

```
inline bool Fibonacci::
check_integrity( int pos ) const
{
    // class scope operator necessary ...
    // unqualified name resolves to this instance!
    if ( ! num_sequence::check_integrity( pos ))
        return false;

    if ( pos > _elems.size() )
        Fibonacci::gen_elems( pos );

    return true;
}
```

The problem with this solution is that, within the base class, check_integrity() is not identified as virtual. This means that each invocation of check_integrity() through a base class pointer or reference resolves to the num_sequence instance. There is no consideration taken of the actual object addressed. For example,

```
void Fibonacci::example()
{
    num_sequence *ps = new Fibonacci( 12, 8 );

    // ok: resolves to Fibonacci::elem() through virtual mechanism
    ps->elem( 1024 );
```

```
        // oops: resolves statically to num_sequence::check_integrity()
        //              based on the type of ps
        ps->check_integrity( pos );
}
```

For this reason, it is not, in general, a good practice to provide nonvirtual member functions with the same name in both the base and the derived class. One conclusion to draw from this might be that all functions within the base class should be declared as virtual. I don't believe this is the correct conclusion, but it does solve the immediate dilemma of our design.

The underlying cause of the dilemma is that the base class instance has been implemented without adequate knowledge of what the derived classes require to check the integrity of their state. Any implementation that proceeds from insufficient knowledge is likely to prove incomplete. But this is different from claiming that the implementation is type-dependent and therefore must be virtual.

Again, the point is that our designs are iterative and must evolve through experience and feedback from users. In this case, the better design solution is to redefine check_integrity() to take two parameters:

```
bool num_sequence::
check_integrity( int pos, int size )
{
    if ( pos <= 0 || pos > max_seq ){
        // same as before ...
    }

    if ( pos > size )
        // gen_elems() is invoked through virtual mechanism
        gen_elems( pos );

    return true;
}
```

In this definition of check_integrity(), gen_elems() is invoked through the virtual mechanism. If check_integrity() is invoked by a Fibonacci class object, the Fibonacci gen_elems() instance is invoked. If check_integrity() is invoked by a Triangular class object, the Triangular gen_elems() instance is invoked, and so on. The new instance might be invoked as follows:

```
int Fibonacci::
elem( int pos )
{
    if ( ! check_integrity( pos, _elems.size() ))
        return 0;
    // ...
}
```

IIt is always a good idea to test an implementation incrementally rather than wait until the entire code base is complete to see whether the darn thing works. Not only does this allow us a sanity check as we proceed, but it also provides the basis for a suite of regression tests that we can run each time we subsequently evolve the design. Here's a small test program to exercise our implementation so far. gen_elems() has been instrumented to display the elements it generates other than the first two:

```
int main()
{
    Fibonacci fib;

    cout << "fib: beginning at element 1 for 1 element: "
        << fib << endl;

    Fibonacci fib2( 16 );
    cout << "fib2: beginning at element 1 for 16 elements: "
        << fib2 << endl;

    Fibonacci fib3( 8, 12 );
    cout << "fib3: beginning at element 12 for 8 elements: "
        << fib3 << endl;
}
```

When the program is compiled and executed, it generates the following output:

```
fib: beginning at element 1 for 1 element: ( 1 , 1 ) 1

fib2: beginning at element 1 for 16 elements:
gen_elems: 2
gen_elems: 3
gen_elems: 5
gen_elems: 8
gen_elems: 13
gen_elems: 21
gen_elems: 34
gen_elems: 55
gen_elems: 89
gen_elems: 144
gen_elems: 233
gen_elems: 377
gen_elems: 610
gen_elems: 987
( 1 , 16 ) 1 1 2 3 5 8 13 21 34 55 89 144 233 377 610 987

fib3: beginning at element 12 for 8 elements:
gen_elems: 1597
gen_elems: 2584
gen_elems: 4181
( 12 , 8 ) 144 233 377 610 987 1597 2584 4181
```

5.6   Using an Inheritance Hierarchy

Let's presume we've defined the five other numeric sequence classes (Pell, Lucas, Square, Triangular, and Pentagonal) in the same manner as the Fibonacci class. We now have a two-level inheritance hierarchy: an abstract num_sequence base class and the six inheriting derived classes. How might we use them?

Here is a simple display() function whose second parameter is ns, a const reference to a num_sequence object.

```
inline void display( ostream &os,
                     const num_sequence &ns, int pos )
{
    os << "The element at position "
       << pos              << " for the "
       << ns.what_am_i() << " sequence is "
       << ns.elem( pos ) << endl;
}
```

Within display(), we call the two virtual functions what_am_i() and elem(). Which instances of these functions are invoked? We cannot say for certain. We know that ns does not refer to an actual num_sequence class object but rather to an object of a class derived from num_sequence. The two virtual function calls are resolved at run-time based on the type of the class object ns refers to. For example, in the following small program I define an object of each derived class in turn and pass it to display():

```
int main()
{
    const int pos = 8;

    Fibonacci fib;
    display( cout, fib, pos );

    Pell pell;
    display( cout, pell, pos );

    Lucas lucas;
    display( cout, lucas, pos );

    Triangular trian;
    display( cout, trian, pos );

    Square square;
    display( cout, square, pos );

    Pentagonal penta;
    display( cout, penta, pos );
}
```

When compiled and executed, this program generates the following output:

```
The element at position 8 for the Fibonacci sequence is 21
The element at position 8 for the Pell sequence is 408
The element at position 8 for the Lucas sequence is 47
The element at position 8 for the Triangular sequence is 36
The element at position 8 for the Square sequence is 64
The element at position 8 for the Pentagonal sequence is 92
```

Notice that this program duplicates the output of our earlier program in Section 4.10. The design of the num_sequence class, however, has changed significantly. The machinery to set, keep track of, and reset the numeric sequence type in the earlier design has been removed. The language provides that support implicitly through the inheritance and the virtual function mechanisms. This object-oriented design is also considerably simpler both to modify and to extend. Unlike our earlier design, adding or removing an existing numeric sequence class requires no invasive changes.

Recall that in our design of the num_sequence base class, we also provided an overloaded instance of the output operator:

```
ostream& operator<<( ostream &os, const num_sequence &ns )
                    { return ns.print( os ); }
```

Because print() is a virtual function, the output operator works with each derived class instance. For example, here's a small program in which I define an object of each numeric sequence and then direct each in turn to the output operator:

```
int main()
{
    Fibonacci  fib( 8 );
    Pell       pell( 6, 4 );
    Lucas      lucas( 10, 7 );
    Triangular trian( 12 );
    Square     square( 6, 6 );
    Pentagonal penta( 8 );
    cout << "fib: "    << fib    << '\n'
         << "pell: "   << pell   << '\n'
         << "lucas: "  << lucas  << '\n'
         << "trian: "  << trian  << '\n'
         << "square: " << square << '\n'
         << "penta: "  << penta  << endl;
};
```

When compiled and executed, the program generates the following output:

```
fib: ( 1 , 8 ) 1 1 2 3 5 8 13 21
pell: ( 4 , 6 ) 12 29 70 169 408 985
lucas: ( 7 , 10 ) 29 47 76 123 199 322 521 843 1364 2207
trian: ( 1 , 12 ) 1 3 6 10 15 21 28 36 45 55 66 78
square: ( 6 , 6 ) 36 49 64 81 100 121
penta: ( 1 , 8 ) 1 5 12 22 35 51 70 92
```

5.7   How Abstract Should a Base Class Be?

Under our current design, the abstract base class provides an interface but does not provide an implementation. Each derived class must not only provide the unique algorithm for generating its elements but also provide support for finding the element, printing the element, maintaining the length and beginning position of the sequence object, and so on. Is this a bad design?

If the designer of the abstract base class is also providing the derived numeric sequence classes and if they are not expected to be added to very often, this design works quite well. If, however, a primary activity is the delivery of new numeric sequence classes and if that activity has been farmed out to individuals who are more comfortable with mathematics than programming, this design complicates the delivery of each derived class.

The following alternative base class design factors implementation support of the shared derived class data into the base class. The interface is unchanged. The program of the preceding section need not be modified, although it must be recompiled. The design change simplifies the work necessary to provide a derived class.

Here is the revised num_sequence base class definition. The two data members — _length and _beg_pos — are now num_sequence data members. We declare them as protected to allow the derived classes direct access to them. The supporting access member functions — length() and beg_pos() — are now also num_sequence class members. We declare them as public to allow the general program read access to these values.

A new data member has also been added to the num_sequence class. _relems, a reference to a vector of integers, refers to the static vector of the derived class. Why is it declared a reference rather than a pointer? As we say in Section 2.3, a reference can never refer to a null object, whereas a pointer may or may not be null. By making it a reference, we spare ourselves from having to check for a null pointer.

A reference data member must be initialized within the constructor's member initialization list and, once initialized, can never be changed to refer to a different object. A pointer data member has neither restriction: We can either initialize it within the constructor or initialize it to null and assign it a valid address later. We choose between making a data member a reference or pointer based on these characteristics.

The base class now has all the information necessary to search and display the elements of the numeric sequence. This also allows us to redefine elem() and print() as public members of num_sequence.

```
class num_sequence {
public:
    virtual ~num_sequence(){}
    virtual const char* what_am_i() const = 0;
```

```
      int                    elem( int pos ) const;
      ostream&               print( ostream &os = cout ) const;

      int                    length()  const { return _length;  }
      int                    beg_pos() const { return _beg_pos; }
      static  int            max_elems()     { return 64; }

  protected:
      virtual void           gen_elems( int pos ) const = 0;
      bool                   check_integrity( int pos, int size ) const;

      num_sequence( int len, int bp, vector<int> &re )
          : _length( len ), _beg_pos( bp ), _relems( re ){}

      int                    _length;
      int                    _beg_pos;
      vector<int>            & _relems;
  };
```

Each derived numeric sequence class now must program only those things unique to it: gen_elems(), which computes the elements of the sequence; what_am_i(), which identifies the sequence; the static vector to hold the sequence elements; and a constructor. The derived sequence class inherits the members for finding the element, printing the element, and maintaining the length and beginning position. For example, here is our revised Fibonacci class definition:

```
class Fibonacci : public num_sequence {
public:
    Fibonacci( int len = 1, int beg_pos = 1 );
    virtual const char* what_am_i() const
            { return "Fibonacci"; }

protected:
    virtual void       gen_elems( int pos ) const;
    static vector<int> _elems;
};
```

Although num_sequence remains an abstract base class, it now provides a partial implementation that is inherited by each derived class.

5.8   Initialization, Destruction, and Copy

Now that num_sequence declares actual data members, we must provide for their initialization. We could leave it to each derived class to initialize these data members, but that's potentially error-prone. A better design is to provide a base class constructor to handle the initialization of all base class members.

Recall that num_sequence is an abstract base class. We cannot define an independent object of its class; rather, the num_sequence serves as a subobject of each derived class object. For this reason, we declare the base class constructor to be a `protected` rather than `public` member.

The initialization of a derived class object consists of the invocation of the base class constructor followed by that of the derived class constructor. It helps to think of the derived class object as consisting of multiple subobjects: a base class subobject initialized by the base class constructor and a derived class subobject initialized by the derived class constructor. In a three-level class hierarchy, such as the AudioBook class of Section 5.1, the derived class consists of three subobjects, each one initialized by its respective constructor.

The design requirements of a derived class constructor are twofold: Not only must it initialize the derived class data members, but it must also supply the expected values to its base class constructor. In our example, the num_sequence base class requires three values that are passed to it using the member initialization list. For example,

```
inline Fibonacci::
Fibonacci( int len, int beg_pos )
         : num_sequence( len, beg_pos, &_elems )

{}
```

If we should overlook the invocation of the num_sequence constructor, the definition of the Fibonacci constructor is flagged as an error. Why? The num_sequence base class requires our explicit invocation of its three-argument constructor. In our design, this is what we want.

Alternatively, we could provide a default num_sequence constructor. We must change _relems to a pointer, however, and add code to verify that it is non-null before each access of the vector:

```
num_sequence::
num_sequence( int len=1, int bp=1, vector<int> *pe=0 )
         : _length( len ), _beg_pos( bp ), _pelems( re ){}
```

Now, if the derived class constructor does not explicitly invoke the base class constructor, the default base class constructor is invoked automatically.

What happens when we initialize one Fibonacci class object with another?

```
Fibonacci fib1( 12 );
Fibonacci fib2 = fib1;
```

If an explicit copy constructor is defined, that instance is invoked. For example, we might define a Fibonacci copy constructor as follows:

```
Fibonacci::Fibonacci( const Fibonacci &rhs )
         : num_sequence( rhs )
{}
```

rhs, the right-hand derived class object, is passed to the base class copy constructor using the member initialization list. What if the base class does not define an explicit copy constructor? Nothing bad happens. Default memberwise initialization is carried out. If an explicit base class copy constructor is defined, it is invoked.

In this case, an explicit Fibonacci copy constructor is unnecessary because the default behavior accomplishes the same results: First the base class subobject is memberwise initialized, followed by the memberwise initialization of the derived class members.

The same is true of the copy assignment operator. If we assign one Fibonacci class object to another and if an explicit copy assignment operator is defined, it is invoked to carry out the assignment. For example, here is how we might define the operator. The only tricky part is to invoke the base class operator explicitly.

```
Fibonacci& Fibonacci::
operator=( const Fibonacci &rhs )
{
    if ( this != &rhs )
        // explicit invocation of the base class operator
        num_sequence::operator=( rhs );

    return *this;
}
```

Again, in this case, an explicit Fibonacci copy assignment operator is unnecessary because the default behavior accomplishes the same results. (Refer to Section 4.2 and Section 4.8 for a discussion of when a copy constructor and a copy assignment operator are necessary.)

The base class destructor is invoked automatically following the invocation of the derived class destructor. We don't need to invoke it explicitly within the derived class destructor.

5.9   Defining a Derived Class Virtual Function

When we define a derived class, we must decide whether to override or inherit each of the base class virtual functions. If we inherit a pure virtual function, the derived class is then also considered an abstract class, and no independent objects of the class can be defined.

If we choose to override the base class instance, the prototype of the derived class instance must match the base class protoype exactly: the parameter list and the return type and whether the virtual function is const or non-const. For example, the following definition of Fibonacci::what_am_i() is not quite right:

```
class Fibonacci : public num_sequence {
public:
```

```
virtual const char* what_am_i() // not quite right ...
        { return "Fibonacci"; }
// ...
};
```

Although the Fibonacci instance of what_am_i() is not quite right, it is not wrong, and that's where the confusion comes in. When I compile it under the Intel C++ compiler, I get the following warning message:

```
warning #653: "const char *Fibonacci::what_am_i()"
        does not match "num_sequence::what_am_i"
        -- virtual function override intended?
```

What is this telling us? It is saying that the derived class declaration of what_am_i() does not exactly match the base class declaration. The base class instance is declared to be a const member function. The derived class instance is a non-const member function. Is this discepancy significant? Unfortunately, it is. Here's a simple illustration:

```
class num_sequence {
public:
   virtual const char* what_am_i() const
           { return "num_sequence\n"; }
};

class Fibonacci : public num_sequence {
public:
   virtual const char *what_am_i()
           { return "Fibonacci\n"; }
};

int main()
{
  Fibonacci b;
  num_sequence p;

  // expect this to generate: Fibonacci
  num_sequence *pp = &b;
  cout << pp->what_am_i();

  cout << b.what_am_i();
  return 0;
}
```

The expected output of this program is two Fibonacci strings. When we compile and execute the program, however, it generates the following unexpected output:

```
num_sequence
Fibonacci
```

The warning message is telling us that the derived class instance is not treated as overriding the base class instance because the two instances do not match exactly. This is a common beginner error and usually proves baffling. That's why I've spent so much time explaining it. The fix is simple; understanding why it is needed is less simple.

Here is a second incorrect redeclaration of what_am_i(). In this case, our return type does not match the return type of the num_sequence instance exactly:

```
class Fibonacci : public num_sequence {
public:
    // incorrect declaration!
    // base class instance returns const char*, not char*
    virtual char* what_am_i(){ return "Fibonacci"; }
    // ...
};
```

The num_sequence instance of what_am_i() returns a const char*. The Fibonacci instance returns a char*. This is simply incorrect and results in a compile-time error.

There is one exception to the exact return type rule: If the base class virtual function returns some base class type, typically a pointer or reference,

```
class num_sequence {
public:
    // derived class instance of clone() can return a
    // pointer to any class derived from num_sequence
    virtual num_sequence *clone()=0;

    // ...
};
```

the derived class instance can return a type that is derived from the base class return type:

```
class Fibonacci : public num_sequence {
public:
    // ok: Fibonacci is derived from num_sequence
    // the virtual keyword in the derived class is optional
    Fibonacci *clone(){ return new Fibonacci( *this ); }

    // ...
};
```

When we are overriding a base class virtual function in the derived class, the virtual keyword is optional. The function is identified as overriding the base class instance based on a comparison of the two function prototypes.

Static Resolution of a Virtual Function

There are two circumstances under which the virtual mechanism does not behave as we expect: (1) within the base class constructor and destructor and (2) when we use a base class object rather than a base class pointer or reference.

When we construct a derived class object, the base class constructor is invoked first. What happens if within the base class constructor a virtual function is called? Should the derived class instance be invoked?

The problem is that the derived class data members are not yet initialized. If the derived class instance of the virtual function is invoked, it is likely to access data members that are uninitialized, and that is not a good thing.

For that reason, within the base class constructor, the derived class virtual functions are never invoked! Within the num_sequence constructor, for example, a call of what_am_i() resolves to the num_sequence instance even if a Fibonacci class object is being defined. The same holds true for virtual functions invoked within the base class destructor.

Consider the following program fragment, which uses the LibMat and AudioBook classes of Section 5.1. Recall that print() is a virtual function of that class hierarchy.

```
void print( LibMat object,
            const LibMat *pointer,
            const LibMat &reference )
{
    // always invokes LibMat::print()
    object.print();

    // always resolved through the virtual mechanism
    // we don't know what instance of print() this invokes
    pointer->print();
    reference.print();
}
```

Polymorphism requires indirection in order to make possible the representation of multiple types within a single object. In C++, only pointers and references of the base class support object-oriented programming.

When we declare an actual object of the base class, such as the first parameter of print(), we allocate enough memory to represent an actual base class object. If we later pass in a derived class object, there simply isn't enough memory available to store the additional derived class data members. For example, when we pass an AudioBook object to print(), as in the following,

```
int main()
{
    AudioBook iWish( "Her Pride of 10",
                     "Stanley Lippman", "Jeremy Irons" );
    gen_elems( iWish, &iWish, iWish );
    // ...
}
```

only the base class LibMat portion of iWish can be copied into the memory reserved for object; Tthe Book and AudioBook subobjects are *sliced* off. pointer and reference are initialized simply with the address of the original iWish object. This is why they can address the complete AudioBook object. (For a more in-depth discussion, see Section 1.3 of [LIPPMAN96a].)

5.10   Run-Time Type Identification

Our implementation of what_am_i() has each class providing a virtual instance that returns a string literal identifying the class:

```
class Fibonacci : public num_sequence {
public:
    virtual const char* what_am_i() const { return "Fibonacci"; }
    // ...
};
```

An alternative design is to provide a single num_sequence instance of what_am_i() that each derived class reuses through inheritance. This design frees each derived class from having to provide its own instance of what_am_i().

One way to implement this might be to add a string member to num_sequence. Each derived class constructor would then pass its class name as an argument to the num_sequence constructor. For example,

```
inline Fibonacci::
Fibonacci( int len, int beg_pos )
            : num_sequence( len, beg_pos, &_elems, "Fibonacci" )

{}
```

An alternative implementation is to use the typeid operator. The typeid operator is part of the run-time type identification (RTTI) language support. It allows us to ask a polymorphic class pointer or reference the actual type of the object it refers to.

```
#include <typeinfo>

inline const char* num_sequence::
what_am_i() const
            { return typeid( *this ).name(); }
```

To use the typeid operator, we must include the typeinfo header file. The typeid operator returns a type_info class object. This object stores type information. There is one associated with each polymorphic class, such as the Fibonacci and Pell derived classes. name() returns a const char* representation of the class name. The expression

```
typeid( *this )
```

returns the type_info class object associated with the actual class type addressed by the this pointer within who_am_i(). The type_info name() member function is invoked through this object, returning the name of the actual class type.

The type_info class also supports equality and inequality comparisons. For example, the following code determines whether ps addresses a Fibonacci class object:

```
num_sequence *ps = &fib;
// ...
if ( typeid( *ps) == typeid( Fibonacci ))
      // ok, ps addresses a Fibonacci class object
```

If we write

```
ps->gen_elems( 64 );
```

we know that the Fibonacci instance of gen_elems() will be invoked. However, although we know from this test that ps addresses a Fibonacci class object, an attempt to invoke the Fibonacci instance of gen_elems() directly through ps results in a compile-time error:

```
// error: ps is not a pointer to Fibonacci
// although we know it currently addresses
// a Fibonacci class object
ps->Fibonacci::gen_elems( 64 );
```

ps does not "know" the type of the object it addresses, even if we and the typeid and virtual function mechanisms do.

To invoke the Fibonacci instance of gen_elems(), we must instruct the compiler to convert ps into a pointer of type Fibonacci. The static_cast operator performs the conversion unconditionally.

```
if ( typeid( *ps) == typeid( Fibonacci ))
{
      Fibonacci *pf = static_cast<Fibonacci*>( ps );
      pf->gen_elems( 64 );
}
```

A static_cast is potentially dangerous because the compiler does not confirm that our conversion is correct. This is why I've couched its use in the truth condition of the typeid operator. A conditional conversion is provided by the dynamic_cast operator:

```
if ( Fibonacci *pf = dynamic_cast<Fibonacci*>( ps ))
      pf->gen_elems( 64 );
```

The dynamic_cast operator is another RTTI operator. It performs a run-time verification that the object addressed by ps is actually of the Fibonacci class type. If it is, the conversion is carried out; pf now addresses the Fibonacci object. If it is not, the dynamic_cast operator returns 0. The if statement condition fails, and the static invocation of the Fibonacci instance of gen_elems() is not carried out.

For a more detailed discussion of the C++ run-time type identification mechanism see Section 19.1 of [LIPPMAN98].

Exercise 5.1

Implement a two-level stack hierarchy. The base class is a pure abstract Stack class that minimally supports the following interface: `pop()`, `push()`, `size()`, `empty()`, `full()`, `peek()`, and `print()`. The two concrete derived classes are LIFO_Stack and Peekback_Stack. The Peekback_Stack allows the user to retrieve the value of any element in the stack without modifying the stack itself.

Exercise 5.2

Reimplement the class hierarchy of Exercise 5.1 so that the base Stack class implements the shared, type-independent members.

Exercise 5.3

A type/subtype inheritance relationship in general reflects an *is-a* relationship: A range-checking ArrayRC is a kind of Array, a Book is a kind of LibraryRentalMaterial, an AudioBook is a kind of Book, and so on. Which of the following pairs reflects an is-a relationship?

```
(a) member function isA_kindOf function
(b) member function isA_kindOf class
(c) constructor isA_kindOf member function
(d) airplane isA_kindOf vehicle
(e) motor isA_kindOf truck
(f) circle isA_kindOf geometry
(g) square isA_kindOf rectangle
(h) automobile isA_kindOf airplane
(i) borrower isA_kindOf library
```

Exercise 5.4

A library supports the following categories of lending materials, each with its own check-out and check-in policy. Organize these into an inheritance hierarchy:

```
book          audio book
record        children's puppet
video         Sega video game
rental book   Sony Playstation video game
CD-ROM book   Nintendo video game
```

6

Programming with Templates

When Bjarne Stroustrup worked out the original C++ language design for templates, he referred to them as *parameterized types*: "parameterized" because they are factored out of the template definition, and "types" because each class or function template typically varies by one or a set of types being operated on or contained. The actual type is later specified by the user.

Stroustrup later changed the name to the more general *template*. A single template definition serves as a prescription for the automatic generation of a unique instance of a function or class based on a user-specified value or type.

Although we have extensively used class templates, such as the vector and string classes, we haven't yet implemented one of our own. We do that in this chapter, walking through the implementation of a binary tree class template.

If you're unfamiliar with the binary tree abstraction, the following is a brief review. A tree consists of nodes and vertices, or links, connecting the nodes. A binary tree maintains two links between nodes, typically called the *left* and *right child*. The tree has a first node called the *root*. Each left or right child may itself serve as root to a subtree. A node without children is called a *leaf* node.

Our binary tree implementation consists of two classes: a BinaryTree class, which holds a pointer to the root, and a BTnode helping class, which holds both the actual value and the left and right child links. It is the type of the node value that we parameterize.

What are the operations our BinaryTree must support? Users must both *insert* and *remove* an element as well as *find* whether an element is present, *clear* all tree elements, and *print* the tree in one of three traversal algorithms: *inorder*, *preorder*, or *postorder*.

In our implementation, the first value inserted into an empty tree becomes the root. Each subsequent value is inserted so that all values less than the root are placed in the root's left subtree. All values greater than the root are placed in the root's right subtree. A value occurs only once within a tree. An occurrence count keeps track of multiple insertions of the same value. For example, given the code sequence

```
BinaryTree<string> bt;
bt.insert( "Piglet" );
```

Piglet becomes the root of our binary tree. Suppose that we next insert Eeyore:

```
bt.insert( "Eeyore" );
```

Because Eeyore is alphabetically less than Piglet, Eeyore becomes the left child of Piglet. Then suppose we next insert Roo:

```
bt.insert( "Roo" );
```

Because Roo is greater than Piglet, Roo becomes the right child of Piglet, and so on. Let's complete our tree by inserting the following elements:

```
bt.insert( "Tigger" );
bt.insert( "Chris" );
bt.insert( "Pooh" );
bt.insert( "Kanga" );
```

The resulting binary tree is pictured in Figure 6.1. In this example, Chris, Kanga, Pooh, and Tigger are leaf nodes.

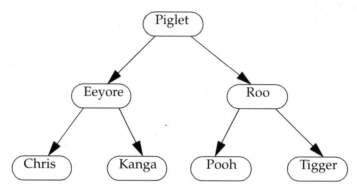

Figure 6.1 Binary Tree after Element Insertion

Each traversal algorithm begins with the root node. In a *preorder* traversal, the node is displayed; then the left child is visited and then the right child. In an *inorder* traversal, the left child is first visited, then the node is displayed, and then the right child is visited. In a *postorder* traversal, the left child is visited; then the right child is visited, and then the node is displayed. For the tree in Figure 6.1, the three traversal algorithms display the nodes as follows:

```
// preorder traversal of Figure 6.1 binary tree
Piglet, Eeyore, Chris, Kanga, Roo, Pooh, Tigger

// inorder traversal of Figure 6.1 binary tree
Chris, Eeyore, Kanga, Piglet, Pooh, Roo, Tigger
```

```
// postorder traversal of Figure 6.1 binary tree
Chris, Kanga, Eeyore, Pooh, Tigger, Roo, Piglet
```

6.1   Parameterized Types

Here is a nontemplate declaration of the BTnode class in which the stored value is a string class object. I call it string_BTnode because we must define other instances that store values of type int, double, and so on.

```
class string_BTnode {
public:
    //  ...
private:
    string _val;
    int _cnt;
    int_BTnode *_lchild;
    int_BTnode *_rchild;
};
```

Without the template mechanism, each type would need its own separately implemented BTnode class, and each would need to be named uniquely.

The template mechanism allows us to separate the type-dependent and invariant portions of our class definition. The code that traverses the tree, inserts and removes nodes, and maintains the occurrence count is the same regardless of the value's type. This code is reused with each instance of the class template.

The value's type stored within each node changes with each instance of the class template, in one case representing a string object, in another an int or double, and so on. In a class template, type dependencies are factored into one or more parameters. In our BTnode class, the type of the data member _val is parameterized:

```
// forward declaration of BTnode class template
template <typename valType>
class BTnode;
```

valType is used within the template class definition as a placeholder. We can give it any name we wish. It serves as a wild card until we specify an actual type. A type parameter can be used anywhere that an actual type, such as int or string, can be used. In the BTnode class, it is used to declare the type of _val:

```
template < typename valType >
class BTnode {
public:
    //  ...
private:
    valType      _val;
    int          _cnt;
```

```
BTnode      *_lchild;
BTnode      *_rchild;
};
```

The BTnode class template collaborates with the BinaryTree class template in the implementation of our abstraction. The BTnode class holds the actual value, the occurrence count, and the pointers to the left and right children. Recall that collaborative class relationships usually require friendship. For each actual type of BTnode class, we want the corresponding BinaryTree instance to be its friend. Here is how we declare that:

```
template <typename Type>
class BinaryTree;  // forward declaration

template <typename valType>
class BTnode {
   friend class BinaryTree<valType>;
   // ...
};
```

To create an instance of the class template, we follow the class template name with an actual type we want to substitute for valType enclosed in angle brackets. For example, to bind valType to type int, we write

```
BTnode< int > bti;
```

Similarly, to bind valType to the class string type, we write

```
BTnode< string > bts;
```

bti and bts represent two definitions of BTnode: one for which _val is defined as an int, and one for which _val is defined as a string. The corresponding BinaryTree string instance is a friend to the BTnode string instance but not to the BTnode int instance.

The BinaryTree class declares one data member, a BTnode pointer to the root node of the tree:

```
template <typename elemType>
class BinaryTree {
public:
    // ...
private:
    // BTnode must be qualified with its template parameter list
    BTnode<elemType> *_root;
};
```

How do we know when to qualify the class template name with its parameter list? The general rule is that within the definition of the class template and its members, the template class name does not need to be qualified. A template class name must otherwise be qualified with its parameter list.

When we specify an actual type for the BinaryTree parameter, such as

```
BinaryTree< string > st;
```

_root becomes a pointer to a BTnode object holding a value of type string. Similarly, when we specify an int type,

```
BinaryTree< int > it;
```

_root becomes a pointer to a BTnode object holding a value of type int.

6.2   The Template Class Definition

Here is a partial definition of our BinaryTree class template:

```
template <typename elemType>
class BinaryTree {
public:
    BinaryTree();
    BinaryTree( const BinaryTree& );
    ~BinaryTree();
    BinaryTree& operator=( const BinaryTree& );

    bool empty() { return _root == 0; }
    void clear();
private:
    BTnode<elemType> *_root;

    // copy a subtree addressed by src to tar
    void copy( BTnode<elemType>*tar, BTnode<elemType>*src );
};
```

Defining an inline member function for a class template is the same as for a non-class template, as the definition of empty() illustrates. The syntax for defining a class template member function outside the class body, however, looks very different, at least at first blush:

```
template <typename elemType>
inline BinaryTree<elemType>::
BinaryTree() : _root( 0 )
{}
```

The member function definition begins with the template keyword and parameter list of the class. The function definition follows that, together with the inline qualifier and class scope operator. The inline qualifier must come after the template keyword and parameter list.

Why is the second occurrence of the BinaryTree name not qualified? After the class scope operator is seen,

```
BinaryTree< elemType >::
```

everything following that is treated as occurring inside the class definition. When we write

```
BinaryTree< elemType >::    // outside class definition
BinaryTree()                // inside class definition
```

the second occurrence of BinaryTree is considered within the class definition and so does not need to be qualified. For example, here are the definitions of the copy constructor, copy assignment operator, and destructor:

```
template <typename elemType>
inline BinaryTree<elemType>::
BinaryTree( const BinaryTree &rhs )
        { copy( _root, rhs._root ); }

template <typename elemType>
inline BinaryTree<elemType>::
~BinaryTree()
        { clear(); }

template <typename elemType>
inline BinaryTree<elemType>&
BinaryTree<elemType>::
operator=( const BinaryTree &rhs )
{
    if ( this != &rhs )
        { clear(); copy( _root, rhs._root ); }
    return *this;
}
```

You probably won't believe me, but after you write a sufficient number of these sorts of definitions, they begin to look almost natural.

6.3   Handling Template Type Parameters

Handling a template type parameter is somewhat more complicated than handling an explicit parameter type. For example, to declare an explicit int parameter to a function, we write

```
bool find( int val );
```

passing it by value. However, to declare an explicit Matrix class parameter to a function, we instead write

```
bool find( const Matrix &val );
```

passing it by reference in order not to generate an unnecessary copy of the Matrix class object. Our program is not wrong if we declare find() as follows:

```
// not wrong, but inefficient
bool find( Matrix val );
```

It simply takes longer to reach the same conclusion and is likely to be criticized by readers of our code, particularly if `find()` is called frequently within the program.

When we manipulate a template type parameter, we don't really know whether the actual type supplied by the user will be a built-in type:

```
BinaryTree<int> bti;
```

In that case the pass by value parameter list of `find()` is preferred. If it is a class type

```
BinaryTree<Matrix> btm;
```

the pass by reference parameter list of `find()` is preferred.

In practice, both built-in and class types are likely to be specified as actual types to the class template. The recommended programming strategy is to treat the template type parameter *as if* it is a class type. As a function parameter, for example, this means that we declare it as a const reference rather than pass it by value.

Within the definition of a constructor, we initialize each type parameter within the member initialization list

```
// preferred initialization method for
// type parameter passed to a constructor
template <typename valType>
inline BTnode<valType>::
BTnode( const valType &val )
    // just in case valType is a class type
    : _val( val )
{
    _cnt = 1;
    _lchild = _rchild = 0;
}
```

rather than within the body of the constructor:

```
template <typename valType>
inline BTnode<valType>::
BTnode( const valType &val )
{
    // not recommended; could be a class type
    _val = val;

    // ok: these types are invariant ...
    _cnt = 1;
    _lchild = _rchild = 0;
}
```

This guarantees optimal performance if the user specifies a class type as the actual type of valType. For example, if I write

```
BTnode<int> btni( 42 );
```

there is no difference in performance between the two forms. However, if I write

```
BTnode<Matrix> btnm( transform_matrix );
```

there is a difference in performance. The assignment of _val in the constructor body requires two steps: (1) The default Matrix constructor is applied to _val before execution of the constructor body, and (2) the copy assignment operator of _val with val is applied within the body. The initialization of _val within the constructor's member initialization list requires only a single step: the copy construction of _val with val.

Again, it is not that our program is wrong either in passing valType by value or in assigning the valType data member within the constructor body. But they do take more time and are considered a sign of an inexperienced C++ programmer.

At this point in learning C++ you shouldn't be overly concerned with efficiency. However, it is useful to point out these two cases because they are common beginner mistakes, and a simple heads-up is usually enough to correct them. Enough said!

6.4   Implementing the Template Class

Each time we insert a new value, we must create a BTnode object, initialize it, and link it somewhere within the tree. We manage the allocation and deallocation of each node explicitly using the new and delete expressions.

insert(), for example, allocates a new BTnode from the program's free store if _root is unset; otherwise, it calls the BTnode insert_value() method to insert the new value into the tree:

```
template <typename elemType>
inline void
BinaryTree<elemType>::
insert( const elemType &elem )
{
    if ( ! _root )
            _root = new BTnode<elemType>( elem );
    else _root->insert_value( elem );
}
```

There are two steps to the operation of the new expression. (1) Memory is requested of the program's free store. If sufficient memory is available, a pointer to the object is returned. (If sufficient memory is not available, a bad_alloc exception is raised. We discuss the C++ exception handling facility in Chapter 7.) (2) If the first step succeeds and an initial value is specified, the object is appropriately initialized. For a class type, as in

```
_root = new BTnode<elemType>( elem );
```

elem is passed to the BTnode constructor. If the allocation step fails, the initialization step is not carried out.

insert_value() is invoked only if a root node is present. The root's left subtree holds values that are less than its value, and the right subtree holds values that are greater. insert_value() recursively invokes itself through either the left or the right child until it finds an unset child to which to attach itself or finds the value already entered. Only one instance of each value is stored in the tree. The BTnode _cnt data member keeps an insertion count. Here is the implementation:

```
template <typename valType>
void BTnode<valType>::
insert_value( const valType &val )
{
    if ( val == _val )
        { _cnt++; return; }

    if ( val < _val )
    {
        if ( ! _lchild )
            _lchild = new BTnode( val );
        else _lchild->insert_value( val );
    }
    else
    {
        if ( ! _rchild )
            _rchild = new BTnode( val );
        else _rchild->insert_value( val );
    }
}
```

The removal of a value is complicated by the need to preserve the order of the tree. The general algorithm is to replace the node with its right child. The left child is then reattached as the leaf node of the right child's left subtree. If there is no right child, the node is replaced with the left child. To simplify the implementation, I've treated the removal of the root node as a special case.

```
template <typename elemType>
inline void
BinaryTree<elemType>::
remove( const elemType &elem )
{
    if ( _root )
    {
        if ( _root->_val == elem )
            remove_root();
        else
            _root->remove_value( elem, _root );
    }
}
```

Both remove_root() and remove_value() reattach the left child as the leaf node of the right child's left subtree. I've factored this operation out into lchild_leaf(), a static member function of the BTnode class:

```
template <typename valType>
void BTnode<valType>::
lchild_leaf( BTnode *leaf, BTnode *subtree )
{
    while ( subtree->_lchild )
            subtree = subtree->_lchild;
    subtree->_lchild = leaf;
}
```

remove_root() resets the root node to one of its children, if a child node is present. If the right child is present, it becomes the new root node; the left child, if present, is reattached either directly or through a call of lchild_leaf(). If the right child is null, _root is set to the left child.

```
template <typename elemType>
void BinaryTree<elemType>::
remove_root()
{
    if ( ! _root ) return;

    BTnode<elemType> *tmp = _root;
    if ( _root->_rchild )
    {
        _root = _root->_rchild;

        // ok, now we must reattach the left child to the
        // bottom of the right child's left subtree
        if ( tmp->_lchild )
        {
            // factor out just for readability
            BTnode<elemType> *lc = tmp->_lchild;
            BTnode<elemType> *newlc = _root->_lchild;
            if ( ! newlc )
                    // no subtree, let's directly attach it
                    _root->_lchild = lc;

            // lchild_leaf() will travel the left subtree
            // looking for a null left child to attach ...
            // lchild_leaf is a static member function
            else BTnode<elemType>::lchild_leaf( lc, newlc );
        }
    }
    else _root = _root->_lchild;

    delete tmp; // ok: now we remove the node previously root
}
```

remove_value() takes two parameters: the value to be deleted, if present, and a pointer to the parent node of the node currently under examination.

```
template <typename valType>
void BTnode<valType>::
remove_value( const valType &val, BTnode *& prev );
```

remove_value()'s parameter list illustrates the two uses of a reference parameter. val is passed as a reference to prevent a potentially expensive copy by value if valType is specified as a class type. Because we don't intend to change val, we pass it as a const.

The second reference parameter is a bit less intuitive. Why are we passing prev as a reference to pointer? Isn't a pointer sufficient? No. Passing a pointer as a parameter allows us to change the object addressed by the pointer but not the address to which the pointer is set. To change the pointer's actual address value, we must add another level of indirection. By declaring prev as a reference to a pointer, we can change both its address value and the value of the object it addresses.

```
template <typename valType>
void BTnode<valType>::
remove_value( const valType &val, BTnode *& prev )
{
    if ( val < _val )
    {
        if ( ! _lchild )
            return;  // not present
        else _lchild->remove_value( val, _lchild );
    }
    else
    if ( val > _val )
    {
        if ( ! _rchild )
            return;  // not present
        else _rchild->remove_value( val, _rchild );
    }
    else
    {
      // ok: found it;
      // reset the tree then delete this node

      if ( _rchild )
      {
         prev = _rchild;
         if ( _lchild )
            if ( ! prev->_lchild )
                  prev->_lchild = _lchild;
            else BTnode<valType>::lchild_leaf(_lchild,prev->_lchild);
      }
      else prev = _lchild;
      delete this;
    }
}
```

We also need a function to remove the entire tree. `clear()` is implemented as a pair of functions: an inline public function and an overloaded private instance that does the real work.

```
template <typename elemType>
class BinaryTree {
public:
    void clear(){ if ( _root ){ clear( _root ); _root = 0; }}
    // ...
private:
    void clear( BTnode<elemType>* );
    // ...
};

template <typename elemType>
void BinaryTree<elemType>::
clear( BTnode<elemType> *pt )
{
    if ( pt ){
        clear( pt->_lchild );
        clear( pt->_rchild );
        delete pt;
    }
}
```

The following program builds the binary tree illustrated in Figure 6.1. A preorder display of the tree is generated in three instances: after the tree is built, after the root node is removed, and after an internal node is removed.

```
#include "BinaryTree.h"
#include <iostream>
#include <string>
using namespace std;

int main()
{
    BinaryTree<string> bt;

    bt.insert( "Piglet" );
    bt.insert( "Eeyore" );
    bt.insert( "Roo" );
    bt.insert( "Tigger" );
    bt.insert( "Chris" );
    bt.insert( "Pooh" );
    bt.insert( "Kanga" );

    cout << "Preorder traversal: \n";
    bt.preorder();

    bt.remove( "Piglet" );
```

```
    cout << "\n\nPreorder traversal after Piglet removal: \n";
    bt.preorder();

    bt.remove( "Eeyore" );

    cout << "\n\nPreorder traversal after Eeyore removal: \n";
    bt.preorder();

    return 0;
}
```

When compiled and executed, the program generates the following output:

```
Preorder traversal:
Piglet  Eeyore  Chris  Kanga  Roo  Pooh  Tigger

Preorder traversal after Piglet removal:
Roo  Pooh  Eeyore  Chris  Kanga  Tigger

Preorder traversal after Eeyore removal:
Roo  Pooh  Kanga  Chris  Tigger
```

Each of the three traversal algorithms — preorder(), inorder(), and postorder() — performs an operation on the current node (in our case, it displays _val) and recursively calls itself on the left and right child. The only difference between the three algorithms is the order in which these actions are carried out:

```
template <typename valType>
void BTnode<valType>::
preorder( BTnode *pt, ostream &os ) const
{
    if ( pt )
    {
        display_val( pt, os );
        if ( pt->_lchild ) preorder( pt->_lchild, os );
        if ( pt->_rchild ) preorder( pt->_rchild, os );
    }
}

template <typename valType>
void BTnode<valType>::
inorder( BTnode *pt, ostream &os ) const
{
    if ( pt )
    {
        if ( pt->_lchild ) inorder( pt->_lchild, os );
        display_val( pt, os );
        if ( pt->_rchild ) inorder( pt->_rchild, os );
    }
}
```

```
template <typename valType>
void BTnode<valType>::
postorder( BTnode *pt, ostream &os ) const
{
    if ( pt ){
        if ( pt->_lchild ) postorder( pt->_lchild, os );
        if ( pt->_rchild ) postorder( pt->_rchild, os );
        display_val( pt, os );
    }
}
```

6.5   A Function Template Output Operator

We'd like to provide an output operator for our BinaryTree class template. For a non-template class, we write

```
ostream& operator<<( ostream&, const int_BinaryTree& );
```

For the class template, we could provide an explicit instance for each generated class definition:

```
ostream& operator<<( ostream&, const BinaryTree<int>& );
```

But that's Sisyphus work: It's tedious, and it never ends. A better solution is to define the output operator as a function template:

```
template <typename elemType>
inline ostream&
operator<<( ostream &os, const BinaryTree<elemType> &bt )
{
    os << "Tree: " << endl;
    bt.print( os );
    return os;
}
```

When we write

```
BinaryTree< string > bts;
cout << bts << endl;
```

an instance of the output operator is generated to support a second parameter of BinaryTree<string>. When we write

```
BinaryTree< int > bti;
cout << bti << endl;
```

an instance of the output operator is generated to support a second parameter of BinaryTree<int>, and so on.

print() is a private member function of the BinaryTree class template (refer to the online code listing for its definition). For the output operator to access print(), it must be made a friend of BinaryTree:

```
template <typename elemType>
class BinaryTree {
    friend ostream& operator<<( ostream&,
                                const BinaryTree<elemType>& );
    // ...
};
```

6.6   Constant Expressions and Default Parameters

Template parameters are not limited only to types, although until now I've limited my discussion to them. We can also declare constant expressions as parameters. For example, our numeric sequence class hierarchy might be redefined as a template class in which the number of elements an object contains is parameterized:

```
template <int len>
class num_sequence {
public:
    num_sequence( int beg_pos=1 );
    // ...
};

template <int len>
class Fibonacci : public NumericSeries<len> {
public:
    Fibonacci( int beg_pos=1 )
        : num_sequence<len>( beg_pos ){}
    // ...
};
```

When a Fibonacci object is created, as in

```
Fibonacci< 16 > fib1;
Fibonacci< 16 > fib2( 17 );
```

instances of both the Fibonacci derived class and the num_sequence base class are generated with len bound to 16. Alternatively, we might parametermize both the length and the beginning position:

```
template < int len, int beg_pos >
class NumericSeries;
```

However, because most class objects begin their range with position 1, this is convenient only if we provide a default value for the position:

```
template <int len, int beg_pos>
class num_sequence { ... };

template <int len, int beg_pos=1>
class Fibonacci : public num_sequence<len,beg_pos>
{ ... };
```

Here is how objects of these classes might be defined:

```
// expands as:
// num_sequence<32,1> *pns1to32 = new Fibonacci<32,1>;
num_sequence<32> *pns1to32  = new Fibonacci<32>;

// overrides default expression parameter value
num_sequence<32,33> *pns33to64 = new Fibonacci<32,33>;
```

Like default function parameter values, the default parameter values are resolved positionally, from right to left. To illustrate how we might actually implement this, I've redefined our num_sequence and Fibonacci base and derived classes of Chapter 5 to use expression parameters:

```
// the num_sequence class definition
// we no longer need to store as data members
// the length and beginning position

template <int len, int beg_pos>
class num_sequence {
public:
    virtual             ~num_sequence(){};
    int                 elem( int pos ) const;
    const char*         what_am_i() const;
    static  int         max_elems(){ return _max_elems; }
    ostream&            print( ostream &os = cout ) const;
protected:
    virtual void        gen_elems( int pos ) const = 0;
    bool                check_integrity( int pos, int size ) const;

    num_sequence( vector<int> *pe ) : _pelems( pe ){}
    static const int _max_elems = 1024;
    vector<int>         *_pelems;
};

// function template output operator definition
template <int len, int beg_pos> ostream&
operator<<( ostream &os, const num_sequence<len,beg_pos> &ns )
        { return ns.print( os ); }

// num_sequence member functions ...
template <int len, int beg_pos>
int num_sequence<len,beg_pos>::
elem( int pos ) const
{
    if ( ! check_integrity( pos, _pelems->size() ))
        return 0;

    return (*_pelems)[ pos-1 ];
}
```

```
template <int length, int beg_pos>
const char* num_sequence<length, beg_pos>::
what_am_i() const
   { return typeid( *this ).name(); }

template <int length, int beg_pos>
bool num_sequence<length, beg_pos>::
check_integrity( int pos, int size ) const
{
   if ( pos <= 0 || pos > max_elems() ){
       cerr << "!! invalid position: " << pos
            << " Cannot honor request\n";
       return false;
   }

   if ( pos > size ) gen_elems( pos );
   return true;
}

template <int length, int beg_pos>
ostream& num_sequence<length, beg_pos>::
print( ostream &os ) const
{
   int elem_pos = beg_pos-1;
   int end_pos = elem_pos + length;

    if ( ! check_integrity( end_pos, _pelems->size() ))
         return os;

     os << "( "
        << beg_pos << " , "
        << length << " ) ";

   while ( elem_pos < end_pos )
         os << (*_pelems)[ elem_pos++ ] << ' ';

   return os;
}

// ok: the Fibonacci class template with default parameter value
template <int length, int beg_pos=1>
class Fibonacci : public num_sequence<length, beg_pos> {
public:
    Fibonacci() : num_sequence<length,beg_pos>( &_elems ){}
protected:
    virtual void      gen_elems( int pos ) const;
    static vector<int> _elems;
};
```

```
// declare the static data member template for Fibonacci
template <int length, int beg_pos>
vector<int> Fibonacci<length,beg_pos>::_elems;

// the Fibonacci class template member functions
template <int length, int beg_pos>
void Fibonacci<length,beg_pos>::
gen_elems( int pos ) const
{
    if ( pos <= 0 || pos > max_elems() )
        return;

    if ( _elems.empty() )
    {
        _elems.push_back( 1 );
        _elems.push_back( 1 );
    }

    if ( _elems.size() < pos )
    {
        int ix = _elems.size();
        int n_2 = _elems[ ix-2 ],
            n_1 = _elems[ ix-1 ];

        int elem;
        for ( ; ix < pos; ++ix )
        {
            elem = n_2 + n_1;
            _elems.push_back( elem );
            n_2 = n_1; n_1 = elem;
        }
    }
}
```

Here is a small program to exercise our implementation. fib1, fib2, and fib3 each represent a different instance of the Fibonacci class template. fib1 has a length of 8 and a default beginning position of 1. fib2 also has a length of 8 but a beginning position of 8. fib3 has a length of 12 and also a beginning position of 8.

```
int main()
{
    Fibonacci<8>   fib1;
    Fibonacci<8,8> fib2;
    Fibonacci<12,8> fib3;

    cout << "fib1: " << fib1 << '\n'
         << "fib2: " << fib2 << '\n'
         << "fib3: " << fib3 << endl;
};
```

When compiled and executed, this generates the following output :

```
fib1: ( 1 , 8 ) 1 1 2 3 5 8 13 21
fib2: ( 8 , 8 ) 21 34 55 89 144 233 377 610
fib3: ( 8 , 12 ) 21 34 55 89 144 233 377 610 987 1597 2584 4181
```

Addresses of functions and objects at global scope are also constant expressions and so can also represent value parameters. For example, here is a numeric sequence class that takes a pointer to a function as its parameter:

```
template <void (*pf)(int pos, vector<int> &seq)>
class numeric_sequence
{
public:
    numeric_sequence( int len, int beg_pos = 1 )
    {
        // sanity check that pf is non-null ...
        if ( ! pf )
            // issue error message and bail out

        _len = len > 0 ? len : 1;
        _beg_pos = beg_pos > 0 ? beg_pos : 1;

        pf( beg_pos+len, _elems );
    }
    // ...
private:
    int         _len;
    int         _beg_pos;
    vector<int> _elems;
};
```

In this example, pf addresses a function that generates pos elements of a particular sequence type within the vector seq. It might be used as follows:

```
void fibonacci( int pos, vector<int> &seq );
void pell( int pos, vector<int> &seq );
// ...
numeric_sequence<fibonacci>  ns_fib( 12 );
numeric_sequence<pell>       ns_pell( 18, 8 );
```

6.7   Template Parameters as Strategy

Our LessThan class function object of Section 4.9 is a natural candidate for transforming into a template class:

```
template <typename elemType>
class LessThan {
public:
    LessThan( const elemType &val ) : _val( val ){}
```

```
bool operator()( const elemType &val ) const
                    { return val < _val; }

void val( const elemType &newval ) { _val = newval; }
elemType val() const { return _val; }
private:
   elemType _val;
};

LessThan<int>    lti( 1024 );
LessThan<string> lts( "Pooh" );
```

A potential problem with this implementation is that it fails if the type supplied by the user does not define a less-than operator. One possible strategy is to provide a second template class with the comparison operator factored out of the class definition. Even if this second class provides the same general semantics as LessThan, however, we must provide a unique name for it because a class template cannot be overloaded based on its parameter list. Let's call this class LessThanPred because the less-than class function object is specified as the default parameter:

```
template <typename elemType, typename Comp = less<elemType> >
class LessThanPred {
public:
   LessThanPred( const elemType &val ) : _val( val ){}
   bool operator()( const elemType &val ) const
                    { return Comp( val, _val ); }

   void val( const elemType &newval ) { _val = newval; }
   elemType val() const { return _val; }
private:
   elemType _val;
};

// alternative function object comparison
class StringLen {
public:
   bool operator()( const string &s1, const string &s2 )
   { return s1.size() < s2.size(); }
};

LessThanPred<int> ltpi( 1024 );
LessThanPred<string, StringLen> ltps( "Pooh" );
```

Alternatively, we might provide a more general name for our function object to indicate that it supports any comparison operation. In this case, it would no longer make sense to provide a default function object:

```
template <typename elemType, typename BinaryComp >
class Compare;
```

Compare applies any `BinaryComp` operation against two objects of the same arbitrary `elemType`.

In Chapter 5, we design an object-oriented numeric sequence class hierarchy. Consider the following alternative design, in which we define a numeric sequence class template with the actual sequence class factored out as a parameter:

```
template <typename num_seq>
class NumericSequence {
public:
    NumericSequence( int len = 1, int bpos = 1 )
                    : _ns( len, bpos ){}

    // this invokes the unknown numeric sequence
    // member functions through a naming discipline:
    // each num_seq parameter class must provide a
    // named function calc_elems(), is_elem(), and so on ...
    void calc_elems( int sz ) const { _ns.calc_elems( sz ); }
    bool is_elem( int elem )  const { return _ns.is_elem( elem ); }

    // ...

private:
    num_seq _ns;
};
```

This template design imposes a naming discipline on the classes used as parameters: Each must provide a named function corresponding to those invoked within the NumericSequence class template, such as `calc_elems()`, `is_elem()`, and so on.

Although this design idiom is somewhat advanced, I thought it worthwhile to show it briefly so that you don't fall into thinking of class template type parameters as representing only element types such as those illustrated in the binary tree implementation and the vector and list container classes of the standard library.

6.8   Member Template Functions

It is also possible to define a member template function. Let's look at an example and then walk through it:

```
class PrintIt {
public:
    PrintIt( ostream &os )
            : _os( os ){}

    // a member template function
    template <typename elemType>
    void print( const elemType &elem, char delimiter = '\n' )
            { _os << elem << delimiter; }
```

```
private:
    ostream& _os;
};
```

PrintIt is a nontemplate class that is initialized to an output stream. It provides a member template `print()` function that writes an object of an arbitrary type to that output stream. By making `print()` a member template function, we can provide a single instance that supports any type for which an instance of the output operator can be applied. Were we to parameterize PrintIt by the type of element we wish to output, we would create a new class template for each distinct type. Under this implementation, there is only a single PrintIt class. Here is how we might use it:

```
int main()
{
    PrintIt to_standard_out( cout );
    to_standard_out.print( "hello" );
    to_standard_out.print( 1024 );

    string my_string( "i am a string" );
    to_standard_out.print( my_string );
}
```

When compiled and executed, this generates the following output:

```
hello
1024
i am a string
```

A template class can also define a member template function. For example, we might parameterize PrintIt by its ostream type while maintaining `print()` as a member template function:

```
template <typename OutStream>
class PrintIt {
public:
    PrintIt( OutStream &os )
            : _os( os ){}

    template <typename elemType>
    void print( const elemType &elem, char delimiter = '\n' )
            { _os << elem << delimiter; }
private:
    ostream& _os;
};
```

Here is our modified program:

```
int main()
{
    PrintIt<ostream> to_standard_out( cout );
    to_standard_out.print( "hello" );
```

```
        to_standard_out.print( 1024 );

        string my_string( "i am a string" );
        to_standard_out.print( my_string );
    }
```

There is a great deal more to be said about templates than I have covered here. For a more detailed look at the C++ template facility, see [LIPPMAN98], Chapter 10 (Function Templates) and Chapter 16 (Class Templates) and [STROUSTRUP97], Chapter 13.

Exercise 6.1

Rewrite the following class definition to make it a class template:

```
        class example {
        public:
            example( double min, double max );
            example( const double *array, int size );
            double& operator[]( int index );
            bool operator==( const example1& ) const;
            bool insert( const double*, int );
            bool insert( double );
            double min() const { return _min; }
            double max() const { return _max; }
            void min( double );
            void max( double );
            int count( double value ) const;
        private:
            int size;
            double *parray;
            double _min;
            double _max;
        };
```

Exercise 6.2

Reimplement the Matrix class of Exercise 4.3 as a template. In addition, extend it to support arbitrary row and column size using heap memory. Allocate the memory in the constructor and deallocate it in the destructor.

Exception Handling

During the implementation of our Triangular_iterator class in Section 4.6, we realized that the iterator can potentially fall into an error state. The _index data member might become set to a value greater than the maximum number of elements stored in the static vector of the Triangular class. On the face of it, this seems an unlikely thing to happen. If it does happen, however, that's bad because the program that is using the value is likely to fail. It's also bad because the programmer using the iterator class has no easy way to recognize or resolve the problem.

As the designer of the iterator class, we can recognize the problem: The iterator is no longer in a valid state and must no longer be used within the program. But we do not know how serious the problem is to the overall program. Only the user of the iterator has that knowledge. Our job is to notify the user. To do this, we use the C++ exception handling facility, the topic of this chapter.

7.1 Throwing an Exception

The exception handling facility consists of two primary components: the recognition and raising of an exception and the eventual handling of the exception. Typically, an exception is raised and handled within various member or nonmember functions. After an exception is raised, normal program execution is suspended. The exception handling facility searches for a portion of the program that is capable of handling the raised exception. After the exception has been handled, program execution resumes in the portion of the program that has handled the exception.

In C++, we raise an exception by using the throw expression:

```
inline void Triangular_iterator::
check_integrity()
{
    if ( _index > Triangular::_max_elems )
        throw iterator_overflow( _index,
                                 Triangular::_max_elems );
```

```
        if ( _index > Triangular::_elems.size() )
            Triangular::gen_elements( _index );
    }
```

The throw expression looks somewhat like a function call. In this example, if _index is greater than _max_elems, an exception object of type iterator_overflow is thrown. The second if statement is never executed, and control does not return to this point in the program after the exception is handled. If _index is less than or equal to _max_elems, no exception is raised, and the program executes as we expect.

What is the exception that gets thrown? An exception is an object of some type. A simple exception object might be an integer or a string:

```
        throw 42;
        throw "panic: no buffer!";
```

Most often, thrown exceptions are class objects of an explicitly provided exception class or exception class hierarchy. For example, here is the definition of the iterator_overflow class:

```
        class iterator_overflow{
        public:
            iterator_overflow( int index, int max )
                    : _index( index ), _max( max ) {}

            int index() { return _index; }
            int max()   { return _max;   }

            void what_happened( ostream &os = cerr ) {
                    os << "Internal error: current index "
                        << _index << " exceeds maximum bound: "
                        << _max;
            }

        private:
            int _index;
            int _max;
        };
```

There is nothing exceptional about the class. We simply define it to store whatever data we wish to carry across program call points to communicate the nature of the raised exception.

The throw expression of our example directly invokes the two-parameter constructor. Alternatively, we can throw an explicit class object:

```
        if ( _index > Triangular::_max_elems ){
            iterator_overflow ex( _index, Triangular::_max_elems );
            throw ex;
        }
```

7.2   Catching an Exception

We catch exception objects by their type using one or a series of catch clauses. A catch clause consists of three parts: the keyword `catch`, the declaration of a single type or single object within parentheses, and a set of statements within curly braces that does the actual handling of the exception. For example, consider the following set of catch clauses:

```
// defined elsewhere ...
extern void log_message( const char* );
extern string err_messages[];
exterm ostream log_file;

bool some_function()
{
    bool status = true;

    // ... we'll get to this part!

    catch( int errno ){
        log_message( err_messages[ errno] );
        status = false;
    }
    catch( const char *str ){
        log_message( str );
        status = false;
    }
    catch( iterator_overflow &iof ){
        iof.what_happened( log_file );
        status = false;
    }

    // last line of function
    return status;
}
```

The following catch clauses handle the three exception objects we threw in the preceding section:

```
throw 42;
throw "panic: no buffer!";
throw iterator_overflow( _index, Triangular::_max_elems );
```

The type of the exception object is compared against the exception declaration of each catch clause in turn. If the types match, the body of the catch clause is executed. For example, when we throw our iterator_overflow object, the three catch clauses are examined in turn. The exception declaration of the third clause matches the type of the exception object, and the associated statements are executed. The what_happened()

member function of our exception class is invoked through iof, the exception object. The const char* return value is passed to some external log_message() function. Following that, status is set to false.

This represents a complete handling of the exception. Normal program execution resumes at the first program statement following the set of catch clauses. In our example, normal program execution begins again with the return of status.

What happens with the throw of the string literal? The matching catch clause this time is the second instance. log_message() is invoked with the str exception object as its argument. status is set to false. Again, the exception is now handled. Control flows past the third catch clause, and normal program execution begins again with the return of status.

It may be that we cannot completely handle an exception. After having logged the message, we might need to rethrow the exception for further handling elsewhere in another catch clause:

```
catch( iterator_overflow &iof )
    {
        log_message( iof.what_happened() );

        // rethrow for another catch clause to handle
        throw;
    }
```

A rethrow expression consists only of the throw keyword. It can occur only within a catch clause. It rethrows the exception object, and the search for a matching catch clause continues.

A catch-all handler allows us to match every exception type. In place of the exception declaration, we specify an *ellipsis*. For example,

```
// matches all exceptions
catch( ... )
{
    log_message( "exception of unknown type" );
    // clean up and exit ...
}
```

7.3   Trying for an Exception

Catch clauses are associated with *try blocks*. A try block begins with the try keyword followed by a sequence of program statements enclosed in braces. The catch clauses are placed at the end of the try block, and they represent the exceptions that are handled if an exception is thrown during execution of the statements within the try block.

For example, the following function looks for elem within a range of elements marked by first, last. The iteration over the range can potentially result in an iterator_overflow exception being thrown, so we place that code within a try block followed by a catch clause that contains an iterator_overflow exception declaration:

```
bool has_elem( Triangular_iterator first,
               Triangular_iterator last, int elem )
{
    bool status = true;

    try
    {
        while ( first != last )
        {
                if ( *first == elem )
                    return status;
                ++first;
        }
    }
    // only exceptions of type iterator_overflow
    // are caught if thrown while the code
    // sequence within the try block is executed
    catch( iterator_overflow &iof )
    {
        log_message( iof.what_happened() );
        log_message( "check if iterators address same container" );
    }

    status = false;
    return status;
}
```

The expression

```
*first
```

invokes the overloaded dereference operator:

```
inline int Triangular_iterator::
operator*()
{
    check_integrity();
    return Triangular::_elems[ _index ];
}
```

That in turn invokes check_integrity():

```
inline void Triangular_iterator::
check_integrity()
{
    if ( _index > Triangular::_max_elems )
        throw iterator_overflow( _index, Triangular::_max_elems );
    // ...
}
```

Let's say that somehow the _index value of last is greater than _max_elems so that at some point the test within check_integrity() evaluates as true and the exception is thrown. What happens?

The exception mechanism looks at the site of the throw expression and asks, has this occurred within a try block? If it has, the catch clauses associated with the try block are examined to see whether there is a catch clause capable of handling the exception. If there is, the exception is handled and normal program execution begins again.

In our example, the throw expression does not occur within a try block. No attempt is made to handle the exception. The remaining statements of the function are not executed. The exception handling mechanism terminates check_integrity(). It resumes its search for a catch clause within the function that invoked check_integrity().

The question is asked again within the overloaded dereference operator: Has the call of check_integrity() occurred within a try block? No. The dereference operator terminates, and the exception mechanism resumes its search within the function that invoked the dereference operator. Has the call

```
*first
```

occurred within a try block? In this case, the answer is yes. The associated catch clause is examined. The exception declaration matches the type of the exception object, and the body of the catch clause is executed. This completes the handling of the exception. Normal program execution resumes with the first statement following the catch clause:

```
// executed if element is not found
// or if iterator_overflow exception is caught
status = false;
return status;
```

What if the chain of function calls is unwound to main() and no appropriate catch clause is found? The language requires that every exception be handled. If no handler is found following examination of main(), the standard library terminate() function is invoked. By default, this terminates the program.

It is up to the programmer to decide how many statements within the function body to place within or outside the try block. If a statement can potentially result in an exception being thrown, not placing it within the try block guarantees that it is not handled within the function. That may or may not be OK. Not every function has to handle every potential exception.

For example, the dereference operator does not place the call of check_integrity() within a try block even though its invocation can result in an exception. Why? It's because the dereference operator is not prepared to handle the exception and can be safely terminated should the exception be thrown.

How do we know whether a function can safely ignore a potential thrown exception? Let's look again at the definition of the dereference operator:

```
inline int Triangular_iterator::
operator*()
{
    check_integrity();
    return Triangular::_elems[ _index ];
}
```

If `check_integrity()` fails, the value of `_index` must be invalid. The evaluation of the return statement is then certainly a bad idea. Should we add a try block to determine the result of invoking `check_integrity()`?

If `check_integrity()` had been implemented to return `true` or `false`, the definition of the dereference operator would need to guard against a `false` return value:

```
return check_integrity()
       ? Triangular::_elems[ _index ]
       : 0;
```

The user, in turn, would need to guard against the dereference operator returning 0.

Because `check_integrity()` throws an exception, these guards are unnecessary. The return statement of the dereference operator is guaranteed to be executed only if no exception is thrown — that is, when it is safe to evaluate the return statement. Otherwise, the function terminates before the statement is ever reached.

Why does the `has_elem()` function of the preceding section couch its dereference of `first` in a try block? It could simply allow the `iterator_overflow` exception to go up to its invoking function. Alternatively, why doesn't `has_elem()` worry about other potential exceptions? For example, it could add a catch-all to handle any exception thrown during its evaluation. The two decisions are flip sides of the same coin.

`has_elem()` provides a specific functionality: to say true or false to whether `elem` is present within the range of elements marked by `first`, `last`. To accomplish this, it iterates across the elements, incrementing `first` until either the element is found or each element has been examined. The dereference and increment of `first` are implementation details of `has_elem()`. The `iterator_overflow` exception is an aspect of that implementation, and I chose to localize it within `has_elem()` because `has_elem()` has the best knowledge of the significance of that exception within the executing program.

The function invoking `has_elem()` must know whether `elem` is present within the range marked off by `first,last`. Knowing that the range itself is invalid is probably important to the project, and that is why we log it. However, it is not something that the function invoking `has_elem()` is likely capable of handling. Therefore, I chose to shield it from the `iterator_overflow` exception.

On the flip side, the implementation of `has_elem()` is too focused on determining whether `elem` is present to be capable of handling all potential exceptions. For example, if the program's heap memory is exhausted, that is something too catastrophic for the implementer of `has_elem()` to take pains over.

When an exception occurs within the try block of a function that is not handled by the associated catch clauses, that function is terminated just as if there had not been a try block present. The search for a catch handler continues up the call chain to the invoking function. Within `has_elem()`, an `iterator_overflow` exception is handled. Are there any potential uncaught exceptions that might be thrown? Our examination of the call chain within `has_elem()` convinces us that there are not.

A common beginner mistake is to confuse C++ exceptions with hardware exceptions, such as a segmentation fault or bus error. For a C++ exception to be thrown, there is a `throw` expression somewhere in the program code that users are able to find.

7.4   Local Resource Management

Consider the following function in which resources are acquired at the start of the function, some processing takes place, and then the resources are released at the end of the function. Given our discussion so far, what is wrong with this function?

```
extern Mutex m;
void f()
{
    // resource acquisition
    int *p = new int;
    m.acquire();

    process( p );

    // freeing up of resources
    m.release();
    delete p;
}
```

The problem is that we cannot guarantee that the resources acquired at the start of the function are ever released. If `process()` or a function invoked within `process()` throws an exception, the two resource-freeing statements following the invocation of `process()` are never executed. This is not an acceptable implementation in the presence of exception handling.

One solution is to introduce a try block and associated catch clause. We'll catch all exceptions, free our resources, and then rethrow the exception:

```
void f()
{
  try {
      // same as above
  }
  catch( ... ) {
      m.release();
      delete p;
```

```
        throw;
    }
}
```

Although this solves our problem, it is not a completely satisfactory solution. We've duplicated the code to free our resources. We've prolonged the search for a handler while we catch the exception, free our resources, and then rethrow the exception. Moreover, the code itself feels considerably more complicated. We'd prefer a less invasive, more autonomous solution. In C++, this usually means defining a class.

Bjarne Stroustrup, the inventor of C++, introduced an idiom for resource management that he describes in the phrase "resource acquisition is initialization." For a class object, initialization occurs within the class constructor. Resource acquisition is accomplished within the constructor of a class. The resource is freed within the destructor. This not only automates resource management but also simplifies our programs:

```
#include <memory>
void f()
{
    auto_ptr<int> p( new int );
    MutexLock ml( m );
    process( p );
    // destructors for p and ml
    // are implicitly invoked here ...
}
```

p and ml are local class objects. If process() executes correctly, the associated class destructors are automatically applied to p and ml before the completion of the function. But what if an exception is thrown during the execution of process()?

All active local class objects of a function are guaranteed to have their destructors applied before termination of the function by the exception handling mechanism. In our example, the destructors for p and ml are guaranteed to be invoked whether or not an exception is thrown.

The MutexLock class might be implemented as follows:[1]

```
class MutexLock {
public:
    MutexLock( Mutex m ) : _lock( m )
        { lock.acquire(); }

    ~MutexLock(){ lock.release(); }
private:
    Mutex &_lock;
};
```

---

[1]   This is based on the excellent article "A Case Study of C++ Design Evolution" by Douglas C. Schmidt in [LIPPMAN96b].

auto_ptr is a template class provided by the standard library. It automates the deletion of objects allocated through the new expression, such as p. To use it, we must include its associated header file, memory:

```
#include <memory>
```

The auto_ptr class overloads the dereference and arrow pointer operators in the same manner as we did with our iterator class in Section 4.6. This allows us to use an auto_ptr object in the same way we would use a pointer. For example,

```
auto_ptr< string > aps( new string( "vermeer" ));
string *ps = new string( "vermeer" );

if (( aps->size() == ps->size()) &&
    ( *aps == *ps ))
        // equal ...
```

For additional discussion of the resource acquisition is initialization idiom, see Section 14.4 of [STROUSTRUP97]. For a more detailed treatment of the auto_ptr class, look at Section 8.4.2 of [LIPPMAN98].

7.5   The Standard Exceptions

If the new expression cannot acquire memory from the program's free store, it throws a bad_alloc exception object. For example,

```
vector<string>*
init_text_vector( ifstream &infile )
{
    vector<string> *ptext = 0;
    try {
        ptext = new vector<string>;
        // open file and file vector
    }
    catch( bad_alloc ) {
        cerr << "ouch. heap memory exhausted!\n";
        // ... clean up and exit
    }
    return ptext;
}
```

Ordinarily, the assignment statement

```
ptext = new vector<string>;
```

allocates the necessary memory, applies the default vector<string> constructor on the heap object, and then assigns the address of that object to ptext.

If the memory to represent a vector<string> object is not available, the default constructor is not invoked, and ptext is not assigned. A bad_alloc exception object is thrown, and control transfers to the associated catch clause following the try block. The exception declaration

```
catch( bad_alloc )
```

does not declare an exception object because we are interested only in catching the exception type and not in actually manipulating the object within the catch clause.[2]

If we wanted to manipulate the bad_alloc exception object, what operations does it support?

The standard library defines an exception class hierarchy rooted by an abstract base class named exception. The exception class declares a virtual function named what() that returns a const char*. Its purpose is to provide a textual description of the exception thrown.

The bad_alloc class is derived from the base exception class. It provides its own instances of what(). Under Visual C++, the bad_alloc instance of what() generates the message *bad allocation*.

We can also derive our iterator_overflow class from the base exception class. To do so, we must include the exception standard header file and provide an instance of what():

```
#include <exception>

class iterator_overflow : public exception {
public:
    iterator_overflow( int index, int max )
             : _index( index ), _max( max )
    {}

    int index() { return _index; }
    int max()   { return _max;   }

    // overrides exception::what()
    const char* what() const;

private:
    int _index;
    int _max;
};
```

The benefit of inheriting iterator_overflow from the standard library exception class hierarchy is that it can now be caught by all code that catches the abstract base exception, including code written before the introduction of the iterator_overflow

---

[2]   To suppress the throw of the bad_alloc exception, we can write
```
        ptext = new (nothrow) vector<string>;
```
   If the new expression fails, it returns 0. Any use of ptext must first check that it is not zero.

class. This means that we don't have to retrofit existing code to know about this or that new exception class type or catch exceptions anonymously using a catch-all. The catch clause

```
catch( const exception &ex )
{
        cerr << ex.what() << endl;
}
```

matches any class derived from exception. It prints *bad allocation* when a bad_alloc exception type is thrown. When an exception type of iterator_overflow is thrown, it prints *Internal error: current index 65 exceeds maximum bound: 64.*

Here is a possible implementation of the iterator_overflow instance of what(). It uses an ostringstream class object to format its output message:

```
#include <sstream>
#include <string>

const char*
iterator_overflow::
what() const
{
    ostringstream ex_msg;
    static string msg;

    // writes the output into the in-memory
    // ostringstream class object,
    // converting the integer values into
    // string representation ...

    ex_msg << "Internal error: current index "
           << _index << " exceeds maximum bound: "
           << _max;

    // extract the string object
    msg = ex_msg.str();

    // extract the const char* representation
    return msg.c_str();
}
```

The ostringstream class supports in-memory output operations on string objects. It is particularly useful when we need to format multiple data types into a string representation. For example, it automatically converts arithmetic objects, such as _index and _max, into their corresponding string representations without our having to concern ourselves about the amount of necessary storage or the algorithm to effect the conversion. The str() member function returns the string object associated with the ostringstream class.

The standard library chose to have what() return a const char* C-style string representation rather than a string class object. This leaves us in an apparent quandary: How do we convert a string class object into a C-style string representation? The string class provides us with the solution: A conversion function, c_str(), that returns a const char* representation of the string is exactly what we need.

To use the ostringstream class, we must include the sstream standard header file:

```
#include <sstream>
```

The iostream library also supports an istringstream input class. It is particularly useful if we need to convert string representations of nonstring data, such as integer values and addresses, into the actual multiple data types. See Section 20.8 of [LIPPMAN98] for a discussion and illustration of the use of the string stream classes.

For a more extensive discussion of the C++ exception handling facility, see Chapter 11 and Section 19.2 of [LIPPMAN98], and Chapter 14 of [STROUSTRUP97]. For a good discussion of exception-safe design and the general issues of class design in the presence of exception handling, see [SUTTER99].

Exercise 7.1

The following function provides absolutely no checking of either possible bad data or possible failure of an operation. Identify all the things that might possibly go wrong within the function (in this exercise, we don't yet worry about possible exceptions raised).

```
int *alloc_and_init( string file_name )
{
    ifstream infile( file_name );
    int elem_cnt;
    infile >> elem_cnt;
    int *pi = allocate_array( elem_cnt );

    int elem;
    int index = 0;
    while ( infile >> elem )
            pi[ index++ ] = elem;

    sort_array( pi, elem_cnt );
    register_data( pi );

    return pi;
}
```

Exercise 7.2

The following functions invoked in alloc_and_init() raise the following exception types if they should fail:

```
allocate_array() noMem
```

```
sort_array()     int
register_data()  string
```

Insert one or more `try` blocks and associated `catch` clauses where appropriate to handle these exceptions. Simply print the occurrence of the error within the `catch` clause.

Exercise 7.3

Add a pair of exceptions to the Stack class hierarchy of Exercise 5.2 to handle the cases of attempting to pop a stack that is empty and attempting to push a stack that is full. Show the modified `pop()` and `push()` member functions.

Appendix A

Exercise Solutions

Exercise 1.4

Try to extend the program: (1) Ask the user to enter both a first and last name, and (2) modify the output to write out both names.

We need two strings for our extended program: one to hold the user's first name and a second to hold the user's last name. By the end of Chapter 1, we know three ways to support this. We can define two individual string objects:

```
string first_name, last_name;
```

We can define an array of two string objects:

```
string usr_name[ 2 ];
```

Or we can define a vector of two string objects:

```
vector<string> usr_name(2);
```

At this point in the text, arrays and vectors have not yet been introduced, so I've chosen to use the two string objects:

```cpp
#include <iostream>
#include <string>
using namespace std;

int main()
{
    string first_name, last_name;
    cout << "Please enter your first name: ";
    cin >> first_name;

    cout << "hi, " << first_name
         << " Please enter your last name: ";

    cin >> last_name;
    cout << '\n';
```

```
                    << "Hello, "
                    << first_name  << ' '  << last_name
                    << " ... and goodbye!\n";
        }
```

When compiled and executed, this program generates the following output (my responses are highlighted in bold):

```
        Please enter your first name: stan
        hi, stan Please enter your last name: lippman

        Hello, stan lippman ... and goodbye!
```

Exercise 1.5

Write a program to ask the user his or her name. Read the response. Confirm that the input is at least two characters in length. If the name seems valid, respond to the user. Provide two implementations: one using a C-style character string, and the other using a string class object.

The two primary differences between a string class object and a C-style character string are that (1) the string class object grows dynamically to accommodate its character string, whereas the C-style character string must be given a fixed size that is (hopefully) large enough to contain the assigned string, and (2) the C-style character string does not know its size. To determine the size of the C-style character string, we must iterate across its elements, counting each one up to but not including the terminating null. The strlen() standard library routine provides this service for us:

```
        int strlen( const char* );
```

To use strlen(), we must include the cstring header file.

However, before we get to that, let's look at the string class implementation. Particularly for beginners, I recommend that the string class be used in favor of the C-style character string.

```
        #include <iostream>
        #include <string>
        using namespace std;

        int main()
        {
            string user_name;

            cout << "Please enter your name: ";
            cin  >> user_name;

            switch ( user_name.size() ){
                case 0:
                    cout << "Ah, the user with no name. "
```

```
                          << "Well, ok, hi, user with no name\n";
                break;

        case 1:
            cout << "A 1-character name? Hmm, have you read Kafka?: "
                     << "hello, " << user_name << endl;
            break;

        default:
            // any string longer than 1 character
            cout << "Hello, " << user_name
                     << " -- happy to make your acquaintance!\n";
            break;
    }
    return 0;
}
```

The C-style character string implementation differs in two ways. First, we must decide on a fixed size to declare user_name; I've arbitrarily chosen 128, which seems more than adequate. Second, we use the the standard library strlen() function to discover the size of user_name. The cstring header file holds the declaration of strlen(). If the user enters a string longer than 127 characters, there will be no room for the terminating null character. To prevent that, I use the setw() iostream manipulator to guarantee that we do not read in more than 127 characters. To use the setw() manipulator, we must include the iomanip header file.

```
#include <iostream>
#include <iomanip>
#include <cstring>
using namespace std;

int main()
{
    // must allocate a fixed size
    const int nm_size = 128;
    char user_name[ nm_size ];
    cout << "Please enter your name: ";
    cin  >> setw( nm_size ) >> user_name;

    switch ( strlen( user_name ))
            {
                // same case labels for 0, 1
                case 127:
                    // maybe string was truncated by setw()
                    cout << "That is a very big name, indeed -- "
                         << "we may have needed to shorten it!\n"
                         << "In any case,\n";

                    // no break -- we fall through ...
```

```
                    default:
                        // the 127 case drops through to here -- no break
                        cout << "Hello, " << user_name
                            << " -- happy to make your acquaintance!\n";
                        break;
                }

        return 0;
    }
```

Exercise 1.6

Write a program to read in a sequence of integers from standard input. Place the values, in turn, in a built-in array and a vector. Iterate over the containers to sum the values. Display the sum and average of the entered values to standard output.

The built-in array and the vector class differ in primarily the same ways as the C-style character string (which is implemented as an array of char elements) and the string class: (1) The built-in array must be of a fixed size, whereas the vector can grow dynamically as elements are inserted, and (2) the built-in array does not know its size. The fixed-size nature of the built-in array means that we must be concerned with potentially overflowing its boundary. Unlike the C-style string, the built-in array has no sentinel value (the null) to indicate its end. Particularly for beginners, I recommend that the vector class be used in favor of the built-in array. Here is the program using the vector class:

```
#include <iostream>
#include <vector>
using namespace std;

int main()
{
    vector<int> ivec;
    int ival;
    while ( cin >> ival )
            ivec.push_back( ival );

    // we could have calculated the sum as we entered the
    // values, but the idea is to iterate over the vector ...
    for ( int sum = 0, ix = 0; ix < ivec.size(); ++ix )
            sum += ivec[ ix ];

    int average = sum / ivec.size();
    cout << "Sum of " << ivec.size()
        << " elements: " << sum
        << ". Average: " << average << endl;
}
```

The primary difference in the following built-in array implementation is the need to monitor the number of elements being read to ensure that we don't overflow the array boundary:

```
#include <iostream>
using namespace std;

int main()
{
    const int array_size = 128;
    int ia[ array_size ];
    int ival, icnt = 0;

    while ( cin >> ival &&
            icnt < array_size )
                ia[ icnt++ ] = ival;

    for ( int sum = 0, ix = 0; ix < icnt; ++ix )
        sum += ia[ ix ];

    int average = sum / icnt;
    cout << "Sum of " << icnt
         << " elements: " << sum
         << ". Average: " << average << endl;
}
```

Exercise 1.7

Using your favorite editor, type two or more lines of text into a file. Write a program to open the file, reading each word into a vector<string> object. Iterate over the vector, displaying it to cout. That done, sort the words using the sort() generic algorithm.

```
#include <algorithm>
sort( container.begin(), container.end() );
```

Then print the sorted words to an output file.

I open both the input and the output file before reading in and sorting the text. I could wait to open the output file, but what would happen if for some reason the output file failed to open? Then all the computations would have been for nothing. (The file paths are hard-coded and reflect Windows conventions. The algorithm header file contains the forward declaration of the sort() generic algorithm.)

```
#include <iostream>
#include <fstream>
#include <algorithm>
#include <string>
#include <vector>

using namespace std;
```

```
int main()
{
    ifstream in_file( "C:\\My Documents\\text.txt"  );
    if ( ! in_file )
       { cerr << "oops! unable to open input file\n"; return -1; }

    ofstream out_file("C:\\My Documents\\text.sort" );
    if ( ! out_file )
       { cerr << "oops! unable to open input file\n"; return -2; }

    string word;
    vector< string > text;
    while ( in_file >> word )
          text.push_back( word );

    int ix;
    cout << "unsorted text: \n";

    for ( ix = 0; ix < text.size(); ++ix )
        cout << text[ ix ] << ' ';
    cout << endl;

    sort( text.begin(), text.end() );

    out_file << "sorted text: \n";
    for ( ix = 0; ix < text.size(); ++ix )
        out_file << text[ ix ] << ' ';
    out_file << endl;

    return 0;
}
```

The input text file consists of the following three lines:

```
we were her pride of ten she named us:
Phoenix, the Prodigal, Benjamin,
and perspicacious, pacific Suzanne.
```

When compiled and executed, the program generates the following output (I've inserted line breaks to display it here on the page):

```
Benjamin, Phoenix, Prodigal, Suzanne.
and her named of pacific perspicacious,
pride she ten the us: we were
```

Exercise 1.8

The switch statement of Section 1.4 displays a different consolation message based on the number of wrong guesses. Replace this with an array of four string messages that can be indexed based on the number of wrong guesses.

The first step is to define the array of string messages in which to index. One strategy is to encapsulate them in a display function that, passed the number of incorrect user guesses, returns the appropriate consolation message. Here is a first implementation. Unfortunately, it is not correct. Do you see the problems?

```cpp
const char* msg_to_usr( int num_tries )
{
    static const char* usr_msgs[] = {
       "Oops! Nice guess but not quite it.",
       "Hmm. Sorry. Wrong again.",
       "Ah, this is harder than it looks, isn't it?",
       "It must be getting pretty frustrating by now!"
    };
    return usr_msgs[ num_tries ];
}
```

The index is off by one. If you flip back to the Section 1.4 switch statement, you'll see that the number of incorrect tries begins with 1 because, after all, we are responding to wrong guesses on the user's part. Our array of responses, however, begins at position 0. So our responses are always one guess more severe than called for.

There are other problems as well. The user can potentially try more than four times and be wrong with each try, although I capped the number of unique messages at 4. If we unconditionally index into the array, a value of 4 or greater will overflow the array boundary. Moreover, we must guard against other potential invalid values such as a negative number.

Here is a second iteration. I've added a new first message in case the user somehow has not yet guessed. I don't expect we'll actually return it, but in this way, the other messages at least are in their "natural" position. I defined a const object to hold a count of the number of entries in the array.

```cpp
const char* msg_to_usr( int num_tries )
{
    const int rsp_cnt = 5;
    static const char* usr_msgs[ rsp_cnt ] = {
       "Go on, make a guess. ",
       "Oops! Nice guess but not quite it.",
       "Hmm. Sorry. Wrong again.",
       "Ah, this is harder than it looks, no?",
       "It must be getting pretty frustrating by now!"
    };
    if ( num_tries < 0 )
        num_tries = 0;
    else
    if ( num_tries >= rsp_cnt )
        num_tries = rsp_cnt-1;
    return usr_msgs[ num_tries ];
}
```

Exercise 2.1

`main()` [in Section 2.1] allows the user to enter only one position value and then terminates. If a user wishes to ask for two or more positions, he must execute the program two or more times. Modify `main()` [in Section 2.1] to allow the user to keep entering positions until he indicates he wishes to stop.

We use a `while` loop to execute the "solicit position, return value" code sequence. After each iteration, we ask the user whether he wishes to continue. The loop terminates when he answers no. We'll jump-start the first iteration by setting the `bool` object more to true.

```
#include <iostream>
using namespace std;

extern bool fibon_elem( int, int& );
int main()
{
    int pos, elem;
    char ch;
    bool more = true;

    while ( more )
    {
        cout << "Please enter a position: ";
        cin  >> pos;

        if ( fibon_elem( pos, elem ))
            cout << "element # " << pos
                 << " is " << elem << endl;
        else
            cout << "Sorry. Could not calculate element # "
                 << pos << endl;

        cout << "would you like to try again? (y/n) ";
        cin >> ch;
        if ( ch != 'y' || ch != 'Y' )
            more = false;
    }
}
```

When compiled and executed, the program generates the following output (my input is highlighted in bold):

```
Please enter a position: 4
element # 4 is 3
would you like to try again? (y/n) y
Please enter a position: 8
element # 8 is 21
```

```
would you like to try again? (y/n) y
Please enter a position: 12
element # 12 is 144
would you like to try again? (y/n) n
```

Exercise 2.2

The formula for the Pentagonal numeric sequence is Pn=n*(3n-1)/2. This yields the sequence 1, 5, 12, 22, 35, and so on. Define a function to fill a vector of elements passed in to the function calculated to some user-specified position. Be sure to verify that the position specified is valid. Write a second function that, given a vector, displays its elements. It should take a second parameter identifying the type of numeric series the vector represents. Write a main() function to exercise these functions.

```cpp
#include <vector>
#include <string>
#include <iostream>
using namespace std;

bool calc_elements( vector<int> &vec, int pos );
void display_elems( vector<int> &vec,
                    const string &title, ostream &os=cout );

int main()
{
    vector<int> pent;
    const string title( "Pentagonal Numeric Series" );

    if ( calc_elements( pent, 0 ))
        display_elems( pent, title );

    if ( calc_elements( pent, 8 ))
        display_elems( pent, title );

    if ( calc_elements( pent, 14 ))
        display_elems( pent, title );

    if ( calc_elements( pent, 138 ))
        display_elems( pent, title );
}

bool calc_elements( vector<int> &vec, int pos )
{
    if ( pos <= 0 || pos > 64 ){
        cerr << "Sorry. Invalid position: " << pos << endl;
        return false;
    }
```

```
    for ( int ix = vec.size()+1; ix <= pos; ++ix )
        vec.push_back( (ix*(3*ix-1))/2 );

    return true;
}

void display_elems( vector<int> &vec,
                    const string &title, ostream &os )
{
    os << '\n' << title << "\n\t";
    for ( int ix = 0; ix < vec.size(); ++ix )
        os << vec[ ix ] << ' ';
    os << endl;
}
```

When compiled and executed, this program generates the following output:

```
Sorry. Invalid position: 0

Pentagonal Numeric Series
        1 5 12 22 35 51 70 92

Pentagonal Numeric Series
        1 5 12 22 35 51 70 92 117 145 176 210 247 287
Sorry. Invalid position: 138
```

Exercise 2.3

Separate the function to calculate the Pentagonal numeric sequence implemented in Exercise 2.2 into two functions. One function should be inline; it checks the validity of the position. A valid position not as yet calculated causes the function to invoke a second function that does the actual calculation.

I factored calc_elements() into the inline calc_elems() that if necessary calls the second function, really_calc_elems(). To test this reimplementation, I substituted the call of calc_elements() in the Exercise 2.2 function with that of calc_elems().

```
    extern void really_calc_elems( vector<int>&, int );
    inline bool calc_elems( vector<int> &vec, int pos )
    {
        if ( pos <= 0 || pos > 64 ){
            cerr << "Sorry. Invalid position: " << pos << endl;
            return false;
        }

        if ( vec.size() < pos )
            really_calc_elems( vec, pos );
        return true;
    }
```

```
void really_calc_elems( vector<int> &vec, int pos )
{
    for ( int ix = vec.size()+1; ix <= pos; ++ix )
        vec.push_back( (ix*(3*ix-1))/2 );
}
```

Exercise 2.4

Introduce a static local vector to hold the elements of your Pentagonal series. This function returns a const pointer to the vector. It accepts a position by which to grow the vector if the vector is not that size as yet. Implement a second function that, given a position, returns the element at that position. Write a main() function to exercise these functions.

```
#include <vector>
#include <iostream>
using namespace std;

inline bool check_validity( int pos )
    { return ( pos <= 0 || pos > 64 ) ? false : true; }

bool pentagonal_elem( int pos, int &elem )
{
    if ( ! check_validity( pos )){
        cout << "Sorry. Invalid position: " << pos << endl;
        elem = 0;
        return false;
    }
    const vector<int> *pent = pentagonal_series( pos );
    elem = (*pent)[pos-1];
    return true;
}

const vector<int>*
pentagonal_series( int pos )
{
    static vector<int> _elems;
    if ( check_validity( pos ) && ( pos > _elems.size() ))
        for ( int ix = _elems.size()+1; ix <= pos; ++ix )
            _elems.push_back( (ix*(3*ix-1))/2 );
    return &_elems;
}

int main(){
    int elem;
    if ( pentagonal_elem( 8, elem ))
        cout << "element 8 is " << elem << '\n';
    if ( pentagonal_elem( 88, elem ))
        cout << "element 88 is " << elem << '\n';
```

```
        if ( pentagonal_elem( 12, elem ))
            cout << "element 12 is " << elem << '\n';

        if ( pentagonal_elem( 64, elem ))
            cout << "element 64 is " << elem << '\n';
    }
```

When compiled and executed, this program generates the following:

```
element 8 is 92
Sorry. Invalid position: 88
element 12 is 210
element 64 is 6112
```

Exercise 2.5

Implement an overloaded set of max() functions to accept (a) two integers, (b) two floats, (c) two strings, (d) a vector of integers, (e) a vector of floats, (f) a vector of strings, (g) an array of integers and an integer indicating the size of the array, (h) an array of floats and an integer indicating the size of the array, and (i) an array of strings and an integer indicating the size of the array. Again, write a main() function to exercise these functions.

```
#include <string>
#include <vector>
#include <algorithm>

using namespace std;

inline int max( int t1, int t2 )
    { return t1 > t2 ? t1 : t2; }

inline float max( float t1, float t2 )
    { return t1 > t2 ? t1 : t2; }

inline string max( const string& t1, const string& t2 )
    { return t1 > t2 ? t1 : t2; }

inline int max( const vector<int> &vec )
    { return *max_element( vec.begin(), vec.end() ); }

inline float max( const vector<float> &vec )
    { return *max_element( vec.begin(), vec.end() ); }

inline string max( const vector<string> &vec )
    { return *max_element( vec.begin(), vec.end() ); }

inline int max( const int *parray, int size )
    { return *max_element( parray, parray+size ); }
```

```
inline float max( const float *parray, int size )
      { return *max_element( parray, parray+size ); }

inline string max( const string *parray, int size )
      { return *max_element( parray, parray+size ); }

int main() {
    string sarray[]={ "we", "were", "her", "pride", "of", "ten" };
    vector<string> svec( sarray, sarray+6 );

    int iarray[]={ 12, 70, 2, 169, 1, 5, 29 };
    vector<int> ivec( iarray, iarray+7 );

    float farray[]={ 2.5, 24.8, 18.7, 4.1, 23.9 };
    vector<float> fvec( farray, farray+5 );

    int imax = max( max( ivec ), max( iarray, 7 ));
    float fmax = max( max( fvec ), max( farray, 5 ));
    string smax = max( max( svec ), max( sarray, 6 ));

    cout << "imax should be 169  -- found: " << imax << '\n'
         << "fmax should be 24.8 -- found: " << fmax << '\n'
         << "smax should be were -- found: " << smax << '\n';
}
```

When compiled and executed, this program generates the following:

```
imax should be 169  -- found: 169
fmax should be 24.8 -- found: 24.8
smax should be were -- found: were
```

Exercise 2.6

Reimplement the functions of Exercise 2.5 using templates. Modify the main() function accordingly.

The nine nontemplate max() functions are replaced by three max() function templates. main() does not require any changes.

```
#include <string>
#include <vector>
#include <algorithm>
using namespace std;

template <typename Type>
inline Type max( Type t1, Type t2 ){ return t1 > t2 ? t1 : t2; }

template <typename elemType>
inline elemType max( const vector<elemType> &vec )
      { return *max_element( vec.begin(), vec.end() ); }
```

```
template <typename arrayType>
inline arrayType max( const arrayType *parray, int size )
        { return *max_element( parray, parray+size ); }

// note: no changes required of main()!
int main() {
    // same as in exercise 2.4
}
```

When compiled and executed, this program generates the same output as the program in Exercise 2.5.

Exercise 3.1

Write a program to read a text file. Store each word in a map. The key value of the map is the count of the number of times the word appears in the text. Define a word exclusion set containing words such as *a*, *an*, *or*, *the*, *and*, and *but*. Before entering a word in the map, make sure it is not present in the word exclusion set. Display the list of words and their associated count when the reading of the text is complete. As an extension, before displaying the text, allow the user to query the text for the presence of a word.

```
#include <map>
#include <set>
#include <string>
#include <iostream>
#include <fstream>
using namespace std;

void initialize_exclusion_set( set<string>& );
void process_file( map<string,int>&, const set<string>&, ifstream& );
void user_query( const map<string,int>& );
void display_word_count( const map<string,int>&, ofstream& );

int main()
{
    ifstream ifile( "C:\\My Documents\\column.txt" );
    ofstream ofile( "C:\\My Documents\\column.map" );
    if ( ! ifile || ! ofile ){
        cerr << "Unable to open file -- bailing out!\n";
        return -1;
    }

    set<string> exclude_set;
    initialize_exclusion_set( exclude_set );

    map<string,int> word_count;
    process_file( word_count, exclude_set, ifile );
    user_query( word_count );
    display_word_count( word_count, ofile );
}
```

```
void initialize_exclusion_set( set<string> &exs ){
    static string _excluded_words[25] = {
        "the","and","but","that","then","are","been",
        "can","a","could","did","for", "of",
        "had","have","him","his","her","its","is",
        "were","which","when","with","would"
    };

    exs.insert( _excluded_words, _excluded_words+25 );
}

void process_file( map<string,int> &word_count,
                   const set<string> &exclude_set, ifstream &ifile )
{
    string word;
    while ( ifile >> word )
    {
        if ( exclude_set.count( word ))
            continue;
        word_count[ word ]++;
    }
}

void user_query( const map<string,int> &word_map )
{
    string search_word;
    cout << "Please enter a word to search: q to quit";
    cin >> search_word;
    while ( search_word.size() && search_word != "q" )
    {
        map<string,int>::const_iterator it;
        if (( it = word_map.find( search_word ))
               != word_map.end() )
            cout << "Found! "  << it->first
                 << " occurs " << it->second
                 << " times.\n";
          else cout << search_word
                    << " was not found in text.\n";
           cout << "\nAnother search? (q to quit) ";
           cin >> search_word;
    }
}

void
display_word_count( const map<string,int> &word_map, ofstream &os )
{
    map<string,int>::const_iterator
                iter = word_map.begin(),
                end_it = word_map.end();
```

```
while ( iter != end_it ){
        os << iter->first  << " ( "
            << iter->second << " )" << endl;
        ++iter;
    }
    os << endl;
}
```

Here is a small piece of text processed by the program. I removed the punctuation from the text because our program does not handle punctuation:

```
MooCat is a long-haired white kitten with large
black patches Like a cow looks only he is a kitty
poor kitty Alice says cradling MooCat in her arms
pretending he is not struggling to break free
```

Here is a snapshot of the interactive session initiated by user_query(). Notice that although *a* occurs two times the text, it is an entry in the excluded word set and is not entered in the map of words found in the text.

```
Please enter a word to search: q to quit Alice
Found! Alice occurs 1 times.

Another search? (q to quit) MooCat
Found! MooCat occurs 2 times.

Another search? (q to quit) a
a was not found in text.

Another search? (q to quit) q
```

Exercise 3.2

Read in a text file — it can be the same one as in Exercise 3.1 — storing it in a vector. Sort the vector by the length of the string. Define a function object to pass to sort(); it should accept two strings and return **true** if the first string is shorter than the second. Print the sorted vector.

Let's begin by defining the function object to pass to sort():

```
class LessThan {
public:
    bool operator()( const string & s1,
                     const string & s2 )
        { return s1.size() < s2.size(); }
};
```

The call to sort looks like this:

```
sort( text.begin(), text.end(), LessThan() );
```

The main program looks like this:

```
int main()
{
    ifstream ifile( "C:\\My Documents\\MooCat.txt" );
    ofstream ofile( "C:\\My Documents\\MooCat.sort" );

    if ( ! ifile || ! ofile ){
        cerr << "Unable to open file -- bailing out!\n";
        return -1;
    }

    vector<string> text;
    string word;

    while ( ifile >> word )
            text.push_back( word );

    sort( text.begin(), text.end(), LessThan() );
    display_vector( text, ofile );
}
```

display_vector() is a function template parameterized on the element type of the vector passed to it to display:

```
template <typename elemType>
void display_vector( const vector<elemType> &vec,
                     ostream &os=cout, int len= 8 )
{
    vector<elemType>::const_iterator
            iter = vec.begin(),
            end_it = vec.end();

    int elem_cnt = 1;
    while ( iter != end_it )
        os << *iter++
                << ( !( elem_cnt++ % len ) ? '\n' : ' ' );
    os << endl;
}
```

The input file is the same text used in Exercise 3.1. The output of this program looks like this:

```
a a a is to in is he
is he not cow her says poor only
Like arms with free break Alice kitty kitty
looks black large white MooCat kitten MooCat patches
cradling pretending struggling long-haired
```

If we want to sort the words within each length alphabetically, we would first invoke sort() with the default less-than operator and then invoke stable_sort(), passing it the LessThan function object. `stable_sort()` maintains the relative order of elements meeting the same sorting criteria.

Exercise 3.3

Define a map for which the index is the family surname and the key is a vector of the children's names. Populate the map with at least six entries. Test it by supporting user queries based on a surname and printing all the map entries.

The map uses a string as an index and a vector of strings for the children's names. This is declared as follows:

```
map< string, vector<string> > families;
```

To simplify the declaration of the map, I've defined a typedef to alias `vstring` as an alternative name for a vector that contains string elements. (You likely wouldn't have thought of this because the typedef mechanism is not introduced until Section 4.6. The typedef mechanism allows us to provide an alternative name for a type. It is generally used to simplify the declaration of a complex type.)

```
#include <map>
typedef vector<string> vstring;
map< string, vstring > families;
```

We get our family information from a file. Each line of the file stores the family name and the name of each child:

```
surname child1 child2 child3 ... childN
```

Reading the file and populating the map are accomplished in `populate_map()`:

```
void populate_map( ifstream &nameFile, map<string,vstring> &families )
{
    string textline;
    while ( getline( nameFile, textline ))
    {
        string fam_name;
        vector<string> child;
        string::size_type
            pos = 0, prev_pos = 0,
            text_size = textline.size();

        // ok: find each word separated by a space
        while ((  pos = textline.find_first_of( ' ', pos ))
                    != string::npos )
        {
            // figure out end points of the substring
            string::size_type end_pos = pos - prev_pos;

            // if prev_pos not set, this is the family name
```

```
                    // otherwise, we are reading the children ...
                    if ( ! prev_pos )
                         fam_name = textline.substr( prev_pos, end_pos );
                    else child.push_back(textline.substr(prev_pos,end_pos));
                    prev_pos = ++pos;
            }

            // now handle last child
            if ( prev_pos < text_size )
                child.push_back(textline.substr(prev_pos,pos-prev_pos));

            if ( ! families.count( fam_name ))
                families[ fam_name ] = child;
            else cerr << "Oops! We already have a "
                      << fam_name << " family in our map!\n";
      }
  }
```

getline() is a standard library function. It reads a line of the file up to the delimiter specified by its third parameter. The default delimiter is the newline character, which is what we use. The line is placed in the ssecond parameter string.

The next portion of the function pulls out, in turn, the family surname and the name of each child. substr() is a string class operation that returns a new string object from the substring delimited by the two position arguments. Finally, the family is entered into the map if one is not already present.

To display the map, we define a display_map() function. It prints entries in this general format:

```
The lippman family has 2 children: danny anna
```

Here is the display_map() implementation:

```
      void display_map( const map<string,vstring> &families, ostream &os )
      {
          map<string,vstring>::const_iterator
                    it = families.begin(),
                    end_it = families.end();

          while ( it != end_it )
          {
              os << "The " << it->first << " family ";
              if ( it->second.empty() )
                  os << "has no children\n";
               else
              { // print out vector of children
                  os   << "has " << it->second.size()  << " children: ";
                  vector<string>::const_iterator
                          iter = it->second.begin(),
                          end_iter = it->second.end();
```

```
                    while ( iter != end_iter )
                        { os << *iter << " "; ++iter; }
                    os << endl;
                }
                ++it;
            }
        }
```

We must also allow users to query the map as to the presence of a family. If the family is present, we display the family name and number of children in the same way that display_map() does for the entire map. (As an exercise, you might factor out the common code between the two functions.) I've named this function query_map().

```
        void query_map( const string &family,
                        const map<string,vstring> &families )
        {
            map<string,vstring>::const_iterator
                it = families.find( family );

            if ( it == families.end() ){
                cout << "Sorry. The " << family
                     << " is not currently entered.\n";
                return;
            }

            cout << "The " << family;
            if ( ! it->second.size() )
                cout << " has no children\n";
            else { // print out vector of children
                cout << " has " << it->second.size() << " children: ";
                vector<string>::const_iterator
                        iter = it->second.begin(),
                        end_iter = it->second.end();
                while ( iter != end_iter )
                    { cout << *iter << " "; ++iter; }
                cout << endl;
            }
        }
```

The main() program is implemented as follows:

```
        int main()
        {
            map< string, vstring > families;
            ifstream nameFile( "C:\\My Documents\\families.txt" );

            if ( ! nameFile ) {
                cerr << "Unable to find families.txt file. Bailing Out!\n";
                return;
            }
```

```
      populate_map( nameFile, families );

      string family_name;
      while ( 1 ){ //!! loop until user says to quit ...
         cout << "Please enter a family name or q to quit ";
         cin >> family_name;
         if ( family_name == "q" )
             break;
         query_map( family_name, families );
      }
      display_map( families );
   }
```

The families.txt file contains the following six entries:

```
lippman danny anna
smith john henry frieda
mailer tommy june
franz
orlen orley
ranier alphonse lou robert brodie
```

When compiled and executed, the program generates the following results. My responses are highlighted in bold.

```
Please enter a family name or q to quit ranier
The ranier family  has 4 children: alphonse lou robert brodie
Please enter a family name or q to quit franz
The franz family  has no children
Please enter a family name or q to quit kafka
Sorry. The kafka family is not currently entered.
Please enter a family name or q to quit q
The franz family has no children
The lippman family has 2 children: danny anna
The mailer family has 2 children: tommy june
The orlen family has 1 children: orley
The ranier family has 4 children: alphonse lou robert brodie
The smith family has 3 children: john henry frieda
```

Exercise 3.4

Write a program to read a sequence of integer numbers from standard input using an istream_iterator. Write the odd numbers into one file using an ostream_iterator. Each value should be separated by a space. Write the even numbers into a second file, also using an ostream_iterator. Each of these values should be placed on a separate line.

To read a sequence of integers from standard input, we define two istream_iterators: one bound to cin, and the second representing end-of-file.

```
istream_iterator<int> in( cin ), eos;
```

Next, we define a vector to hold the elements read:

```
vector< int > input;
```

To perform the reading, we use the copy() generic algorithm:

```
#include <iterator>
#include <vector>
#include <iostream>
#include <algorithm>
using namespace std;

int main()
{
    vector< int > input;
    istream_iterator in( cin ), eos;

    copy( in, eos, back_inserter( input ));

    // ...
}
```

The back_inserter() is necessary because copy() uses the assignment operator to copy each element. Because input is empty, the first element assignment would cause an overflow error. back_inserter() overrides the assignment operator. The elements are now inserted using push_back().

We partition the elements into even and odd using the partition() generic algorithm and an even_elem function object that evaluates to true if the value is even:

```
class even_elem {
public:
    bool operator()( int elem )
        { return elem%2 ? false : true; }
};

vector<int>::iterator division =
        partition( input.begin(), input.end(), even_elem() );
```

We need two ostream_iterators: one for the even number file and one for the odd number file. We first open two files for output using the ofstream class:

```
#include <fstream>
ofstream even_file( "C:\\My Documents\\even_file" ),
            odd_file( "C:\\My Documents\\odd_file" );

if ( ! even_file || ! odd_file )
{
    cerr << "arghh!! unable to open the output files. bailing out!";
    return -1;
}
```

We bind our two ostream_iterators to the respective ofstream objects. The second string argument indicates the delimiter to output following the output of each element.

```
ostream_iterator<int> even_iter( even_file, "\n" ),
                      odd_iter( odd_file, " " );
```

Finally, we use the copy() generic algorithm to output the partitioned elements:

```
copy( input.begin(), division, even_iter );
copy( division, input.end(), odd_iter );
```

For example, I entered the following sequence of numbers:

     2 4 5 3 9 5 2 6 8 1 8 4 5 7 3

At that point, even_file contained the following values: 2 4 4 8 8 6 2, whereas odd_file contained these values: 5 9 1 3 5 5 7 3. The partition() algorithm does not preserve the order of the values. If preserving the order of the values is important, we would instead use the stable_partition() generic algorithm. Both the stable_sort() and stable_partition() algorithms maintain the elements' relative order.

Exercise 4.1

Create a Stack.h and a Stack.suffix, where suffix is whatever convention your compiler or project follows. Write a main() function to exercise the full public interface, and compile and execute it. Both the program text file and main() must include Stack.h:

```
#include "Stack.h"
```

The header file for our Stack class contains the necessary header file inclusions and the actual class declaration:

```
#include <string>
#include <vector>
using namespace std;

class Stack {
public:
    bool    push( const string& );
    bool    pop ( string &elem );
    bool    peek( string &elem );
    bool    empty() const { return _stack.empty(); }
    bool    full()  const { return _stack.size() == _stack.max_size(); }
    int     size()  const { return _stack.size(); }

private:
    vector<string> _stack;
};
```

The Stack program text file contains the definition of the push(), pop(), and peek() member functions. Under Visual C++, the file is named Stack.cpp. It must include the Stack class header file.

```
#include "Stack.h"
bool Stack::pop( string &elem ){
    if ( empty() ) return false;
    elem = _stack.back();
    _stack.pop_back();
    return true;
}

bool Stack::peek( string &elem ){
    if ( empty() ) return false;
    elem = _stack.back();
    return true;
}

bool Stack::push( const string &elem ){
    if ( full() ) return false;
    _stack.push_back( elem );
    return true;
}
```

Here is a small program to exercise the Stack class interface. It reads in a sequence of strings from standard input, pushing each one onto the stack until either end-of-file occurs or the stack is full:

```
int main() {
    Stack st;
    string str;

    while ( cin >> str && ! st.full() )
            st.push( str );

    if ( st.empty() ) {
        cout << '\n' << "Oops: no strings were read -- bailing out\n ";
        return 0;
    }
    st.peek( str );
    if ( st.size() == 1 && str.empty() ) {
        cout << '\n' << "Oops: no strings were read -- bailing out\n ";
        return 0;
    }
    cout << '\n' << "Read in " << st.size() << " strings!\n"
        << "The strings, in reverse order: \n";

    while ( st.size() )
       if ( st.pop( str ))
            cout << str << ' ';

    cout << '\n' << "There are now " << st.size()
        << " elements in the stack!\n";
}
```

To test the program, I typed in the last sentence of the James Joyce novel, *Finnegans Wake*. The following is the output generated by the program (my input is in bold):

```
A way a lone a last a loved a long the
Read in 11 strings!
The strings, in reverse order:
the long a loved a last a lone a way A
There are now 0 elements in the stack!
```

Exercise 4.2

Extend the Stack class to support both a find() and a count() operation. find() returns true or false depending on whether the value is found. count() returns the number of occurrences of the string. Reimplement the main() of Exercise 4.1 to invoke both functions.

We implement these two functions simply by using the corresponding generic algorithms of the same names:

```
#include <algorithm>
bool Stack::find( const string &elem ) const {
   vector<string>::const_iterator end_it = _stack.end();
   return ::find( _stack.begin(), end_it, elem ) != end_it;
}

int Stack::count( const string &elem ) const
     { return ::count( _stack.begin(), _stack.end(), elem ); }
```

The global scope operator is necessary for the invocation of the two generic algorithms. Without the global scope operator, for example, the unqualified invocation of find() within find() recursively invokes the member instance of find()! The Stack class declaration is extended to include the declarations of these two functions:

```
class Stack {
public:
   bool   find( const string &elem ) const;
   int    count( const string &elem ) const;

   // ... everything else the same ...
};
```

The program now inquires of the user which word she would like to search for and reports whether it is within the stack and, if so, how many times it occurs:

```
int main()
{
   Stack st;
   string str;
   while ( cin >> str && ! st.full() )
           st.push( str );
```

```
        // check for empty stack as before ...

        cout << '\n' << "Read in " << st.size() << " strings!\n";
        cin.clear(); // clear end-of-file set ...

        cout << "what word to search for? ";
        cin  >> str;

        bool found = st.find( str );
        int  count = found ? st.count( str ) : 0;

        cout << str << (found ? " is " : " isn\'t " ) << "in the stack. ";
        if ( found )
            cout << "It occurs " << count << " times\n";
    }
```

Here is an interactive execution of the program. The items highlighted in bold are what I entered:

```
        A way a lone a last a loved a long the
        Read in 11 strings!
        what word to search for? a
        a is in the stack. It occurs 4 times
```

Exercise 4.3

Consider the following global data:

```
        string program_name;
        string version_stamp;
        int version_number;
        int tests_run;
        int tests_passed;
```

Write a class to wrap around this data.

Why might we wish to do this? By wrapping these global objects within a class, we encapsulate their direct access within a small set of functions. Moreover, the names of the objects are now hidden behind the scope of the class and cannot clash with other global entities. Because we wish only a single instance of each global object, we declare each one to be a static class member as well as the member functions that access them.

```
        #include <string>
        using std::string;

        class globalWrapper {
        public:
            static int tests_passed()      { return _tests_passed; }
            static int tests_run()         { return _tests_run; }
```

```
        static int version_number()   { return _version_number; }
        static string version_stamp() { return _version_stamp; }
        static string program_name()  { return _program_name; }

        static void tests_passed( int nval )  { _tests_passed = nval; }
        static void tests_run( int nval )     { _tests_run = nval; }

        static void version_number( int nval )
                { _version_number = nval; }

        static void version_stamp( const string& nstamp )
                { _version_stamp = nstamp; }

        static void program_name( const string& npn )
                { _program_name = npn; }

    private:
        static string  _program_name;
        static string  _version_stamp;
        static int     _version_number;
        static int     _tests_run;
        static int     _tests_passed;
    };

    string globalWrapper::_program_name;
    string globalWrapper::_version_stamp;
    int globalWrapper::_version_number;
    int globalWrapper::_tests_run;
    int globalWrapper::_tests_passed;
```

Exercise 4.4

A user profile consists of a login, the actual user name, the number of times logged
on, the number of guesses made, the number of correct guesses, the current level —
one of beginner, intermediate, advanced, guru — and the percentage correct (this
latter may be computed or stored). Provide a UserProfile class. Support input and
output, equality and inequality. The constructors should allow for a default user
level and default login name of "guest." How might you guarantee that each guest
login for a particular session is unique?

```
        class UserProfile {
        public:
            enum uLevel { Beginner, Intermediate, Advanced, Guru };

            UserProfile( string login, uLevel = Beginner );
            UserProfile();

            // default memberwise initialization and copy sufficient
```

```cpp
    // no explicit copy constructor or copy assignment operator
    // no destructor necessary ...

    bool operator==( const UserProfile& );
    bool operator!=( const UserProfile &rhs );

    // read access functions
    string login() const { return _login; }
    string user_name() const { return _user_name; }
    int login_count() const { return _times_logged; }
    int guess_count() const { return _guesses; }
    int guess_correct() const { return _correct_guesses; }
    double guess_average() const;
    string level() const;

    // write access functions
    void reset_login( const string &val ){ _login = val; }
    void user_name( const string &val ){ _user_name = val; }

    void reset_level( const string& );
    void reset_level( uLevel newlevel ) { _user_level = newlevel; }

    void reset_login_count( int val ){ _times_logged = val; }
    void reset_guess_count( int val ){ _guesses = val; }
    void reset_guess_correct( int val ){ _correct_guesses = val; }

    void bump_login_count( int cnt=1 ){ _times_logged += cnt; }
    void bump_guess_count( int cnt=1 ){ _guesses += cnt; }
    void bump_guess_correct(int cnt=1){ _correct_guesses += cnt;}
 private:
    string _login;
    string _user_name;
    int    _times_logged;
    int    _guesses;
    int    _correct_guesses;
    uLevel _user_level;

    static map<string,uLevel> _level_map;
    static void init_level_map();
    static string guest_login();
};

inline double UserProfile::guess_average() const
{
    return _guesses
        ? double(_correct_guesses) / double(_guesses) * 100
        : 0.0;
}
```

```
inline UserProfile::UserProfile( string login, uLevel level )
    : _login( login ),   _user_level( level ),
      _times_logged( 1 ), _guesses( 0 ), _correct_guesses( 0 ){}

#include <cstdlib>

inline UserProfile::UserProfile()
    : _login( "guest" ), _user_level( Beginner ),
      _times_logged( 1 ), _guesses( 0 ), _correct_guesses( 0 )
{
    static int id = 0;
    char buffer[ 16 ];

    // _itoa() is a Standard C library function
    // turns an integer into an ascii representation
      _itoa( id++, buffer, 10 );

    // add a unique id during session to guest login
    _login += buffer;
}

inline bool UserProfile::
operator==( const UserProfile &rhs )
{
    if ( _login == rhs._login &&
         _user_name == rhs._user_name )
              return true;
    return false;
}

inline bool UserProfile::
operator !=( const UserProfile &rhs ){ return ! ( *this == rhs ); }

inline string UserProfile::level() const {
    static string _level_table[] = {
           "Beginner", "Intermediate", "Advanced", "Guru" };
    return _level_table[ _user_level ];
}

ostream& operator<<( ostream &os, const UserProfile &rhs )
{ // output of the form: stanl Beginner 12 100 10 10%
    os << rhs.login() << ' '
       << rhs.level() << ' '
       << rhs.login_count() << ' '
       << rhs.guess_count() << ' '
       << rhs.guess_correct() << ' '
       << rhs.guess_average() << endl;
    return os;
}
```

```
        // overkill ... but it allows a demonstration ...
        map<string,UserProfile::uLevel> UserProfile::_level_map;

        void UserProfile::init_level_map(){
            _level_map[ "Beginner" ] = Beginner;
            _level_map[ "Intermediate" ] = Intermediate;
            _level_map[ "Advanced" ] = Advanced;
            _level_map[ "Guru" ] = Guru;
        }

        inline void UserProfile::reset_level( const string &level ){
            map<string,uLevel>::iterator it;
            if ( _level_map.empty() )
                init_level_map();

            // confirm level is a recognized user level ...
            _user_level =
                (( it = _level_map.find( level )) != _level_map.end() )
                     ? it->second : Beginner;
        }

        istream& operator>>( istream &is, UserProfile &rhs )
        {   // yes, this assumes the input is valid ...
            string login, level;
            is >> login >> level;

            int lcount, gcount, gcorrect;
            is >> lcount >> gcount >> gcorrect;
            rhs.reset_login( login );
            rhs.reset_level( level );

            rhs.reset_login_count( lcount );
            rhs.reset_guess_count( gcount );
            rhs.reset_guess_correct( gcorrect );

            return is;
        }
```

Here is a small program to exercise our UserProfile class:

```
        int main()
        {
            UserProfile anon;
            cout << anon; // test out output operator

            UserProfile anon_too; // to see if we get unique id
            cout << anon_too;

            UserProfile anna( "AnnaL", UserProfile::Guru );
            cout << anna;
```

```
        anna.bump_guess_count( 27 );
        anna.bump_guess_correct( 25 );
        anna.bump_login_count();
        cout << anna;

        cin >> anon; // test out input operator
        cout << anon;
    }
```

When compiled and executed, this program generates the following output (my responses are highlighted in bold):

```
guest0 Beginner 1 0 0 0
guest1 Beginner 1 0 0 0
AnnaL Guru 1 0 0 0
AnnaL Guru 2 27 25 92.5926
robin Intermediate 1 8 3
robin Intermediate 1 8 3 37.5
```

Exercise 4.5

Implement a 4x4 Matrix class supporting at least the following general interface: addition and multiplication of two Matrix objects, a print() member function, a compound += operator, and subscripting supported through a pair of overloaded function call operators, as follows:

```
float& operator()( int row, int column );
float  operator()( int row, int column ) const;
```

Provide a default constructor taking an optional 16 data values and a constructor taking an array of 16 elements. You do not need a copy constructor, copy assignment operator, or destructor for this class (these are required in Chapter 6 when we reimplement the Matrix class to support arbitrary rows and columns).

```
#include <iostream>
typedef float elemType; // for transition into a template

class Matrix
{
    // friends are not affected by the access level they are
    // declared in. I like to place them at class beginning
    friend Matrix operator+( const Matrix&, const Matrix& );
    friend Matrix operator*( const Matrix&, const Matrix& );

public:
    Matrix( const elemType* );
    Matrix( elemType=0.,elemType=0.,elemType=0.,elemType=0.,
            elemType=0.,elemType=0.,elemType=0.,elemType=0.,
            elemType=0.,elemType=0.,elemType=0.,elemType=0.,
            elemType=0.,elemType=0.,elemType=0.,elemType=0. );
```

```
    // don't need copy constructor, destructor,
    // or copy assignment operator for the Matrix class

    // simplifies transition to general matrix
    int rows() const { return 4; }
    int cols() const { return 4; }

    ostream& print( ostream& ) const;
    void operator+=( const Matrix& );

    elemType operator()( int row, int column ) const
           { return _matrix[ row ][ column ]; }

    elemType& operator()( int row, int column )
           { return _matrix[ row ][ column ]; }
private:
    elemType _matrix[4][4];
};

inline ostream& operator<<( ostream& os, const Matrix &m )
       { return m.print( os ); }

Matrix operator+( const Matrix &m1, const Matrix &m2 ){
    Matrix result( m1 );
    result += m2;
    return result;
}
Matrix operator*( const Matrix &m1, const Matrix &m2 ){
    Matrix result;
    for ( int ix = 0; ix < m1.rows(); ix++ )
        for ( int jx = 0; jx < m1.cols(); jx++ ){
                result( ix, jx ) = 0;
                for ( int kx = 0; kx < m1.cols(); kx++ )
                     result( ix, jx ) += m1( ix, kx ) * m2( kx, jx );
            }
    return result;
}

void Matrix::operator+=( const Matrix &m ){
    for ( int ix = 0; ix < 4; ++ix )
        for ( int jx = 0; jx < 4; ++jx )
            _matrix[ix][jx] += m._matrix[ix][jx];
}

ostream& Matrix::print( ostream &os ) const {
    int cnt = 0;
    for ( int ix = 0; ix < 4; ++ix )
        for ( int jx = 0; jx < 4; ++jx, ++cnt ){
            if ( cnt &&  !( cnt % 8 )) os << endl;
```

```
                    os << _matrix[ix][jx] << ' ';
          }
     os << endl;
     return os;
}

Matrix::Matrix( const elemType *array ){
    int array_index = 0;
    for ( int ix = 0; ix < 4; ++ix )
         for ( int jx = 0; jx < 4; ++jx )
              _matrix[ix][jx] = array[array_index++];
}

Matrix::Matrix(
        elemType a11, elemType a12, elemType a13, elemType a14,
        elemType a21, elemType a22, elemType a23, elemType a24,
        elemType a31, elemType a32, elemType a33, elemType a34,
        elemType a41, elemType a42, elemType a43, elemType a44 )
{
    _matrix[0][0] = a11; _matrix[0][1] = a12;
    _matrix[0][2] = a13; _matrix[0][3] = a14;
    _matrix[1][0] = a21; _matrix[1][1] = a22;
    _matrix[1][2] = a23; _matrix[1][3] = a24;
    _matrix[2][0] = a31; _matrix[2][1] = a32;
    _matrix[2][2] = a33; _matrix[2][3] = a34;
    _matrix[3][0] = a41; _matrix[3][1] = a42;
    _matrix[3][2] = a43; _matrix[3][3] = a44;
}
```

Here is a small program that exercises a portion of the Matrix class interface:

```
int main()
{
    Matrix m;
    cout << m << endl;

    elemType ar[16]={
       1., 0., 0., 0., 0., 1., 0., 0.,
       0., 0., 1., 0., 0., 0., 0., 1. };

    Matrix identity( ar );
    cout << identity << endl;

    Matrix m2( identity );
    m = identity;
    cout << m2 << endl; cout << m  << endl;

    elemType ar2[16] = {
       1.3, 0.4, 2.6, 8.2, 6.2, 1.7, 1.3, 8.3,
       4.2, 7.4, 2.7, 1.9, 6.3, 8.1, 5.6, 6.6 };
```

```
        Matrix m3( ar2 ); cout << m3 << endl;
        Matrix m4 = m3 * identity; cout << m4 << endl;
        Matrix m5 = m3 + m4; cout << m5 << endl;
        m3 += m4; cout << m3 << endl;
    }
```

When compiled and executed, this program generates the following output:

```
0 0 0 0 0 0 0 0
0 0 0 0 0 0 0 0

1 0 0 0 0 1 0 0
0 0 1 0 0 0 0 1

1 0 0 0 0 1 0 0
0 0 1 0 0 0 0 1

1 0 0 0 0 1 0 0
0 0 1 0 0 0 0 1

1.3 0.4 2.6 8.2 6.2 1.7 1.3 8.3
4.2 7.4 2.7 1.9 6.3 8.1 5.6 6.6
1.3 0.4 2.6 8.2 6.2 1.7 1.3 8.3
4.2 7.4 2.7 1.9 6.3 8.1 5.6 6.6

2.6 0.8 5.2 16.4 12.4 3.4 2.6 16.6
8.4 14.8 5.4 3.8 12.6 16.2 11.2 13.2

2.6 0.8 5.2 16.4 12.4 3.4 2.6 16.6
8.4 14.8 5.4 3.8 12.6 16.2 11.2 13.2
```

Exercise 5.1

Implement a two-level stack hierarchy. The base class is a pure abstract Stack class that minimally supports the following interface: pop(), push(), size(), empty(), full(), peek(), and print(). The derived classes are LIFO_Stack and Peekback_Stack. The Peekback_Stack allows the user to retrieve the value of any element in the stack without modifying the stack itself.

The two derived classes implement the actual element container using a vector. To display the vector, I use a const_reverse_iterator. This supports traversing the vector from the back to the front.

```
        #include <string>
        #include <iostream>
        #include <vector>
        using namespace std;

        typedef string elemType;
```

```
class Stack {
public:
    virtual ~Stack(){}
    virtual bool pop( elemType& ) = 0;
    virtual bool push( const elemType& ) = 0;
    virtual bool peek( int index, elemType& ) = 0;

    virtual int  top() const = 0;
    virtual int  size() const = 0;

    virtual bool empty() const = 0;
    virtual bool full() const = 0;
    virtual void print( ostream& =cout ) const = 0;
};

ostream& operator<<( ostream &os, const Stack &rhs )
    { rhs.print(); return os; }

class LIFO_Stack : public Stack {
public:
   LIFO_Stack( int capacity = 0 ) : _top( 0 )
       { if ( capacity ) _stack.reserve( capacity ); }
   int  size()  const { return _stack.size(); }
   bool empty() const { return ! _top; }
   bool full()  const { return size() >= _stack.max_size(); }
   int  top()   const { return _top; }
   void print( ostream &os=cout ) const;

   bool pop(  elemType &elem );
   bool push( const elemType &elem );
   bool peek( int, elemType& ){ return false; }
private:
   vector< elemType > _stack;
   int _top;
};

bool LIFO_Stack::pop( elemType &elem ){
    if ( empty() ) return false;
    elem = _stack[ --_top ];
    _stack.pop_back();
    return true;
}

bool LIFO_Stack::push( const elemType &elem ){
    if ( full() ) return false;
    _stack.push_back( elem );
    ++_top;
    return true;
}
```

```
void LIFO_Stack::print( ostream &os=cout ) const {
   vector<elemType>::const_reverse_iterator
          rit = _stack.rbegin(),
          rend = _stack.rend();

   os << "\n\t";
   while ( rit != rend )
          os << *rit++ << "\n\t";

   os << endl;
}
```

The implementation of the Peekback_Stack duplicates that of LIFO_Stack except for the implementation of peek():

```
bool Peekback_Stack::
peek( int index, elemType &elem )
{
    if ( empty() )
        return false;

    if ( index < 0 || index >= size() )
        return false;

    elem = _stack[ index ];
    return true;
}
```

Here is a small program that exercises the inheritance hierarchy. The nonmember peek() instance accepts an abstract Stack reference and invokes the virtual peek() member function, which is unique to each derived class.

```
void peek( Stack &st, int index )
{
    cout  << endl;
    string t;
    if ( st.peek( index, t ))
         cout << "peek: " << t;
    else cout << "peek failed!";
    cout << endl;
}

int main()
{
    LIFO_Stack st;
    string str;
    while ( cin >> str && ! st.full() )
           st.push( str );

    cout << '\n' << "About to call peek() with LIFO_Stack" << endl;
```

```
        peek( st, st.top()-1 );
        cout << st;

        Peekback_Stack pst;

        while ( ! st.empty() ){
            string t;
            if ( st.pop( t ))
                pst.push( t );
        }

        cout << "About to call peek() with Peekback_Stack" << endl;
        peek( pst, pst.top()-1 );
        cout << pst;
    }
```

When compiled and executed, this program generates the following output:

```
    once upon a time
    About to call peek() with LIFO_Stack
    peek failed!

        time
        a
        upon
        once

      About to call peek() with Peekback_Stack
      peek: once

        once
        upon
        a
        time
```

Exercise 5.2

**Reimplement the class hierarchy of Exercise 5.1 so that the base Stack class imple-
ments the shared, type-independent members.**

The reimplementation of the class hierarchy illustrates a concrete class hierarchy; that
is, we replace our pure abstract Stack class with our implementation of LIFO_Stack,
renaming it Stack. Although Stack serves as a base class, it also represents actual
objects within our applications. Thus it is termed a concrete base class.
Peekback_Stack is derived from Stack. In this implementation, it inherits all the members of Stack except peek(), which it overrides. Only the peek() member function and
the destructor of Stack are virtual. The definitions of the member functions are the
same and are not shown.

```
class Stack {
public:
    Stack( int capacity = 0 ): _top( 0 )
    {
        if ( capacity )
            _stack.reserve( capacity );
    }
    virtual ~Stack(){}

    bool pop( elemType& );
    bool push( const elemType& );
    virtual bool peek( int, elemType& )
            { return false; }

    int  size()  const { return _stack.size(); }
    int  top()   const { return _top; }

    bool empty() const { return ! _top; }
    bool full()  const { return size() >= _stack.max_size(); }
    void print( ostream&=cout );

protected:
    vector<elemType> _stack;
    int _top;
};

class Peekback_Stack : public Stack {
public:
    Peekback_Stack( int capacity = 0 )
        : Stack( capacity ) {}

    bool peek( int index, elemType &elem );
};
```

Exercise 5.3

A type/subtype inheritance relationship in general reflects an *is-a* relationship: A range-checking ArrayRC is a kind of Array, a Book is a kind of LibraryRentalMaterial, an AudioBook is a kind of Book, and so on. Which of the following pairs reflects an is-a relationship?

        (a) member function isA_kindOf function

This reflects an is-a relationship. A member function is a specialized instance of a function. Both have a return type, a name, a parameter list, and a definition. In addition, a member function belongs to a particular class, may or may not be a virtual, const, or static member function, and so on. Inheritance correctly models the relationship.

(b) `member function isA_kindOf class`

This does not reflect an is-a relationship. A member function has a class that it is a member of, but it is not a specialized instance of a class. Inheritance incorrectly models the relationship.

(c) `constructor isA_kindOf member function`

This reflects an is-a relationship. A constructor is a specialized instance of a member function. A constructor must be a member function; however, it has specialized characteristics. Inheritance correctly models the relationship.

(d) `airplane isA_kindOf vehicle`

This reflects an is-a relationship. An airplane is a kind of vehicle. A vehicle is an abstract class. Airplane is also an abstract class and subsequently is likely to be inherited from. Inheritance correctly models the relationship.

(e) `motor isA_kindOf truck`

This does not reflect an is-a relationship. A motor is part of a truck. A truck has a motor. Inheritance incorrectly models the relationship.

(f) `circle isA_kindOf geometry`

This reflects an is-a relationship. A circle is a specialized instance of geometry — of 2D geometry. Geometry is an abstract base class. Circle is a concrete specialization of geometry. Inheritance correctly models the relationship.

(g) `square isA_kindOf rectangle`

This reflects an is-a relationship. Like a circle, a rectangle is a specialized instance of geometry. A square is a further specialization — a rectangle in which each side is equal. Inheritance correctly models the relationship.

(h) `automobile isA_kindOf airplane`

This is neither a has-a nor an is-a relationship. Both an automobile and an airplane are kinds of vehicles. Inheritance incorrectly models the relationship.

(i) `borrower isA_kindOf library`

This does not reflect an is-a relationship. A borrower is an object (or component) of a library. A library has one or more borrowers. A borrower is a member of a library but is not a kind of library! Inheritance incorrectly models the relationship.

Exercise 5.4

A library supports the following categories of lending materials, each with its own check-out and check-in policy. Organize these into an inheritance hierarchy:

book	audio book
record	children's puppet
video	Sega video game

```
rental book   Sony Playstation video game
CD-ROM book   Nintendo video game
```

An inheritance hierarchy moves from the most abstract to the most specific. In this example, we are given concrete instances of materials loaned by a library. Our task is twofold. First, we must group common abstractions: the four book abstractions and the three video game abstractions. Second, we must provide additional classes that can serve as an abstract interface for the concrete instances. This must be done at two levels: at the level of each family of concrete classes, such as our books, and at the level of the entire library lending hierarchy.

For example, Sega, Sony Playstation, and Nintendo video games are specific instances of video games. To tie them together, I've introduced an abstract video game class. I've designated the book class as a concrete base class with the three other kinds of books as specialized instances. Finally, we need a root base class of our library lending materials.

In the following hierarchy, each tab represents an inheritance relationship. For example, audio, rental, and CD-ROM are inherited from book, which in turn is inherited from the abstract library_lending_material.

```
library_lending_material
    book
        audio book
        rental book
        CD-ROM book
    children's puppet
    record
    video
    video game
        Sega
        Sony Playstation
        Nintendo
```

Exercise 6.1

Rewrite the following class definition to make it a class template:

```
class example {
public:
    example( double min, double max );
    example( const double *array, int size );

    double& operator[]( int index );
    bool operator==( const example1& ) const;

    bool insert( const double*, int );
    bool insert( double );

    double min() const { return _min; }
```

```
        double max() const { return _max; }

        void min( double );
        void max( double );

        int count( double value ) const;
    private:
        int     _size;
        double *_parray;
        double _min;
        double _max;
};
```

To transform the example class into a template, we must identify and factor out each dependent data type. _size, for example, is of type int. Might that vary with different user-specified instances of example? No. _size is an invariant data member that holds a count of the elements addressed by _parray. _parray, however, may address elements of varying types: int, double, float, string, and so on. We want to parameterize the data type of the members _parray, _min, and _max, as well as the return type and signature of some of the member functions.

```
template <typename elemType>
class example {
public:
        example( const elemType &min, const elemType &max );
        example( const elemType *array, int size );

        elemType& operator[]( int index );
        bool operator==( const example1& ) const;

        bool insert( const elemType*, int );
        bool insert( const elemType& );

        elemType min() const { return _min; };
        elemType max() const { return _max; };

        void min( const elemType& );
        void max( const elemType& );

        int count( const elemType &value ) const;
    private:
        int       _size;
        elemType *_parray;
        elemType _min;
        elemType _max;
};
```

Because elemType now potentially represents any built-in or user-defined class, I declare the formal parameters as const references rather than pass them by value.

Exercise 6.2

Reimplement the Matrix class of Exercise 5.3 as a template. In addition, extend it to support arbitrary row and column size using heap memory. Allocate the memory in the constructor and deallocate it in the destructor.

The primary work of this exercise is to add general row and column support. We introduce a constructor that takes a row and a column size as arguments. The body of the constructor allocates the necessary memory from the program's free store:

```
Matrix( int rows, int columns )
      : _rows( rows ), _cols( columns )
{
    int size = _rows * _cols;
    _matrix = new elemType[ size ];
    for ( int ix = 0; ix < size; ++ix )
        _matrix[ ix ] = elemType();
}
```

elemType is the template parameter. _matrix is now an elemType pointer that addresses the heap memory allocated through the new expression.

```
template <typename elemType>
class Matrix {
public:
    // ...
private:
    int        _rows;
    int        _cols;
    elemType *_matrix;
};
```

It is not possible to specify an explicit initial value for which to set each element of the Matrix. The potential actual types that might be specified for elemType are simply too diverse. The language allows us, rather, to specify a default constructor:

```
_matrix[ ix ] = elemType();
```

For an int, this becomes int() and resolves to 0. For a float, this becomes float() and resolves to 0.0f. For a string, this becomes string() and invokes the default string constructor, and so on.

We must add a destructor to delete the heap memory acquired during the class object's construction:

```
~Matrix(){ delete [] _matrix; }
```

We also must provide a copy constructor and a copy assignment operator now. Default memberwise initialization and copy are no longer sufficient when we allocate memory in a constructor and deallocate it in a destructor. Under the default behavior, the _matrix pointer member of both class objects now addresses the same heap memory. This becomes particularly nasty if one object is destroyed while the other object continues to be active within the program: Its underlying matrix has been deleted! One solution is to *deep copy* the underlying matrix so that each class object addresses a separate instance:

```
template <typename elemType>
Matrix<elemType>::Matrix( const Matrix & rhs )
{
    _rows = rhs._rows; _cols = rhs._cols;
    int mat_size = _rows * _cols;
    _matrix = new elemType[ mat_size ];
    for ( int ix = 0; ix < mat_size; ++ix )
            _matrix[ ix ] = rhs._matrix[ ix ];
}

template <typename elemType>
Matrix<elemType>& Matrix<elemType>::operator=( const Matrix &rhs )
{
    if ( this != &rhs ){
            _rows = rhs._rows; _cols = rhs._cols;
            int mat_size = _rows * _cols;
            delete [] _matrix;
            _matrix = new elemType[ mat_size ];
            for ( int ix = 0; ix < mat_size; ++ix )
                    _matrix[ ix ] = rhs._matrix[ ix ];
    }

    return *this;
}
```

Here is the full class declaration and the remaining member functions:

```
#include <iostream>
template <typename elemType>
class Matrix
{
    friend Matrix<elemType>
        operator+( const Matrix<elemType>&, const Matrix<elemType>& );

    friend Matrix< elemType >
        operator*( const Matrix<elemType>&, const Matrix<elemType>& );

public:
    Matrix( int rows, int columns );
    Matrix( const Matrix& );
    ~Matrix();
    Matrix& operator=( const Matrix& );

    void operator+=( const Matrix& );
```

```
        elemType& operator()( int row, int column )
            { return _matrix[ row * cols() + column ]; }

        const elemType& operator()( int row, int column ) const
            { return _matrix[ row * cols() + column ]; }

        int rows() const { return _rows; }
        int cols() const { return _cols; }

        bool same_size( const Matrix &m ) const
            { return rows() == m.rows() && cols() == m.cols(); }

        bool comfortable( const Matrix &m ) const
            { return ( cols() == m.rows() ); }

        ostream& print( ostream& ) const;

protected:
    int   _rows;
    int   _cols;
    elemType *_matrix;
};

template <typename elemType>
inline ostream&
operator<<( ostream& os, const Matrix<elemType> &m )
    { return m.print( os ); }

// end of Matrix.h

template <typename elemType>
Matrix< elemType >
operator+( const Matrix<elemType> &m1, const Matrix<elemType> &m2 )
{
    // make sure m1 & m2 are same size
    Matrix<elemType> result( m1 );
    result += m2;
    return result;
}

template <typename elemType>
Matrix<elemType>
operator*( const Matrix<elemType> &m1, const Matrix<elemType> &m2 )
{
    // m1's columns must equal m2's rows ...
    Matrix<elemType> result( m1.rows(), m2.cols() );
    for ( int ix = 0; ix < m1.rows(); ix++ ) {
        for ( int jx = 0; jx < m1.cols(); jx++ ) {
            result( ix, jx ) = 0;
```

```
                for ( int kx = 0; kx < m1.cols(); kx++ )
                    result( ix, jx ) += m1( ix, kx ) * m2( kx, jx );
            }
        }
        return result;
    }

    template <typename elemType>
    void Matrix<elemType>::operator+=( const Matrix &m ){
        // make sure m1 & m2 are same size
        int matrix_size = cols() * rows();
        for ( int ix = 0; ix < matrix_size; ++ix )
            ( *( _matrix + ix )) += ( *( m._matrix + ix ));
    }

    template <typename elemType>
    ostream& Matrix<elemType>::print( ostream &os ) const {
        int col = cols();
        int matrix_size = col * rows();
        for ( int ix = 0; ix < matrix_size; ++ix ){
            if ( ix % col == 0 ) os << endl;
            os << ( *( _matrix + ix )) << ' ';
        }
        os << endl;
        return os;
    }
```

Here is a small program to exercise our Matrix class template:

```
    int main()
    {
        ofstream log( "C:\\My Documents\\log.txt" );
        if ( ! log )
            { cerr << "can't open log file!\n"; return; }

        Matrix<float> identity( 4, 4 );
        log << "identity: " << identity << endl;
        float ar[16]={ 1., 0., 0., 0., 0., 1., 0., 0.,
                       0., 0., 1., 0., 0., 0., 0., 1. };

        for ( int i = 0, k = 0; i < 4; ++i )
            for ( int j = 0; j < 4; ++j )
                identity( i, j ) = ar[ k++ ];
        log <<  "identity after set: " << identity << endl;

        Matrix<float> m( identity );
        log << "m: memberwise initialized: " << m << endl;

        Matrix<float> m2( 8, 12 );
        log << "m2: 8x12: " <<  m2  << endl;
```

```
    m2 = m;
    log << "m2 after memberwise assigned to m: "
        << m2 << endl;

    float ar2[16]={ 1.3, 0.4, 2.6, 8.2, 6.2, 1.7, 1.3, 8.3,
                    4.2, 7.4, 2.7, 1.9, 6.3, 8.1, 5.6, 6.6 };

    Matrix<float> m3( 4, 4 );
    for ( int ix = 0, kx = 0; ix < 4; ++ix )
        for ( int j = 0; j < 4; ++j )
            m3( ix, j ) = ar2[ kx++ ];

    log << "m3: assigned random values: " << m3 << endl;

    Matrix<float> m4 = m3 * identity; log << m4 << endl;
    Matrix<float> m5 = m3 + m4; log << m5 << endl;

    m3 += m4; log << m3 << endl;
}
```

When compiled and executed, the program generates the following output:

```
identity:
0 0 0 0
0 0 0 0
0 0 0 0
0 0 0 0

identity after set:
1 0 0 0
0 1 0 0
0 0 1 0
0 0 0 1

m: memberwise initialized:
1 0 0 0
0 1 0 0
0 0 1 0
0 0 0 1

m2: 8x12:
0 0 0 0 0 0 0 0 0 0 0 0
0 0 0 0 0 0 0 0 0 0 0 0
0 0 0 0 0 0 0 0 0 0 0 0
0 0 0 0 0 0 0 0 0 0 0 0
0 0 0 0 0 0 0 0 0 0 0 0
0 0 0 0 0 0 0 0 0 0 0 0
0 0 0 0 0 0 0 0 0 0 0 0
0 0 0 0 0 0 0 0 0 0 0 0
```

```
m2 after memberwise assigned to m:
1 0 0 0
0 1 0 0
0 0 1 0
0 0 0 1

m3: assigned random values:
1.3 0.4 2.6 8.2
6.2 1.7 1.3 8.3
4.2 7.4 2.7 1.9
6.3 8.1 5.6 6.6

1.3 0.4 2.6 8.2
6.2 1.7 1.3 8.3
4.2 7.4 2.7 1.9
6.3 8.1 5.6 6.6

2.6 0.8 5.2 16.4
12.4 3.4 2.6 16.6
8.4 14.8 5.4 3.8
12.6 16.2 11.2 13.2

2.6 0.8 5.2 16.4
12.4 3.4 2.6 16.6
8.4 14.8 5.4 3.8
12.6 16.2 11.2 13.2
```

Exercise 7.1

The following function provides absolutely no checking of either possible bad data or the possible failure of an operation. Identify all the things that might possibly go wrong within the function (in this exercise, we don't yet worry about possible exceptions raised).

```cpp
int *alloc_and_init( string file_name )
{
    ifstream infile( file_name );
    int elem_cnt;
    infile >> elem_cnt;
    int *pi = allocate_array( elem_cnt );

    int elem;
    int index = 0;
    while ( infile >> elem )
            pi[ index++ ] = elem;

    sort_array( pi, elem_cnt );
    register_data( pi );
```

```
        return pi;
    }
```

The first error is a type violation: The ifstream constructor requires a const char* and not a string. To retrieve the C-style character string representation, we invoke the c_str() string member function:

```
    ifstream infile( file_name.c_str() );
```

Following the definition of infile, we should check that it opened successfully:

```
    if ( ! infile ) // open failed ...
```

If infile did open successfully, the third statement executes but may not succeed. For example, if the file contained text, the attempt to place an element in elem_cnt fails. Alternatively, it is possible for the file to be empty.

```
    if ( ! infile ) // gosh, the read failed
```

Whenever we deal with pointers, we must be concerned as to whether they actually address an object. If allocate_array() was unable actually to allocate the array, pi is initialized to 0. We must test that:

```
    if ( ! pi ) // geesh, allocate_array() didn't really
```

The assumption of the program is that elem_cnt represents a count of the elements contained within the file. index is unlikely to overflow the array. However, we cannot guarantee that index is never greater than elem_cnt unless we check.

Exercise 7.2

The following functions invoked in alloc_and_init() raise the following exception types if they should fail:

```
    allocate_array() noMem
    sort_array()     int
    register_data()  string
```

Insert one or more try blocks and associated catch clauses where appropriate to handle these exceptions. Simply print the occurrence of the error within the catch clause.

Rather than surround each individual function invocation with a separate try block, I have chosen to surround the entire set of calls with a single try block that contains three associated catch clauses:

```
    int *alloc_and_init( string file_name )
    {
        ifstream infile( file_name.c_str() );
        if ( ! infile )return 0;

        int elem_cnt;
```

```
        infile >> elem_cnt;
        if ( ! infile ) return 0;

        try {
           int *pi = allocate_array( elem_cnt );
           int elem;
           int index = 0;
           while ( infile >> elem && index < elem_cnt )
                     pi[ index++ ] = elem;

           sort_array( pi, elem_cnt );
           register_data( pi );
        }
        catch( const noMem &memFail ) {
              cerr << "alloc_and_init(): allocate_array failure!\n"
                  << memFail.what() << endl;
              return 0;
        }
        catch( int &sortFail ) {
              cerr << "alloc_and_init(): sort_array failure!\n"
                     << "thrown integer value: " << sortFail << endl;
              return 0;
        }
        catch( string &registerFail ) {
              cerr << "alloc_and_init(): register_data failure!\n"
                     << "thrown string value: "
                      << registerFail << endl;
              return 0;
        }
        return pi; // reach here only if no throw occurred ...
    }
```

Exercise 7.3

Add a pair of exceptions to the Stack class hierarchy of Exercise 6.2 to handle the cases of attempting to pop a stack that is empty and attempting to push a stack that is full. Show the modified pop() and push() member functions.

We'll define a PopOnEmpty and a PushOnFull pair of exception classes to be thrown, respectively, in the pop() and push() Stack member functions. These classes no longer need to return a success or failure value:

```
        void pop( elemType &elem )
        {
            if ( empty() )
                  throw PopOnEmpty();
            elem = _stack[ --_top ];
            _stack.pop_back();
        }
```

```
void push( const elemType &elem ){
    if ( ! full() ){
        _stack.push_back( elem );
        ++_top;
        return;
    }
    throw PushOnFull();
}
```

To allow these two Stack class exceptions to be caught in components that do not explicitly know about PopOnEmpty and PushOnFull exception classes, the class exceptions are made part of a StackException hierarchy that is derived from the standard library logic_error class.

The logic_error class is derived from exception, which is the root abstract base class of the standard library exception class hierarchy. This hierarchy declares a virtual function what() that returns a const char* identifying the exception that has been caught.

```
class StackException : public logic_error {
public:
    StackException( const char *what ) : _what( what ){}
    const char *what() const { return _what.c_str(); }
protected:
    string _what;
};

class PopOnEmpty : public StackException {
public:
    PopOnEmpty() : StackException( "Pop on Empty Stack" ){}
};

class PushOnFull : public StackException {
public:
    PushOnFull() : StackException( "Push on Full Stack" ){}
};
```

Each of the following catch clauses handles an exception of type PushOnFull:

```
catch( const PushOnFull &pof )
    { log( pof.what() ); return; }

catch( const StackException &stke )
    { log( stke.what() ); return; }

catch( const logic_error &lge )
    { log( lge.what() ); return; }

catch( const exception &ex )
    { log( ex.what() ); return; }
```

Appendix B

Generic Algorithms Handbook

Each generic algorithm, with the fistful of exceptions that make the rule, begins with a pair of iterators that marks the range of elements within the container over which to traverse. The range begins with the first iterator and ends with but does *not* include the second:

```
const int array_size = 7;
int iarray[array_size] = { 1, 10, 8, 4, 3, 14, 8 };
vector<int> vec( iarray, iarray+ array_size );

vector<int>::iterator it = find( vec.begin(), vec.end(), value );
int *pi = find( iarray, iarray+array_size, value );
```

The algorithms are generally overloaded to support two versions: one that uses either the built-in equality or the less-than operator of the underlying element type, and a second one that accepts either a function object or a pointer to function providing an alternative implementation of that operator. For example, by default sort() orders the container elements using the less-than operator. To override that, we can pass in the predefined greater-than function object:

```
sort( vec.begin(), vec.end() );
sort( vec.begin(), vec.end(), greater<int>() );
```

Other algorithms, however, are separated into two uniquely named instances; the predicate instance in each case ends with the suffix _if, as in find_if(). For example, to find an element less than 10, we might write

```
find_if( vec.begin(), vec.end(), bind2nd( less<int>, 10 ))
```

Many of the algorithms that modify the container they are applied to come in two flavors: an in-place version that changes the container, and a version that returns a copy of the container with the changes applied. For example, there is both a replace() and a replace_copy() algorithm. The copy version always contains _copy in its name. It accepts a third iterator that points to the first element of the container in which to copy the modified elements. By default, the copy is achieved by assignment. We can use one of three inserter adapters to override the assignment semantics and have the elements instead inserted. (See Section 3.9 for a discussion and examples.)

As programmers, we must quickly be able to look up which algorithms are available and how they are generally used. That is the purpose of this handbook.[1] The following built-in arrays, vectors, and lists are used as arguments to the algorithms:

```
int ia[8]={ 1, 3, 6, 10, 15, 21, 28, 36 };
vector<int> ivec( ia, ia+8 );
list<int> ilist( ia, ia+8 );

string sa[10] = { "The", "light", "untonsured", "hair",
    "grained", "and", "hued", "like", "pale", "oak" };
vector<string> svec( sa, sa+10 );
list<string> slist( sa, sa+10 );
```

Each listing provides a brief description of the algorithm, indicates the header file that must be included (either algorithm or numeric), and provides one or two usage examples.

accumulate()
By default, adds the container elements to an initial value specified by the third argument. A binary operation can be passed in to override the default addition.

```
#include <numeric>

iresult = accumulate( ia, ia+8, 0);
iresult = accumulate( ilist.begin(), ilist.end(), 0, plus<int>() );
```

adjacent_difference()
By default, creates a new sequence in which the value of each new element, other than the first one, represents the difference of the current and the preceding element. Given the sequence {0,1,1,2,3,5,8}, the new sequence is {0,1,0,1,1,2,3}. A binary operation can be passed in to override subtraction. For example, times<int> yields the sequence {0,0,1,2,6,15,40}. The third argument is an iterator that addresses the container into which to copy the results.

```
#include <numeric>

adjacent_difference( ilist.begin(), ilist.end(), iresult.begin() );
adjacent_difference( ilist.begin(), ilist.end(), iresult.begin(),
                     times<int>() );
```

---

1 This handbook is an abridged and recast version of the C++ Primer Appendix, which provides a program example and discussion of each generic algorithm. Here I've listed a subset of the algorithms that are, in my opinion, the most frequently used.

adjacent_find()

By default, looks for the first adjacent pair of duplicate elements. A binary operator can override the built-in equality operator. Returns an iterator that addresses the first element of the pair.

```
#include <algorithm>
class TwiceOver {
public:
    bool operator() ( int val1, int val2 )
        { return val1 == val2/2 ? true : false; }
};

piter = adjacent_find( ia, ia+8 );
iter  = adjacent_find( vec.begin(), vec.end(), TwiceOver() );
```

binary_search()

Assumes that the container is sorted by the less-than operator. If the container is sorted by some other ordering relationship, the binary operator must be passed in. The algorithm returns true or false.

```
#include <algorithm>
found_it = binary_search( ilist.begin(), ilist.end(), value );
found_it = binary_search( vec.begin(), vec.end(), value,
                          greater<int>() );
```

copy()

Copies the elements of one container into a second container.

```
#include <algorithm>
ostream_iterator<int>  ofile( cout, " " );
copy( vec.begin(), vec.end(), ofile );

vector<string> target( svec.size() );
copy( svec.begin(), svec.end(), target.begin() );
```

copy_backward()

Behaves the same as copy() except that the elements are copied in the reverse order.

```
#include <algorithm>
copy_backward( svec.begin(), svec.end(), target.begin() );
```

count()

Returns a count of the number of elements within the container equal to value.

```
#include <algorithm>
cout << value << " occurs "
     << count( svec.begin(), svec.end(), value )
     << " times in string vector.\n";
```

count_if()

Returns a count of the number of times the operator evaluated as true.

```
#include <algorithm>
class Even {
public:
    bool operator()( int val ){ return !( val%2 ); }
};

ires = count_if( ia, ia+8, bind2nd(less<int>(),10) );
lres = count_if( ilist.begin(), ilist_end(), Even() );
```

equal()

Returns true if the two sequences are equal for the number of elements contained within the first container. By default, the equality operator is used. Alternatively, a binary function object or pointer to function can be supplied.

```
#include <algorithm>
class EqualAndOdd{
public:
    bool operator()( int v1, int v2 )
        { return ((v1==v2) && (v1%2)); }
};

int ia1[] = { 1,1,2,3,5,8,13 };
int ia2[] = { 1,1,2,3,5,8,13,21,34 };
res = equal( ia1, ia1+7, ia2 ); // true
res = equal( ia1, ia1+7, ia2, equalAndOdd() ); // false
```

fill()

Assigns a copy of value to each element within the container.

```
#include <algorithm>
fill( ivec.begin(), ivec.end(), value );
```

fill_n()

Assigns a copy of value to count elements within the container.

```
#include <algorithm>
fill_n( ia, count, value );
fill_n( svec.begin(), count, string_value );
```

find()

The elements within the container are compared for equality with value. If a match is found, the search ends. find() returns an iterator to the element. If no match is found, container.end() is returned.

```
#include <algorithm>
piter = find( ia, ia+8, value );
iter  = find( svec.begin(), svec.end(), "rosebud" );
```

find_end()

This algorithm takes two iterator pairs. The first pair marks the container to be searched. The second pair marks a sequence to match against. The elements within the first container are compared for the last occurrence of the sequence using either the equality operator or the specified binary operation. If a match is found, an iterator addressing the first element of the matched sequence is returned; otherwise, the iterator marking the end of the first container is returned. For example, given the character sequence Mississippi and a second sequence ss, find_end() returns an iterator to the first s of the second ss sequence.

```
#include <algorithm>
int ia[ 17 ] = { 7,3,3,7,6,5,8,7,2,1,3,7,6,3,8,4,3 };
int seq[ 3 ] = { 3, 7, 6 };

// found_it addresses ia[10]
found_it = find_end( ia, ia+17, seq, seq+3 );
```

find_first_of()

find_first_of() accepts two iterator pairs. The first pair marks the elements to search. The second pair marks a collection of elements to search for. For example, to find the first vowel in the character sequence synesthesia, we define our second sequence as aeiou. find_first_of() returns an iterator to the first instance of an element of the sequence of vowels, in this case pointing to the first e. If the first sequence does not contain any of the elements, an iterator that addresses the end of the first sequence is returned. An optional fifth parameter allows us to override the default equality operator with any binary predicate operation.

```
#include <algorithm>
string s_array[] = { "Ee", "eE", "ee", "Oo", "oo", "ee" };
string to_find[] = { "oo", "gg", "ee" };

// returns first occurrence of "ee" -- &s_array[2]
found_it = find_first_of( s_array, s_array+6,
                          to_find, to_find+3 );
```

find_if()

The elements within the container are compared for equality with the specified binary operation. If a match is found, the search ends. find_if() returns an iterator to the element. If no match is found, container.end() is returned.

```
#include <algorithm>
find_if( vec.begin(), vec.end(), LessThanVal(ival) );
```

for_each()

for_each() takes a third parameter that represents an operation that is applied to each element in turn. The operation cannot modify the elements (we can use transform() for that). Although the operation may return a value, that value is ignored.

```cpp
#include <algorithm>
template <typename Type>
    void print_elements( Type elem ) { cout << elem << " "; }

for_each( ivec.begin(), ivec.end(), print_elements );
```

generate()

generate() fills a sequence by applying the specified generator.

```cpp
#include <algorithm>
class GenByTwo {
public:
    void operator()(){
        static int seed = -1; return seed += 2; }
};
list<int> ilist( 10 );

// fills ilist: 1 3 5 7 9 11 13 15 17 19
generate( ilist.begin(), ilist.end(), GenByTwo() );
```

generate_n()

generate_n() fills a sequence by applying n successive invocations of the generator.

```cpp
#include <algorithm>
class gen_by_two {
public:
    gen_by_two( int seed = 0 ) : _seed( seed ){}
    int operator()() { return _seed += 2; }
private:
    int _seed;
};
vector<int> ivec( 10 );

// fills ivec: 102 104 106 108 110 112 114 116 118 120
generate_n( ivec.begin(), ivec.size(), gen_by_two(100) );
```

includes()

includes() returns true if every element of the second sequence is contained within the first sequence; otherwise, it returns false. Both sequences must be sorted, either by the default less-than operator or by the same operation passed as an optional fifth parameter.

```cpp
#include <algorithm>
```

```
    int ia1[] = { 13, 1, 21, 2, 0, 34, 5, 1, 8, 3, 21, 34 };
    int ia2[] = { 21, 2, 8, 3, 5, 1 };

    // includes must be passed sorted containers
    sort( ia1, ia1+12 ); sort( ia2, ia2+6 );
    res = includes( ia1, ia1+12, ia2, ia2+6 ); // true
```

inner_product()

`inner_product()` accumulates the product of two sequences of values, adding them in turn to a user-specified initial value. For example, given the two sequences {2,3,5,8} and {1,2,3,4}, the result is the sum of the product pairs (2*1)+(3*2)+(5*3)+(8*4). If we provide an initial value of 0, the result is 55.

A second version allows us to override the default addition operation and the default multiply operation. For example, if we use the same sequence but specify subtraction and addition, the result is the difference of the following addition pairs: (2+1)-(3+2)-(5+3)-(8+4). If we provide an initial value of 0, the result is -28.

```
    #include <numeric>
    int ia[] = { 2, 3, 5, 8 };
    int ia2[] = { 1, 2, 3, 4 };
    int res = inner_product( ia, ia+4, ia2, 0);

    vector<int> vec( ia, ia+4 );
    vector<int> vec2( ia2, ia2+4 );

    res = inner_product( vec.begin(), vec.end(), vec2.begin(), 0,
                         minus<int>(), plus<int>() );
```

inplace_merge()

`inplace_merge()` takes three iterator parameters: `first`, `middle`, and `last`. Two input sequences are marked by [`first`,middle] and [`middle`,last] (`middle` marks 1 past the last element of the first sequence). These sequences must be consecutive. The resulting sequence overwrites the two ranges beginning at `first`. An optional fourth parameter allows us to specify an ordering operation other than the default less-than operator.

```
    #include <algorithm>
    int ia[20] = { 29,23,20,17,15,26,51,12,35,40,
                   74,16,54,21,44,62,10,41,65,71 };

    int *middle = ia+10, *last = ia+20;

    // 12 15 17 20 23 26 29 35 40 51 10 16 21 41 44 54 62 65 71 74
    sort( ia, middle ); sort( middle, last );

    // 10 12 15 16 17 20 21 23 26 29 35 40 41 44 51 54 62 65 71 74
    inplace_merge( ia, middle, last );
```

iter_swap()

Swaps the values contained within the elements addressed by two iterators.

```
#include <algorithm>
typedef list<int>::iterator iterator;
iterator it1 = ilist.begin(), it2 = ilist.begin()+4;
iter_swap( it1, it2 );
```

lexicographical_compare()

By default, the less-than operator is applied, although an optional fifth option allows us to provide an alternative ordering operation. Returns true if the first sequence is less than or equal to the second sequence.

```
#include <algorithm>
class size_compare {
public:
    bool operator()( const string &a, const string &b ) {
        return a.length() <= b.length();
    }
};
string sa1[] = { "Piglet", "Pooh",  "Tigger" };
string sa2[] = { "Piglet", "Pooch", "Eeyore" };

// false: 'c' less than 'h'
res = lexicographical_compare( sa1, sa1+3, sa2, sa2+3 );

list<string> ilist1( sa1, sa1+3 );
list<string> ilist2( sa2, sa2+3 );

// true: Pooh < Pooch
res = lexicographical_compare(
        ilist1.begin(), ilist1.end(),
        ilist2.begin(), ilist2.end(), size_compare() );
```

max(), min()

Returns the larger (or smaller) of the two elements. An optional third argument allows us to provide an alternative comparison operation.

max_element(), min_element()

Returns an iterator pointing to the largest (or smallest) value within the sequence. An optional third argument allows us to provide an alternative comparison operation.

```
#include <algorithm>
int mval = max( max( max( max( ivec[4],  ivec[3] ),
                            ivec[2] ),ivec[1] ),ivec[0] );

mval = min( min( min( min( ivec[4], ivec[3] ),
                        ivec[2] ),ivec[1] ),ivec[0] );
```

```
vector<int>::const_iterator iter;
iter = max_element( ivec.begin(), ivec.end() );
iter = min_element( ivec.begin(), ivec.end() );
```

merge()

Combines two sorted sequences into a single sorted sequence addressed by the fifth iterator. An optional sixth argument allows us to indicate an ordering other than the default less-than operator.

```
#include <algorithm>
int ia[12]  =  {29,23,20,22,17,15,26,51,19,12,35,40};
int ia2[12] = {74,16,39,54,21,44,62,10,27,41,65,71};

vector<int> vec1( ia, ia+12 ),  vec2( ia2, ia2+12 );
vector<int> vec_result(vec1.size()+vec2.size());

sort( vec1.begin(), vec1.end(), greater<int>() );
sort( vec2.begin(), vec2.end(), greater<int>() );

merge( vec1.begin(), vec1.end(),
       vec2.begin(), vec2.end(),
       vec_result.begin(), greater<int>() );
```

nth_element()

nth_element() reorders the sequence so that all elements less than the nth element occur before it and all elements that are greater occur after it. For example, given

```
int ia[] = { 29,23,20,22,17,15,26,51,19,12,35,40 };
```

an invocation of nth_element() marking ia+6 as nth (it has a value of 26)

```
nth_element( ia, ia+6, &ia[12] );
```

yields a sequence in which the seven elements less than 26 are to its left, and the four elements greater than 26 are to its right:

```
{ 23,20,22,17,15,19,12,26,51,35,40,29 }
```

The elements on either side of the nth element are not guaranteed to be in any particular order. An optional fourth parameter allows us to indicate a comparison other than the default less-than operator.

partial_sort(), partial_sort_copy()

partial_sort() accepts three parameters — first, middle, and last — and an optional fourth parameter that provides an alternative ordering operation. The iterators first and middle mark the range of slots available to place the sorted elements of the container (middle is 1 past the last valid slot). The elements stored beginning at middle through last are unsorted. For example, given the array

```
int ia[] = {29,23,20,22,17,15,26,51,19,12,35,40 };
```

an invocation of `partial_sort()` marking the sixth element as `middle`

```
partial_sort( ia, ia+5, ia+12 );
```

yields the sequence in which the five smallest elements are sorted:

```
{ 12,15,17,19,20,29,23,22,26,51,35,40 }
```

The elements from `middle` through `last-1` are not placed in any particular order, although all their values fall outside the sequence actually sorted.

partial_sum()

Creates a new sequence in which, by default, the value of each new element represents the sum of all the previous elements up to its position. For example, given the sequence {0,1,1,2,3,5,8}, the new sequence is {0,1,2,4,7,12,20}. The fourth element, for example, is the partial sum of the three previous values (0,1,1) plus its own (2), yielding a value of 4. An optional fourth parameter allows the user to specify an alternative operation to apply.

```
#include <numeric>
int ires[7], ia[7] = { 1, 3, 4, 5, 7, 8, 9 };
vector<int> vres(7), vec( ia, ia+7 );

// partial_sum(): 1 4 8 13 20 28 37
partial_sum( ia, ia+7, ires );

//partial sum using times<int>(): 1 3 12 60 420 3360 30240
partial_sum(vec.begin(),vec.end(),vres.begin(),times<int>());
```

partition(), stable_partition()

`partition()` reorders the elements based on the true/false evaluation of a unary operation. All the elements that evaluate as true are placed before the elements that evaluate as false. For example, given the sequence {0,1,2,3,4,5,6} and a predicate that tests for elements that are even, the true and false element ranges are {0,2,4,6} and {1,3,5}. Although all the even elements are guaranteed to be placed before any of the odd elements, the relative position of the elements within the reordering is not guaranteed to be preserved. `stable_partition()` guarantees to preserve the relative order of the elements within the container.

```
#include <algorithm>

class even_elem {
public:
    bool operator()( int elem )
        { return elem%2 ? false : true; }
};

int ia[] = { 29,23,20,22,17,15,26,51,19,12,35,40 };
vector<int> vec( ia, ia+12 );
```

```
// partition based on whether element is even:
//   40 12 20 22 26 15 17 51 19 23 35 29
stable_partition( vec.begin(), vec.end(), even_elem() );
```

random_shuffle()

By default, random_shuffle() reorders the elements randomly based on its own algorithm. An optional third parameter allows us to pass in a random-number-generating operation that must return a value of type double within the interval [0,1].

```
#include <algorithm>
random_shuffle( ivec.begin(), ivec.end() );
```

remove(), remove_copy()

remove() separates out all instances of a value within the sequence. It does not actually erase the matched elements (the container's size is preserved). Rather, each non-matching element is assigned in turn to the next free slot. The returned iterator marks 1 past the new range of elements.

For example, consider the sequence {0,1,0,2,0,3,0,4}. Let's say that we wish to remove all 0 values. The resulting sequence is {1,2,3,4,0,3,0,4}. The 1 is copied into the first slot, the 2 into the second slot, the 3 into the third slot, and the 4 into the fourth slot. The 0 at the fifth slot represents the *leftover* of the algorithm. The returned iterator addresses that slot. Typically, this iterator is then passed to erase(). (The built-in array is not suited to the remove() algorithm because it cannot be resized easily. For this reason, the remove_copy() is the preferred algorithm for use with an array.)

```
#include <algorithm>

int ia[] = { 0, 1, 0, 2, 0, 3, 0, 4, 0, 5 };
vector<int> vec( ia, ia+10 );

// vector after remove, without applying erase():
// 1 2 3 4 5 3 0 4 0 5
vec_iter = remove( vec.begin(), vec.end(), 0 );

// vector after erase(): 1 2 3 4 5
vec.erase( vec_iter, vec.end() );

int ia2[5];
// ia2: 1 2 3 4 5
remove_copy( ia, ia+10, ia2, 0 );
```

remove_if(), remove_copy_if()

remove_if() removes all elements within the sequence for which the predicate operation evaluates as true. Otherwise, remove_if() and remove_copy_if() behave the same as remove() and remove_copy() — see the earlier discussion.

```
#include <algorithm>

class EvenValue {
public:
    bool operator()( int value ) {
        return value % 2 ? false : true; }
};

int ia[] = { 0, 1, 1, 2, 3, 5, 8, 13, 21, 34 };
vector<int> vec( ia, ia+10 );

iter = remove_if( vec.begin(), vec.end(), bind2nd(less<int>(),10) );
vec.erase( iter, vec.end() ); // sequence now: 13 21 34

int ia2[10]; // ia2: 1 1 3 5 13 21
remove_copy_if( ia, ia+10,ia2, EvenValue() );
```

replace(), replace_copy()

replace() replaces all instances of old_value with new_value within the sequence.

```
#include <algorithm>
string oldval( "Mr. Winnie the Pooh" );
string newval( "Pooh" );
string sa[] = { "Christopher Robin", "Mr. Winnie the Pooh",
                "Piglet", "Tigger", "Eeyore" };

vector<string> vec( sa, sa+5 );

// Christopher Robin Pooh Piglet Tigger Eeyore
replace( vec.begin(), vec.end(), oldval, newval );

vector<string> vec2;

// Christopher Robin Mr. Winnie the Pooh Piglet Tigger Eeyore
replace_copy( vec.begin(), vec.end(),
              inserter(vec2,vec2.begin()), newval, oldval );
```

replace_if(), replace_copy_if()

replace_if() replaces all elements within the sequence with new_value for which the predicate comparison operation evaluates as true.

```
#include <algorithm>
int new_value = 0;
int ia[] = { 0, 1, 1, 2, 3, 5, 8, 13, 21, 34 };
vector<int> vec( ia, ia+10 );

// new sequence:  0 0 0 0 0 0 0 13 21 34
replace_if( vec.begin(), vec.end(),
            bind2nd(less<int>(),10), new_value );
```

reverse(), reverse_copy()

Reverses the order of elements in a container.

```
#include <algorithm>
list<string> slist_copy( slist.size() );

reverse( slist.begin(), slist.end() );
reverse_copy( slist.begin(), slist.end(), slist_copy.begin() );
```

rotate(), rotate_copy()

rotate() is passed three iterators: first, middle, and last. It exhanges the two ranges marked by the iterators first, middle-1 and middle, last-1. For example, given the following C-style character string "boohiss!!",

```
char ch[] = "boohiss!!";
```

To change it to "hissboo!!", the call to rotate() looks like this:

```
rotate( ch, ch+3, ch+7 );
```

Here is another example:

```
#include <algorithm>
int ia[] = { 1, 3, 5, 7, 9, 0, 2, 4, 6, 8, 10 };
vector<int> vec( ia, ia+11 ), vec2(11);
```

In this first invocation, we exchange the last six elements, beginning with 0, with the first five elements, beginning with 1:

```
// rotate on middle element(0) : 0 2 4 6 8 10 1 3 5 7 9
rotate( ia, ia+5, ia+11 );
```

In this second invocation, we exchange the last two elements, beginning with 8, with the first nine elements, beginning with 1:

```
// rotate on next to last element(8): 8 10 1 3 5 7 9 0 2 4 6
rotate_copy( vec.begin(), vec.end()-2, vec.end(), vec2.begin() );
```

search()

Given two sequences, search() returns an iterator that addresses the first position in the first sequence in which the second sequence occurs. If the subsequence does not occur, an iterator that addresses the end of the first sequence is returned. For example, within Mississippi, the subsequence iss occurs twice, and search() returns an iterator to the start of the first instance. An optional fifth parameter allows the user to override the default equality operator.

```
#include <algorithm>

char str[25] = "a fine and private place";
char substr[4]  = "ate";
int *piter = search( str,str+25,substr,substr+4 );
```

search_n()

search_n() looks for the first occurrence of n instances of a value within a sequence. In the following example, we search str for two occurrences of the character o in succession, and an iterator to the first o of moose is returned. If the subsequence is not present, an iterator that addresses the end of the first sequence is returned. An optional fifth parameter allows the user to override the default equality operator.

```
#include <algorithm>
const char oh    = 'o';

char str[ 26 ]  = "oh my a mouse ate a moose";
char *found_str = search_n( str, str+26, 2, oh );
```

set_difference()

set_difference() constructs a sorted sequence of the elements present in a first sequence but not present in a second. For example, given the two sequences {0,1,2,3} and {0,2,4,6}, the set difference is {1,3}. All the set algorithms (three additional algorithms follow) take five iterators: The first two mark the first sequence, and the second two mark the second sequence. The fifth iterator marks the position of the container into which to copy the elements. The algorithm presumes that the sequences are sorted using the less-than operator; an optional sixth argument allows us to pass in an alternative ordering operation.

set_intersection()

set_intersection() constructs a sorted sequence of the elements present in both sequences. For example, given the two sequences {0,1,2,3} and {0,2,4,6}, the set intersection is {0,2}.

set_symmetric_difference()

set_symmetric_difference() constructs a sorted sequence of the elements that are present in the first sequence but not present in the second, and those elements present in the second sequence are not present in the first. For example, given the two sequences {0,1,2,3} and {0,2,4,6}, the set symmetric difference is {1,3,4,6}.

set_union()

set_union() constructs a sorted sequence of the element values contained within the two sequences. For example, given the two sequences {0,1,2,3} and {0,2,4,6}, the set union is {0,1,2,3,4,6}. If the element is present in both containers, such as 0 and 2 in the example, the element of the first container is copied.

```
#include <algorithm>
string str1[] = { "Pooh", "Piglet", "Tigger", "Eeyore" };
string str2[] = { "Pooh", "Heffalump", "Woozles" };
```

```
            set<string> set1( str1, str1+4 ),
                        set2( str2, str2+3 );

            // holds result of each set operation
            set<string> res;

            //set_union(): Eeyore Heffalump Piglet Pooh Tigger Woozles
            set_union( set1.begin(), set1.end(),
                       set2.begin(), set2.end(), inserter(res,res.begin()));

            res.clear(); // empties the container of elements

            // set_intersection(): Pooh
            set_intersection( set1.begin(), set1.end(), set2.begin(),
                              set2.end(), inserter( res,res.begin() ));

            res.clear();

            // set_difference(): Eeyore Piglet Tigger
            set_difference( set1.begin(), set1.end(), set2.begin(),
                            set2.end(), inserter( res, res.begin() ));

            res.clear();

            // set_symmetric_difference():
            //    Eeyore Heffalump Piglet Tigger Woozles
            set_symmetric_difference( set1.begin(), set1.end(), set2.begin(),
                                      set2.end(), inserter( res, res.begin() ));
```

sort(), stable_sort()

By default, sorts the elements in ascending order using the less-than operator. An optional third parameter allows us to pass in an alternative ordering operation. stable_sort() preserves the relative order of elements within the container. For example, imagine that we have sorted our words alphabetically and now wish to order them by word length. To do this, we pass in a function object LessThan that compares two strings by length. Were we to use sort(), we would not be guaranteed to preserve the alphabetical ordering.

```
            #include <algorithm>
            stable_sort( ia, ia+8 );
            stable_sort( svec.begin(), svec.end(), greater<string>() );
```

transform()

The first version of transform() invokes the unary operator passed to it on each element in the sequence. For example, given a sequence {0,1,1,2,3,5} and a function object Double, which doubles each element, the resulting sequence is {0,2,2,4,6,10}.

The second version invokes the binary operator passed to it on the associated elements of a pair of sequences. For example, given the sequences {1,3,5,9} and {2,4,6,8}, and a function object AddAndDouble that adds the two elements and then doubles their sum, the resulting sequence is {6,14,22,34}. The resulting sequence is copied into the container pointed to by either the third iterator of the first version or the fourth iterator of the second.

```
#include <algorithm>
int double_val( int val ) { ·return val + val; }
int difference( int val1, int val2 ) { return abs( val1 - val2 ); }

int ia[]  = { 3, 5, 8, 13, 21 };
vector<int> vec( 5 ), vec2( 5 );

// first version: 6 10 16 26 42
transform( ia, ia+5, vec.begin(), double_val );

// second version: 3 5 8 13 21
transform( ia, ia+5, vec.begin(), vec2.begin(), difference );
```

unique(), unique_copy()

All consecutive groups of elements containing either the same value (using the equality operator) or evaluating as true when passed an optional alternative comparison operation are collapsed into a single element. In the word *Mississippi*, the *semantic* result is "Misisipi." Because the three *i*'s are not consecutive, they are not collapsed, nor are the two pairs of *s*'s. To guarantee that all duplicated elements are collapsed, we would first sort the container.

As with remove(), the container's actual size is not changed. Each unique element is assigned in turn to the next free slot, beginning with the first element of the container. In our example, the *physical* result is "Misisipippi," where the character sequence *ppi* represents the leftover piece of the algorithm. The returned iterator marks the beginning of the refuse. Typically this iterator is then passed to erase(). (Because the built-in array does not support the erase() operation, unique() is less suitable for arrays; unique_copy() is more appropriate.)

```
#include <algorithm>
int ia[] = { 0, 1, 0, 2, 0, 3, 0, 4, 0, 5 };
vector<int> vec( ia, ia+10 );

sort( vec.begin(), vec.end() );
iter = unique( vec.begin(), vec.end() );
vec.erase( vec_iter, vec.end() ); // vec: 0 1 2 3 4 5

int ia2[10];
sort( ia, ia+10 );
unique_copy( ia, ia+10, ia2 );
```

Index

Addison-Wesley Computer and Engineering Publishing Group

How to Interact with Us

1. Visit our Web site

http://www.awl.com/cseng

When you think you've read enough, there's always more content for you at Addison-Wesley's web site. Our web site contains a directory of complete product information including:

- Chapters
- Exclusive author interviews
- Links to authors' pages
- Tables of contents
- Source code

You can also discover what tradeshows and conferences Addison-Wesley will be attending, read what others are saying about our titles, and find out where and when you can meet our authors and have them sign your book.

2. Subscribe to Our Email Mailing Lists

Subscribe to our electronic mailing lists and be the first to know when new books are publishing. Here's how it works: Sign up for our electronic mailing at **http://www.awl.com/cseng/mailinglists.html**. Just select the subject areas that interest you and you will receive notification via email when we publish a book in that area.

3. Contact Us via Email

cepubprof@awl.com
Ask general questions about our books.
Sign up for our electronic mailing lists.
Submit corrections for our web site.

bexpress@awl.com
Request an Addison-Wesley catalog.
Get answers to questions regarding
your order or our products.

innovations@awl.com
Request a current Innovations Newsletter.

webmaster@awl.com
Send comments about our web site.

mikeh@awl.com
Submit a book proposal.
Send errata for an Addison-Wesley book.

cepubpublicity@awl.com
Request a review copy for a member of the media
interested in reviewing new Addison-Wesley titles.

We encourage you to patronize the many fine retailers who stock Addison-Wesley titles. Visit our online directory to find stores near you or visit our online store: **http://store.awl.com/** or call **800-824-7799**.

Addison Wesley Longman
Computer and Engineering Publishing Group
One Jacob Way, Reading, Massachusetts 01867 USA
TEL 781-944-3700 • FAX 781-942-3076